T0327580

Bullying and Harassment at Work

An Innovative Approach to Understanding and Prevention

David D. Van Fleet

Professor Emeritus, W. P. Carey School of Business, Arizona State University, USA

Ella W. Van Fleet

Founder and Owner (Retired), Professional Business Associates, Scottsdale, AZ, USA

NEW HORIZONS IN MANAGEMENT

 Edward Elgar
PUBLISHING

Cheltenham, UK • Northampton, MA, USA

Published by
Edward Elgar Publishing Limited
The Lypiatts
15 Lansdown Road
Cheltenham
Glos GL50 2JA
UK

Edward Elgar Publishing, Inc.
William Pratt House
9 Dewey Court
Northampton
Massachusetts 01060
USA

Paperback edition 2023

A catalogue record for this book
is available from the British Library

Library of Congress Control Number: 2022934688

This book is available electronically in the **Elgar**online
Business subject collection
http://dx.doi.org/10.4337/9781803923284

ISBN 978 1 80392 327 7 (Hardback)
ISBN 978 1 80392 328 4 (eBook)
ISBN 978 1 0353 2040 0 (Paperback)

Printed and bound by CPI Group (UK) Ltd, Croydon, CR0 4YY

Bullying and Harassment at Work

NEW HORIZONS IN MANAGEMENT

Series Editor: Professor Sir Cary Cooper, *50th Anniversary Professor of Organizational Psychology and Health at Alliance Manchester Business School, University of Manchester, UK and President of the Chartered Institute of Personnel and Development and British Academy of Management*

This important series makes a significant contribution to the development of management thought. This field has expanded dramatically in recent years and the series provides an invaluable forum for the publication of high quality work in management science, human resource management, organizational behaviour, marketing, management information systems, operations management, business ethics, strategic management and international management.

The main emphasis of the series is on the development and application of new original ideas. International in its approach, it will include some of the best theoretical and empirical work from both well-established researchers and the new generation of scholars.

Titles in the series include:

This work is dedicated to all those who have experienced unacceptable behavior at work from co-workers, managers/supervisors, or even suppliers/customers.

This book is based on the research and opinions of the authors and is meant as a source of valuable information for the reader. However, it is not meant as a substitute for direct legal assistance. If such assistance is required, the services of a competent professional should be sought.

The anecdotes, mini-cases, and longer cases in each chapter are based on surveys and correspondence by the authors and their earlier work, E. W. Van Fleet & D. D. Van Fleet, *Violence at Work: What Everyone Should Know*, Charlotte, NC: Information Age Publishing, 2014.

Contents

Figures, tables and forms

FIGURES

TABLES

FORMS

About the authors

Drs. David and Ella Van Fleet have a combined total of over 75 years in teaching and research on management and organizations. David taught management, organizational behavior, leadership, and human relations management. Ella taught entrepreneurship, small business management, communication, and marketing. Having entered the business world in the 1960s, the Van Fleets have had the opportunity to observe and experience many changes in the ways in which organizations, government, and society in general view workplace behavior. They draw upon their research and their lengthy and impressive careers to provide examples, analyses and recommendations for dealing with bullying and harassment.

In addition to their many publications authored individually or with others, the Van Fleets have also authored the following articles together: Baseballs or Cricket Balls: On the Meanings of Bullying and Harassment (*Journal of Human Resource and Sustainability Studies*, 2018); Towards a Behavioral Description of Managerial Bullying (*Employee Responsibilities and Rights Journal*, 2012); Preventing Workplace Violence: The Violence Volcano Metaphor (*Journal of Applied Management and Entrepreneurship*, 2007); Internal Terrorists: The Terrorists Inside Organizations (*Journal of Managerial Psychology*, 2006); Terrorism and the Workplace: Concepts and Recommendations (in *Dysfunctional Behavior in Organizations*, JAI Press, 1998); and Workplace Violence: Moving Toward Minimizing Risks (Project Minerva publication, funded by OSHA,1996).

Among the several books they have completed are *Violence at Work: What Everyone Should Know* (Charlotte, NC: Information Age Publishing, 2014); *The Violence Volcano: Reducing the Threat of Workplace Violence* (Charlotte, NC: Information Age Publishing, 2010); and *Workplace Survival: Dealing with Bad Bosses, Bad Workers, Bad Jobs* (Frederick, MD: PublishAmerica, 2007).

David and Ella have also served on the Workplace Violence Prevention and Intervention Committee (WVPI) from 2009 through 2011. The WVPI is a committee of ASIS International (formerly the American Society for Industrial Security) and SHRM (the Society for Human Resource Management), that is tasked with developing national Workplace Violence Prevention and Intervention Standards.

Preface

Bullying and harassment – especially sexual harassment – as well as other unacceptable workplace behaviors pose problems for organizations. Numerous books and articles have been written about bullying, and the same is true for harassment. Human resource professionals may be uncertain as to which topic should be addressed, as examples of bullying and harassment yield numerous behaviors or incidents that are essentially the same. As a result, writing distinct policy statements is almost certain to cause confusion when policymakers and legislators need to reach a consensus.

Indeed, organizational policies and federal laws typically single out and attempt to define the two separately when, in fact, they may be more alike than different. It is time to move toward a recognition that organizations should address them at the same time, in the same way. This book is a first step toward educating everyone to move in that direction.

Following an analysis of articles dealing with bullying and harassment, bullying and harassment are treated as approximately equal to each other (hence, B≈H). Then a unique framework (V-REEL®) is presented for analyzing the organization's internal environment as it might influence bullying and/or harassment. Finally, there is a discussion of what constitutes, rather than what differentiates, bullying and harassment and, more importantly, what can be done now to try to eradicate it. The book should be used to educate everyone and anyone – individually or in schools, colleges or organizational training programs.

It should be noted that the focus of this book is on dysfunctional behavior that could impact an organization's reputation and possibly its bottom line and not on what is legal versus illegal. It is up to lawyers and legislators to wrestle with issues of legality. The concern here is with people in organizations – ensuring that they are treated with dignity and respect for the benefit of all.

EDUCATIONAL FEATURES

This book is intended to be educational when used by individuals or groups in classroom settings. To ensure the educational impact, there are several specific features:

- To get the reader to focus on the material, each chapter begins by asking readers to write down their thoughts before beginning the chapter.
- At the end of the chapter, readers are asked to review what they had written before reading the chapter and to reflect on the material they have just covered.
- Each chapter has numerous anecdotes that provide real-world examples of the material being presented.
- Each chapter has a mini case to help focus the reader on situations that might occur.
- Each chapter has several questions at the end to help readers review the material.
- Each chapter has one or more "action" items, usually a form to complete about the material in the chapter as it pertains to their organization. These are full-page so that they are convenient and useful for photocopying for individual or group use.
- In addition, each chapter has two cases designed for group discussions regarding the kinds of incidents discussed throughout the book.
- To aid readers even further, additional material is presented: an example of the sort of *survey* that might be used to assess conditions in the organization, a *glossary* of important terms, a *bibliography* of useful references, and a *listing* of EEOC, Health and Human Services, Offices of Tribal Affairs, and U.S. Human Rights Watch organization locations or contact information.

SPEAKING UP

Studies have shown that few of those who suffer harassment ever file a complaint. Hopefully, using the material and the framework of this book, more of those who are bullied or harassed will have the courage to speak up and address the problem.

Acknowledgments

The authors are indebted to the many individuals who responded to surveys and emails as we investigated bullying and harassment in workplaces and workplace violence. Many of those individuals spent considerable time detailing incidents for our use. In addition, the authors acknowledge the many helpful comments and suggestions on earlier drafts provided by our endorsers, as well as those of Marsha E. Rule, Esquire, and Richard Morrison, Principal at Transformation Solutions Group.

1. Bullying and harassment

When you think of bullying, what comes to mind? How about harassment? Write down what you feel are good definitions or descriptions of each of these so that you can keep them in mind as you read this chapter.

INTRODUCTION

Bullying and harassment are types of behaviors that unfortunately have become increasingly significant problems in our workplaces (Carbo & Hughes, 2010; Crothers & Lipinski, 2014; Einarsen et al., 2011; Parzefall & Salin, 2010; Rayner & Cooper, 2006; Rayner & Keashley, 2005). Because of the frequency of these behaviors and the costs associated with them, it is important to educate ourselves and others to distinguish these behaviors. We need to recognize them when we display them so that we can learn to avoid them. We also need to educate others so that they can avoid them. And of course, we need to see that all organizations take action to reduce or hopefully eliminate these unproductive types of behavior.

As noted in the Preface, the focus of this book is on dysfunctional behavior that could impact an organization's reputation and possibly its bottom line and not on what is legal versus illegal. It is up to lawyers and legislators to wrestle with issues of legality. Our concern is with people in organizations – ensuring that they are treated with dignity and respect for the benefit of all.

Bullying

Bullying can take many forms. One list consists of over 30 forms (ERC, 2013):

1. Aggression
2. Belittling
3. Blocking advancement or growth
4. Campaigning
5. Coercion
6. Constant change and inconsistency
7. Creating a feeling of uselessness
8. Criticism
9. Deceit

10. Diversion
11. Embarrassment
12. Ignoring
13. Impossible or changing expectations
14. Intimidation
15. Intrusion
16. Isolation/exclusion
17. Minimization
18. Mood swings
19. Offensive communication
20. Pitting employees against each other
21. Projection of blame
22. Punishment
23. Rationalization
24. Removal of responsibility
25. Revenge
26. Seduction
27. Shame and guilt
28. Taking credit
29. Threats
30. Undermining work
31. Withholding information

Given the length of this list, it should come as no surprise that at least 11% of workers are bullied in the workplace (Sansone & Sansone, 2015). It may be that as many as one out of five worldwide are exposed to bullying in their workplaces (Rayner et al., 2002). One study found that over 40% of workers in the United States had experienced at least one instance of psychological aggression (e.g., bullying or harassment) in one year (Schat et al., 2006). A 2019 report found that 94% of surveyed employees indicated that they had experienced workplace bullying with just over 51% indicating that the perpetrator was a boss or manager (Robinson, 2019). A more recent study found that 69% of women and 63% of men have personally become victims of workplace bullying although it was a co-worker rather than a manager who was identified as the perpetrator in 52% of the instances (Woolf, 2021). Regardless of which source of information you use, it is apparent that bullying in the workplace is a major problem facing organizations.

  Price (2021) suggests that bullying at work is identified by numerous specific behaviors. Those behaviors are intimidation, ignoring, condescension, constantly changing expectations, lying, taking credit, talking over you, gossiping, destructive criticism, disrespecting your time, dismissing your concerns, secrecy, lack of support, humiliation, misgendering you, favoritism, removal of duties, micromanagement, unwelcome sexual advances, blocking promotions, making fun of you, gaslighting, and, of course, physical violence. While this is a long list, you may be able to add to it based on your own experiences or observations. As you think about your own experiences, maybe you have had or seen a supervisor like this one:

SETS IMPOSSIBLE DEADLINES

My supervisor sets deadlines for me that are really impossible to meet and when I request information that might help me meet the deadlines, I get nothing useful. She usually just says "look it up"; or, if someone else is around to hear her put me down, she says, "Oh, no, here comes Mr. DoLittle." When I miss a deadline, ask for clarification of an assignment, or make any statements with which she disagrees, she says she is making a note of it to use when performance review time comes. She is setting me up for a bad review or maybe even an excuse to get rid of me.

Another recent report concluded that among employed Americans, 39% suffer abusive conduct at work, another 22% witness it, 61% are affected by it, and 73% are aware that workplace bullying happens (Namie, 2021, p. 6). That report also noted that 67% of perpetrators are men who usually target other men, but that women perpetrators choose women targets 65% of the time (p. 12). And further, it concluded that bosses are the most frequent perpetrators (p. 14).

Harassment

Harassment is similar to bullying; however, frequently harassment involves a sexual component. Again, many forms exist (Swartz Swidler LLC, 2019):

1. Harassment based on race
2. Harassment based on gender
3. Harassment based on religion
4. Harassment based on disability
5. Harassment based on sexual orientation
6. Age-related harassment
7. Personal harassment
8. Physical harassment
9. Power harassment
10. Psychological harassment
11. Online harassment

12. Retaliation harassment
13. Sexual harassment
14. Quid pro quo sexual harassment
15. Harassment by third parties
16. Verbal harassment

In addition, one study suggests that 32.8% of women reported experiencing at least one form of harassment based on the extent to which they did not meet traditionally held stereotypes of femininity (Main, 2021). Another study suggests that 25% to 75% of women report having been sexually harassed at some point in their careers (Seiner, 2021). And another recent study indicates that, in the workplace, 45% of respondents indicated that discrimination and harassment were prevalent issues for employers (Littler® Annual Employer Survey Report, 2021). So, harassment and particularly sexual harassment like bullying is a significant problem in the workplace that must be addressed.

Harassment from a legal perspective is governed by state laws, which vary by state (USLegal.com, 2021). Harassment is unwelcomed contact that becomes "unlawful where (1) enduring the offensive conduct becomes a condition of continued employment, or (2) the conduct is severe or pervasive enough to create a work environment that a reasonable person would consider intimidating, hostile, or abusive" (EEOC.gov, 2021). However, as noted earlier, our concern is not with what is or is not unlawful but rather with what impacts the dignity and respect of all members of organizations.

One law firm provides a long list of possible forms of harassment including discriminatory harassment based on race, gender, religion, disability, sexual orientation or age: and other forms, such as personal, physical, power, psychological, or verbal harassment. They also note that harassment could be online harassment, retaliation harassment, sexual harassment, quid pro quo sexual harassment, and even harassment by third parties (Swartz Swidler LLC, 2019).

On the other hand, Yahnke (2018) identified different types of harassment at work. Included were discrimination, personal, physical, power, psychological, online, retaliation, sexual, quid pro quo, third party, and verbal. Each of these, of course, could involve variations in the manner in which it would actually take place. But they capture a lot of the different forms of harassment. Schooley (2020) has a shorter list. She lists verbal, psychological, digital (cyberbullying), physical, and sexual harassment.

A study conducted by the U.S. Department of the Interior (Table 1.1) indicates that harassment has been shown to be associated with a variety of personal characteristics. Among those are age (the young or old), race (minorities), religion (those who are different from that of the perpetrator), or disability (physical or psychological). The study also suggested that the harassment tends to occur as frequently as three times a month. Interestingly,

Table 1.1   *Recent harassment rates*

Basis of harassment	Percentage experiencing harassment	Average times per month
Age	20.5	3.0
Racial/ethnic	9.3	3.0
Religious	7.1	2.9
Disability	6.1	3.2

Source: U.S. Department of the Interior, Work Environment Survey, January–March 2017.

it is age that is the group with the highest frequency of harassment. The young may be teased about their lack of experience while the elderly are harassed as being no longer relevant.

The number of charges filed with the EEOC gradually declined from 1997 until 2020 (Table 1.2) both in total and for sexual harassment. The percentage of charges based on race also has been declining. However, the percentage of harassment charges based on sex has remained fairly constant. Nevertheless, a recent study suggests that 38% of women and 14% of men have reported experiencing some form of sexual harassment at work (Kearl et al., 2019). The number of charges can be misleading because many women and men do not file complaints despite the fact that "25% to 85% of all American women experienced sexual harassment in the workplace in 2019" (Vuleta, 2021b).

As shown in Figure 1.1, women experience bullying, harassment and unwanted attention based on sex. Men, on the other hand, experience slightly more verbal abuse but considerably more humiliating behavior, and especially physical violence. More recently, 35% of workers feel they have been harassed at work with the most common forms being gender/sex (50%), race/ethnicity (17%), religion (15%), sexual orientation (13%) and age (14%) (Hiscox, 2018).

Understanding these statistics is not as easy as it may seem. Different definitions may have been employed in these and other studies. In addition, social media, in its various forms, provides opportunities for such behaviors in ways that did not exist in the past (Mainiero & Jones, 2013; Lucero et al., 2013). In an effort to distinguish bullying from isolated bad behavior, Britain reportedly stated that bullying occurs only when the conduct is persistent and frequent, lasting more than six months, and occurring at least once a week (Montalbán & Durán, 2005).

TERMS USED

Nevertheless, bullying and harassment may go by a variety of terms like deviance, aggression and antisocial behavior (Griffin & Lopez, 2005). Some of the

Table 1.2   *Harassment and sexual harassment charges filed with EEOC,*
                   1997–2020

Year	Total charges	% of charges based on sex	% of charges based on race	Harassment charges	Sexual harassment charges
1997	80,680	30.7	36.2	n/a	16,245
1998	79,591	30.7	36.2	n/a	15,442
1999	77,444	30.9	37.3	n/a	15,131
2000	79,896	31.5	36.2	n/a	15,592
2001	80,840	31.1	35.8	n/a	15,562
2002	84,442	30.2	35.4	n/a	14,626
2003	81,293	30.0	35.1	n/a	13,634
2004	79,432	30.5	34.9	n/a	13,222
2005	75,428	30.6	35.5	n/a	12,688
2006	75,768	30.7	35.9	n/a	12,104
2007	82,792	30.1	37.0	n/a	12,565
2008	95,402	29.7	35.6	n/a	13,930
2009	93,277	30.0	36.0	n/a	12,783
2010	99,922	29.1	35.9	27,356	11,852
2011	99,947	28.5	35.4	27,270	11,517
2012	99,412	30.5	33.7	26,777	13,359
2013	93,727	29.5	35.3	26,756	10,712
2014	88,778	29.3	35.0	26,820	10,208
2015	89,385	29.5	34.7	27,893	10,019
2016	91,503	29.4	35.3	28,216	9,805
2017	84,254	30.4	33.9	26,978	9,614
2018	76,418	32.3	32.2	26,699	11,342
2019	72,675	32.4	33.0	26,221	11,283
2020	67,448	31.7	32.7	24,221	9,671

Source: Charge statistics (charges filed with EEOC).

more common terms used to describe these behaviors are abusive management, aggressive management, dark side behaviors, emotional abuse, incivility, misbehavior, misconduct, psychological violence, sexual harassment and mobbing (for more complete sets of terms, see Grigoryan & Honnen-Weisdorn, 2019; Vardi & Weitz, 2016; Einarsen et al., 2002; Davenport et al., 2005).

Mobbing is a very unique form of bullying or harassment in that it involves dysfunctional behavior by a group. Sometimes referred to as "group bullying," mobbing in the workplace involves groups of people targeting a co-worker.

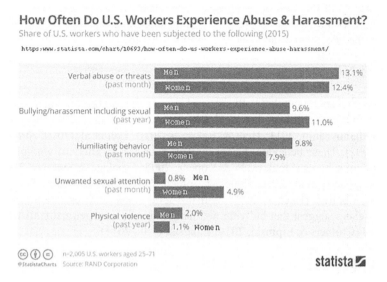

Figure 1.1   Comparison of abuse and harassment experienced between men and women

The group tries to isolate a particular person or humiliates him or her, or even acts aggressively toward them (e.g., pushing, shoving, bumping) (Cornoiu & Gyorgy, 2013; Keim & McDermott, 2010). Mobbing is particularly vile as it involves multiple individuals bullying or harassing an individual (Mulder et al., 2017; Montalbán & Durán, 2005). The group members may attempt to pass off the individual's work as their own. They may accuse the individual of things that he or she did not do. They try to create an intolerable environment for the individual. Tactics of mobbing may include the following (Peterson, 2019):

• Verbal aggression, including insults and sarcastic remarks;
• Ignoring suggestions, failing to provide feedback or other forms of stonewalling;
• Leaving the target's name off memos or emails, failing to notify the target of an important meeting, excluding him or her socially, or even relocating the target's workplace to a poor or distant location;
• Spreading gossip about the target – false information or true information that is embarrassing to the target;
• Resorting to physical aggression if the group members feel safe in doing so.

Regardless of the term or label used, such behaviors are unacceptable in the workplace and should be prevented from happening and quickly corrected when they do occur (Van Fleet & Van Fleet, 2014b).

EXTENT

Researchers point out that bullying and harassment have been found in numerous countries throughout the world (Chan et al., 2019; Saguy, 2011; Rosenthal & Budjanovcanin, 2011; Hoel & Einarsen, 2010; Loh et al., 2010; Smith et al., 2002). These behaviors have also been found in a variety of workplaces, including schools (Smokowski & Kopasz, 2005; Espelage & Swearer, 2003), nursing (Berry et al., 2016; Houck & Colbert, 2016), National Parks (Fonseca, 2017), libraries (Hecker, 2007), and fast-food stores and restaurants. Some researchers suggest that bullying and harassment occur in virtually all workplaces (Crothers & Lipinski, 2014; Einarsen et al., 2011).

IMPACT

Clearly, the types of behaviors that have been discussed are bad for both organizations and their members. Bullying and harassment have impacts on targets, witnesses and their organizations (Rayner et al., 2002). One study compared the impact of psychological aggression with that of sexual harassment and found that the effects of psychological aggression and bullying were significantly more severe than the effects of sexual harassment on outcome variables, such as job satisfaction, stress, anger and health (Lapierre et al., 2005).

Individuals can be impacted in terms of their health, including depression, anxiety and insomnia. Those who observe such behaviors can also be impacted. They may suffer lowered morale and productivity and, indeed, may seek employment elsewhere if they feel the organization is not acting to correct the situation. All employees may feel an increase in their life stress. And, of course, such behaviors can result in significant costs to the organization (Figure 1.2), including legal, medical, lowered productivity, emotional well-being, morale, turnover and burnout (Gumbus & Lyons, 2011; Needham, 2003).

The impact of bullying on an individual's health could be substantial. The effects could include insomnia, anxiety, depression, digestive disorders, musculoskeletal problems and cardiovascular illness. At the workgroup level, the effects may be decreases in motivation, morale, productivity or job satisfaction. It can also lead to a reluctance to report problems or to offer suggestions for improvement. Finally, organizations may experience skilled employees leaving, absenteeism increasing, more workers' compensation claims, a diminution of

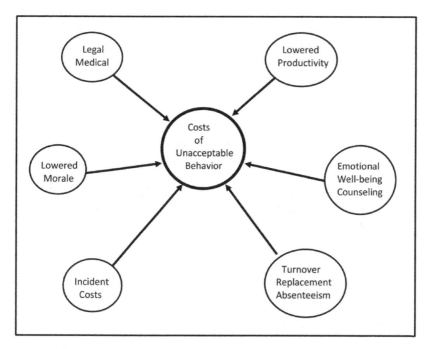

Figure 1.2　　Costs of unacceptable behavior

the quality of services performed, a damaged reputation, and difficulty in attracting highly qualified employees (Unknown, 2017).

One form of harassment, sexual, is particularly costly to individuals and organizations. For example, one study using risk premium analysis to calculate the statistical value of harassment (SVH) determined in 2017 that the costs of sexual harassment were $7.6 million (Hersch, 2018). In Australia, for instance, another estimate was that in that same year organizations lost $2.6 billion in productivity due to sexual harassment, with almost a third of that resulting from turnover (Deloitte, 2019, p. 5). It was also estimated that absenteeism accounted for 28% of costs with managerial time at 24% (Deloitte Access Economics, 2019, p. 5).

A Google search for examples of bullying and a search for examples of harassment yields numerous behaviors or incidents that are the same. Employing varying uses of the terms is almost certain to wreak havoc when policymakers and legislators need to reach a consensus, as when attempting to write distinct policy statements. Indeed, organizational policies and federal laws typically single out and attempt to define the two separately when, in fact, they may be more alike than different. If these two terms, bullying and harassment, do, in fact, describe behaviors that are significantly different, then distinct policy or legislative statements may be necessary (Miller & Mondschein, 2012).

Consider the case of Carl. Is he being bullied or harassed? Or both? It may depend on whom you ask.

EVERYONE IS YELLING AT ME

Every time I turn around, it seems like someone is yelling at me. No matter what I say or do, no matter how well I do my job, someone cusses me out. I don't know why I get picked on this way. Every once in a while, someone else gets yelled at, but I get it several times a day and from just about everyone. I complained to my boss, but he said, "Carl, don't waste my time with your whining. Take it or get another job." No help there so I'm unsure what I can or should do.

Carl's case exemplifies the problem of trying to reach a clear and unambiguous definition of bullying and harassment – which is it? Consider another example, the case of Mary and a co-worker who does not appreciate Mary's humor.

MARY'S JOKES AREN'T FUNNY

Mary did it again! What's with her and her sarcastic comments and stupid jokes. She just seems to enjoy watching me when my face turns red or when everybody sees that I don't know what to say. It might not be so bad if anyone else was the butt of her jokes, but it always seems to be me. I've spoken to her about it, and she says, "You just can't take a joke." That's basically what our supervisor says, too. She says Mary is just joking, so don't be so uptight about it.

If you were Mary's co-worker, might you consider Mary's little jokes as bullying? Or as harassing? This seems to be harassment, but given the co-worker's response, it could certainly be considered bullying as well.

In one study of bullying, we found that "negative managerial behavior directed at a particular employee, especially in the presence of others, is highly likely to be seen as bullying" (Van Fleet & Van Fleet, 2012, p. 210). The managerial adage to "praise in public and punish in private" is based on the recognition that public criticism is notoriously damaging not just to the individual being subjected to it but also to others who observe the incident.

PUBLIC DISCIPLINE IS NOT WORKING

Discipline in our group is not handled privately. If a group member is disciplined for any reason, everyone including those outside the group is made aware of it. The reason, according to management, is to make an example of anyone's mistakes so that others will not make the same mistake. However, it is embarrassing and degrading and hasn't seemed to reduce mistakes. Instead, everyone tries to hide any mistakes to avoid being called out.

One striking point in this chapter is that many of the terms used to describe bullying are the same as many of the terms used to describe harassment. Are they really just variations on the same theme? Are they just two ways of talking about the same issue? The next chapter explores these questions in more detail.

MINI CASE: WORK DISRUPTIONS

I work for an organization that has a different kind of harasser. My supervisor gets anonymous notes discrediting me or other workers. He says he doesn't pay attention to the notes, but I'm not so sure.

At other times, personal equipment would not work. We would discover that the phone was disconnected or the cable for the printer was somehow unplugged, or the network connection wouldn't work, and we'd find the cable there unplugged. Documents were also impacted. Sometimes *they* were merely misplaced but other times they disappeared altogether.

In an effort to deal with whoever is doing this, several of us are taking turns at coming to work early, working a bit late, and taking turns for lunch and breaks. This seems to work but it is a pain so I don't know how long we can keep it up.

1. Is this harassment or is it bullying?
2. What do you think needs to be done?
3. Should you ask your manager to videotape the after-hours visitor?

THINK ABOUT THIS CHAPTER AGAIN

Look at the definitions or descriptions you wrote down at the beginning of this chapter. How might you change those now? Then take a few minutes to prepare responses to the following questions and actions. In particular, human resource instructors and students should do this to be better prepared to deal with B≈H issues. Make your responses as if you are working in an organization. The responses should then be discussed by all students or participants.

Introductory Questions

1.   What forms of bullying and harassment exist in your organization? Try to be specific (use the form in the *Actions section* below).
2.   What specific actions have you or your organization taken to reduce these forms?
3.   Cite at least five of the seven different costs of these forms to your organization.

Introductory Actions

1.   Draft policy statements specific to your organization.
2.   Use the following form to record your responses to Introductory Question #1 in the *Questions section* above. Be as specific as possible and indicate (1) what the behavior was that you observed or experienced, (2) who the perpetrator was, (3) who the target was, and (4) whether it was bullying or harassment.

The form is on a separate page to enable photocopying for classroom or individual use.

INSTRUCTIONS FOR FORM 1

Bullying and Harassment in my Organization

> *Behavior Column*: Briefly describe what happened – the behavior.
> *Perp. Column*: Perpetrator or Offender was (E) an employee/worker, (M) a manager, or (O) someone else (supplier or customer).
> *Targ. Column*: Target or Victim was (E) an employee/worker, (M) manager, or (O) someone else (supplier or customer).
> *The B or H column*: (B) if you feel the behavior was bullying, (H) if you feel it was harassment, or (BH) if you feel it could be either or both.

CHAPTER 1 CASES

These cases are based on actual situations with identifying names and locations changed or omitted. While anyone would benefit from reading and thinking about these cases, they are best used in a group context where different individual perspectives could be bought forth.

Form 1   *Bullying and harassment in my organization*

BULLYING AND HARASSMENT IN MY ORGANIZATION			
The behavior	Perp.	Targ.	B or H
1.			
2.			
3.			
4.			
5.			
6.			

Case 1.1: Hypercritical Boss

Jane is a 45-year-old woman, married with two grown children. They live in a suburban community near a large city. Years ago, after receiving a college degree in business administration from a nearby university, she began working in the payroll department of a sizable company in the city. Over the years, she has gradually worked her way up to a lead or supervisory position. While she still does some payroll work, she has finally been put in charge of the employees in one section of the department. She thoroughly enjoys her work and is well respected by the members of her group even though most of them are quite a bit younger than she is. She is rightfully proud of her work and that of the group under her.

Then along came George. Jane described him: "George was the kind of boss who is really a backward boss – a double sob! He likes to stand by my desk and turn red in the face while pointing out any minute error he could see as well as some he couldn't see. His style was to criticize, repeat the criticism, and then summarize the criticism once more for all to hear." He soon began applying the same tactics directly to members of Jane's staff. Jane has become just one more case of psychological aggression at work.

Jane says, "I spoke with him about his going directly to my staff but got nowhere, so I took the issue up with his manager, noting that his behavior was impacting the performance of both my staff and me. I told his manager that people are starting to get frustrated and disgruntled and might begin leaving the company if George continues to go unchecked." That manager responded, "I'll be retiring soon, and I need him to provide some continuity after I leave. I will speak to him, though." But nothing changed.

Jane's staff looked to her for help. She told them, "I've spoken to George and gotten nowhere. I've now also taken the matter to his boss, but his boss lacks both the management skills and the intestinal fortitude to do anything about him. She says the company needs him to replace her when she retires. I don't know what to tell you other than just grin and bear it or pack it in and leave."

Jane then consulted with her husband about the situation. He said essentially the same thing she had told her staff – grin and bear it or leave. However, he also noted, "Now that the kids are grown, we don't really need the additional income from your job. And we've got a good-sized nest egg put away to cover emergencies." Shortly thereafter, Jane and one other person left the company.

1. To what sort of psychological aggression is Jane being subjected?
2. How would you label that behavior?
3. What do you think Jane should have done in this situation?
4. What would you do if you were in Jane's situation?
5. How might an organization prevent this sort of situation in the future?

Case 1.2: Supervisor Intimidated

Donald is a nice young man but the few friends he has all say that he is a bit dull and boring. When they go out for a few drinks, he is careful not to drink too much but he nevertheless frequently acts like he has had one too many. He is good-looking, he is well mannered, he dresses impeccably, and he carries himself well. He has a relatively low-paying and rather routine office job in a major corporation. He handles incoming calls, helps to manage the filing system, greets clients and visitors on occasion, does some routine word processing, and helps keep the breakroom clean. Although he struggled academically, taking over six years to earn a bachelor's degree, he nevertheless managed to receive an MBA (Master of Business Administration) from an online program.

Including his supervisor, Donald is the only person in the office with an MBA. After he got the degree, he had it nicely framed. He then put it in his work area for everyone to see and made a point of calling it to their attention. Soon thereafter, he began to change. He began to act as if he were the only one who knew how to do anything, calling attention to his "higher" education.

One of the first noticeable changes was how he interacted with his supervisor. He began to intimidate his supervisor by being oversensitive and overly dramatic. His supervisor states, "He walks out of meetings if he doesn't get his way. He seems to be either on the verge of tears or so angry that it concerns me, so I meet with him privately to calm him down. I try to explain that he isn't some sort of target and that people do listen to what he has to say. However, he seems to think that having an MBA means that he is always right and that everyone else is wrong. He just doesn't listen to anyone else's point of view. But given his repeating behavior, I'm not sure I'm getting through to him."

His co-workers have voiced their feelings about Donald. "He has become mister bigshot and will report other employees to managers for the smallest things that bother him. If he isn't happy, no one else is going to be happy. It's his way or the highway, and he doesn't hesitate to call attention to his having a degree that no one else has. He is like a bully on whose bad side you don't want to be on." In order to avoid having to help anyone with their questions, he would wear headphones so he had a reason to shut everyone out, pretending he could not hear them. He always had to be recognized for every little thing he did, or he threw a fit. Most people stayed away from him or pretended to be his friend to his face to avoid being tattled about or told on. They knew he could find a reason to get them into trouble.

1. What sort of psychological aggression is Donald displaying in this case?
2. How would you label that behavior?

3. What do you think Donald's supervisor should do in this situation? What should his co-workers do?
4. What do you think Donald's supervisor will do in this situation?
5. How might the organization prevent this sort of situation in the future?

2.   What is B≈H?

Have your views of bullying and harassment changed as a result of what you read in the previous chapter? Using your current ideas, changed or not, write down what you now feel are good definitions of both bullying and harassment. Keep those definitions in mind as you read this chapter.[1]

INTRODUCTION

Bullying and Harassment seem to be regarded as different forms of unacceptable behavior. But they also may be regarded as similar, in that both are viewed as unacceptable behaviors in the workplace. Think about your understanding of those two terms and consider this incident.

COORDINATOR PICKS ON ME

During a major weather event, my coordinator called my home and told me I was really needed at work. He assured me that others were already there to help. So, I battled the weather to show up; but when I got there, I found out that I was the only person there. I had to figure out how to fix the issue with no help. Very stressful. This was not the first time this sort of thing has happened. He seems to take pleasure in picking on me over and over again. When will I learn to just say no?

Is the coordinator Bullying this person or is he Harassing him? Are Bullying and Harassment really different or just different labels for the same thing? Because they do seem so similar, a more careful examination would be helpful. Thus, in an attempt to determine whether the words Bullying and Harassment describe significantly different behaviors, content analysis was employed (Van Fleet, White, & Van Fleet, 2018).

CONTENT ANALYSIS

Content analysis is a well-established research tool that is typically used to determine relationships among words, given the presence of certain words, themes or concepts within a qualitative data set (Riffe et al., 2005). As such, content analysis has the potential to be a useful method in understanding how Bullying and Harassment are alike or different. Content analysis consists of both quantitative (focused on counting and measuring) and qualitative (focused on interpreting and understanding) components (Luo, 2021). It has been described as being a systematic, replicable technique for compressing many words of text into a few content categories based on explicit rules of coding. It has also been described as a technique for making inferences by systematically and objectively identifying specified characteristics of messages (Stemler, 2000).

A major reason for using content analysis is that it enables the use of data sets consisting of very large numbers of words (Roberts, 1997). There are several other advantages to the use of content analysis (Luo, 2019). It involves unobtrusive data collection so there is no direct involvement of participants who could bias the results. It is readily replicable by other researchers by using the same database and following the same methodology. And it is flexible in that it can be performed at any time, in any location and at a low cost. As such, it enables researchers to identify and describe relationships among the words in the data set. Content analysis also allows inferences to be made. These inferences can then be substantiated using other data collection methods (Stemler, 2000).

To conduct content analysis, Symphony Software© (www.activejava.com) was employed. Symphony© is a software tool from Active Java that is used for organizing, analyzing and reporting text analyses. Its primary use has been to gather opinions or identify underlying themes from multiple sources of text. This technique allowed the researchers to determine whether scholars were using similar or different words when writing about Bullying and Harassment. More specifically, Symphony© allows the construction of "word clouds" (a visual representation of word frequency; Atenstaedt, 2012) that could then corroborate findings from the clouds with multidimensional scaling (MDS).

The data set that was used consisted of articles listed in the 2016 edition of the Social Science Citation Index online (Van Fleet et al., 2018). First, all articles dealing with Bullying were identified using both titles and abstracts. Then those concerning Harassment were similarly identified. To be even more inclusive, articles dealing with Abusive Management or Abusive Supervision, in general, were included (Tepper et al., 2011). The Bullying search yielded 4,667 citations. The Harassment search added 5,086 more words. The Abusive Management or Supervision search did not add much as it contributed only 392 more words. After removing non-applicable words (e.g., articles, prepositions, proper names, specific geographic locations, and terms associated purely with research methods such as logit and intercorrelations), a final data set consisting of 14,129 unique words was used for the analysis.

IDENTIFYING WORD CLOUDS

Word clouds (also known as text clouds or tag clouds) are figures in which the size of each word indicates its frequency or importance (Abulaish et al., 2013). They work in a straightforward way: The more a specific word appears in a database of text, the bigger and bolder it appears in the word cloud (DaPaolo & Wilkinson, 2014). A word cloud, then, is a group of words depicted in different sizes. Using different fonts, more frequent words appear larger than words that occur less often (Scott & Wolfe, 2016).

Clouds are more qualitative than quantitative, in that they do not tell how many more times a word appears than another but rather only indicate that one word appears more often than another (Tessem et al., 2015). The bigger and bolder the word appears, the more often it's mentioned within a given text and the more important it is. Thus, word clouds can compare and contrast different pieces of text to find the wording similarities between them (Atenstaedt, 2012; Edyburn, 2010).

Bullying Word Cloud

The words most clearly associated with Bullying were *behave, experience, social, target, relate, violence, associate, age, self* and *effect*. Bullying also includes *name-calling, physically pushing* and *shoving*, or *verbally threatening*. Interestingly, *harass* and *abuse* do not appear among the 50 most frequent words in the Bullying word cloud. An examination of the word cloud indicated that Bullying refers to actions being done by someone more powerful emotionally, physically, or organizationally.

Harassment Word Cloud

The words most clearly associated with Harassment were *male, female, behave, experience, social, sex, respond, gender, relate, race* and *women*. The Harassment word cloud also includes *labeling, name-calling*, or *threatening to label* the target in some way. *Bully* and *abuse* both appear among the 50 most frequent words in the Harassment word cloud. Harassment also was associated with *organizations* and *workplaces*. Harassment may also be associated with *violent actions*, including *suicide*. Non-Sexual Harassment is likely to be perceived as behavior that is repeated over some period of unstated time, such as *stalking* and *getting revenge*.

When scholars write about Bullying, Harassment is only infrequently mentioned. On the other hand, when writing about Harassment, Bullying is frequently mentioned, perhaps suggesting that Harassment is the more inclusive concept. But the results also indicate that Bullying and Harassment are more alike than they are different. However, when the focus is on children instead of adults, Bullying is the word most often used.

Harassment can result from an individual being unhappy with a co-worker, particularly if one has "turned in" the other. As indicated in this instance, the disclosure may seem mild, but its impact may be great.

CO-WORKER COMMENTS CAN LEAD TO TROUBLE

Ever since I told our supervisor that Joe was taking advantage of our relatively lax schedules by coming late and leaving early, Joe has been on my case. All I did was casually mention it to the coordinator, but given Joe's reaction, you'd think I had filed some sort of formal complaint. He is determined to get even, and he means to do that by harassing me to death. In the future, I'll just keep my mouth shut rather than incur someone else's wrath.

Because Harassment is recurring and impacts the person's work, it could also be considered Bullying. Recurring behaviors may be subtle but nevertheless detrimental to work performance. Harry is one co-worker who seems to have made himself the No.1 Pest while everyone else ignores him.

HARRY, MY CO-WORKER PEST

It's really hard for me to concentrate on my work because of Harry. He seems to be everywhere I turn – constantly coming by my work area, turning up in the break room when I'm there, and pestering me about trivial matters mostly not connected to our work. I don't think he is coming on to me as he has never suggested having lunch or dinner; and, thankfully, he hasn't bothered me at home either. But his constant presence at work is getting to me.

Harry's motives aren't clear. They don't have to be. While his behavior is clearly impacting this co-worker, a casual observer may not even see a problem here. Many supervisors would brush off complaints about Harry with comments like "live with it" or "It's no big deal. Just ignore him and get to work." In doing so, the supervisor compounds the problem and becomes part of it going forward.

Entire Set Word Cloud

A word cloud of the complete set of words was developed. Bully was the central word but Harass was nearby. Other nearby words were *behave, experience, victim, self, associate, relate, social, sex, peer* and *work*. Somewhat surprisingly, *abuse* and *aggressive* are more distant. Frequency of occurrence in and of itself is not sufficient to fully understand the relationship between the words Bullying and Harassment. Both words occurred frequently in the information set used. The more important issue is how often are they used together? To answer that question, a further analysis was necessary.

Action Words Analysis

Because these incidents seem common and unclear as to whether they represent Bullying or Harassment, an examination of numerous words associated with action or the result of action was conducted.

Action Words examined were *aggressive, assault, behave, bully, harass, participate, respond, stalk, suicide, tease, trauma, target, violence* and *violent*. Interestingly, no words indicating *repetition* or *repeated actions* occurred, indicating that *repetition* is not a necessary component of either Bullying or Harassment, although repetition could clearly make things worse for the victim. Repetition by one perpetrator can lead to others following suit.

MANAGER'S BEHAVIOR COPIED BY WORKERS

My supervisor has been constantly commenting on things I do or don't do. She says my clothes are too casual for our office. She ridicules me for anything and everything. Recently, she said I shouldn't eat so much fast food. Now co-workers have picked up on her comments and suggest that I am "a bit heavy" and should cut down on the number of calories I get. My weight does not impact my job performance, so why is it anyone else's business?

In examining action-oriented words, Bullying involves mostly *physical actions*, although *verbal actions* are also noted. Harassment frequently refers to *sexual references* and also words involving *labeling, name-calling*, or *threatening to label the target*.

Because of the sizable overlap between Bullying and Harassment, a final word cloud was obtained *for the complete set* of words. *Bully* was the central word, with *harass* close by. *Abuse* and *aggressive* also appear but are seen as more distant. But the frequency of occurrence is not the full story. A more interesting question is how often are they used together. To understand that involved multidimensional scaling.

MULTIDIMENSIONAL SCALING

Multidimensional scaling (MDS) is a method of exploratory data analysis in which large amounts of data are condensed into a relatively simple spatial map so that important relationships are identified (Cox & Cox, 2008). It results in a visual representation of distances or similarities between sets of objects. The distance between pairs of points corresponds to the dissimilarity or similarity between the words in the database (Gronau & Lee, 2020). MDS is an especially useful technique for researchers because it can reveal like and unlike words. MDS, then, can represent measurements of similarity (or dissimilarity) among pairs of objects as distances between points of a multidimensional space.

Borg and Groenen (2005) indicate that MDS serves four purposes:

1. To represent similarity or dissimilarity of information as distances between words in order to make the information accessible for visual inspection and exploration.
2. To allow testing to distinguish among different objects of interest.
3. To discover the dimensions that underlie elements of similarity and dissimilarity.
4. To present a psychological model that explains judgments of dissimilarity.

The first two purposes are the most important ones in developing any distinctions between Bullying and Harassment. The distinction would help to determine if snide comments are bullying or harassment.

SNIDE REMARKS HURT

I've put up with snide comments for years, but recently a new foreman has emboldened my co-workers. They not only comment on my accent but have used the N-word when I can overhear them gossiping. I asked the foreman to do something about it and he said, "That's the nature of the world today so either put up with it or get out." So, I then went to his boss, who said he'd look into it. That was months ago and nothing has happened. I'm getting so depressed that I have thought about suicide.

MDS is particularly useful for dealing with either nominal or ordinal data (Chabowski et al., 2015; Hout et al., 2013; Jaworska & Chupetlovska-Anastasova, 2009). MDS can be used to identify similarities or a sense of "sameness" or similarity among groups of items such as words. As used here, it can assist in interpreting results reported in published articles (Mugavin, 2008; Cox & Cox, 2001). "More formally, MDS refers to a set of statistical techniques that are used to reduce the complexity of a data set, permitting visual appreciation of the underlying relational structures contained therein" (Hout et al., 2013, p. 93).

The MDS results in this study suggest that *bully, harass, violence, women* and *suicide* are clustered, with *aggressive, target* and *cyberbullying* close by (Van Fleet et al., 2018). *Work, workplace, discriminate* and *race* are also clustered with another nearby cluster of *public, management, job, worker, employee, organization* and *organizable*. Interestingly, *nurse* appeared by itself near the word *bully*. Bully(ing) and Harass(ment) appear quite close to one another, suggesting that they frequently occur together and share many words in common, including *aggressive, target, cyberbullying, race, discrim-inate, work* and *workplace*. They are separated only by words such as *women, violence* and *suicide*, which suggests that those are key terms in differentiating Bullying and Harassment.

The MDS results also noted that the words *management, job, work, employee, organization* and *organizable* are related and also very close to *race* and *discriminate*.

So, when an incident like the following occurs, one may need to examine the personal characteristics, including the race of the worker and boss.

MY BOSS OVERLOADS ME WITH WORK

I don't know if my boss hates me or thinks I'm wonderful because he is constantly overloading me with jobs, many of which are beyond my current pay grade. Maybe he thinks he is helping me develop, or maybe he thinks I'll get fed up with it and quit. I can't always do the jobs and have to get help from my co-workers to complete them. But that doesn't seem to matter to the boss. I just feel that I'm being asked to do more than anyone else.

A few observations and definitions seem appropriate to summarize here:

- Improper (bad) behavior refers to any form of intentional (as opposed to accidental) behavior that is potentially injurious to individuals or the organization (Griffin & Lopez, 2005).
- Improper physical behavior is more likely to be termed Bullying.
- Improper behavior directed toward children is usually identified as Bullying, although increasingly, Adult Bullying is being recognized (Lutgen-Sandvik, 2013; Howard et al., 2016).

- Improper managerial behavior involving verbal criticism done publicly is Bullying (Van Fleet & Van Fleet, 2012).
- Improper behavior involving name-calling or related actions is labeled Harassment. Improper behavior involving sexual content is Sexual Harassment (Boland, 2005).

NOW WHAT?

As illustrated by the incidents noted in this chapter and the preceding one, the two concepts of Bullying and Harassment are so interrelated that you may not know when or if Bullying transforms into Harassment or vice versa. The relevant and important question is: Does it matter what label is used? If a particular behavioral incident is described, some will label it as Bullying and some as Harassment, but the label is not what is important – the behavior is what is important.

So, this book concentrates on unacceptable behaviors in the workplace with the intent of understanding those behaviors regardless of definitions or labels that might be applied to those behaviors. The concern is to identify behaviors that are unacceptable regardless of one's position in the company. Thus, in addition to workplace behaviors associated with Bullying and Harassment, unacceptable behavior, in general, will be discussed. Behaviors involving co-workers, managers, or even third parties will be examined. Then a unique way will be presented to assist individuals and organizations in identifying the forces that contribute to unacceptable behavior and those forces that help to reduce such behavior. Finally, the role that legislation and regulations play in dealing with and hopefully reducing these sorts of behaviors will be noted.

Therefore, Bullying and Harassment will be addressed but with no further effort to differentiate them. Toward that end, those kinds of behavior will be referred to using a shorthand expression B≈H (pronounced simply by the letters "BH") to note that Bullying and Harassment are approximately the same but also to include other similar forms of dysfunctional behavior. To make clear the similarities, specific illustrations of real-world characteristics of unacceptable workplace behavior (B≈H) will be included as well as what to do about them. The more closely employers look at such abusive behavior, the more they will come to realize that there are steps that they can take to either eliminate or significantly reduce the incidence of those in their organizations.

Academics, researchers, lawyers and human resource professionals quibble over precise definitions (Crawshaw, 2009). Much of this is precisely because politicians are trying to develop legislation. In the past, the primary sources available to them were limited to organizations such as:

* Society for Human Resource Management;
* Occupational Safety & Health Administration;
* U.S. Department of Labor;
* U.S. Equal Employment Opportunity Commission;
* U.S. Department of Education, Office for Civil Rights;
* U.S. Department of Justice, Civil Rights Division;
* National Institutes of Health;
* Human Resource Division of the Academy of Management;
* Regional and/or state agencies or affiliate organizations to the national ones.

While these are commendable sources, organizations should use the following definition so that there is only a need for a single policy. As a result of prior work on bullying and harassment, then, the following inclusive definition is proposed:

> *B≈H refers to verbal or physical conduct that explicitly or implicitly affects an individual's health, unreasonably interferes with an individual's work performance, or creates an intimidating, hostile, or offensive work environment.* (Based on Van Fleet et al., 2018, p. 144.)

Thus, B≈H is a shorthand way of referring to dysfunctional words and behaviors that includes but is not limited to bullying and harassment at the workplace.

Based on this research, it is recommended that a group (e.g., committee, task force) of managers and non-managers develop a single policy. That policy should begin with a statement much like the following.

> This organization endeavors to create and maintain an environment in which people are treated with dignity, decency and respect. That environment shall be characterized by mutual trust and the absence of intimidation, oppression and exploitation. The organization will not in any instance tolerate bullying, discrimination, harassment, unlawful behavior of any kind, or B≈H. B≈H refers to words and behaviors that comprise inappropriate pressure, coercion or intimidation. Through enforcement of this policy and by training and educating its employees, the organization will seek to prevent, correct, and discipline behavior that violates this policy.

The policy statement should then provide detailed specifics and examples as to what behaviors would be covered (using examples from the group's personal experiences or those in this book), how individuals should report incidents (see Chapter 8), what should be done if such a report is made (see Chapter 9), and the consequences to the perpetrator if true and to the person making a claim if it is false (see Chapter 9).

Whether your organization has one policy or two or more, to eradicate B≈H everyone in the organization will need to be educated and trained. That training should include the types, forms, examples and recommendations that are covered in the following chapters (see Chapter 9 for details).

MINI CASE: GET OTHERS TO DO THEIR WORK

Tom manipulates his supervisor and others to get them to do his work for him. When he is with his supervisor, he is all smiles and charming. But when he is with a co-worker, he works himself up to a frenzy, making them feel that they are not doing their part when it really is him not doing his part. He leaves early and takes a long lunch hour. He doesn't want to do the work and just puts it off, knowing that his co-workers will complete it.

He takes credit for the work of the group but accepts no blame if something is wrong. He will agree with the supervisor and imply that he just couldn't convince his co-workers about it. He will no doubt soon be in management because he seems to have no conscience and he is an expert at getting others to do his work.

1.   Is Tom a bully or not?
2.   What can an organization do with people like Tom?
3.   What can the targeted or molested employee do to convince the perpetrator not to ask him for help?
4.   What suggestions can you give co-workers for "Just saying no" when asked for help?

THINK ABOUT THIS CHAPTER AGAIN

As with the last chapter, look at the definitions or descriptions you wrote down at the beginning of this chapter. Then take a few minutes to prepare responses to the following questions and actions. In particular, managers and human resource professionals should do this to be better prepared to handle B≈H in their organizations. Make your responses as if you are working in an organization. The responses should then be discussed by all students or participants.

B≈H: Questions

1.   As in the previous chapter, what B≈H exists in your organization? Try to be specific (see form below under *B≈H Actions*).

2. Again, what specific actions have you personally taken in an effort to reduce B≈H?
3. What specific actions has your organization taken to reduce B≈H?
4. In your view, at what point does *bullying* transform into *harassment* or vice versa?

B≈H: Actions

1. Draft a single policy statement that is specific to your organization.
2. Expanding on what you did in the previous chapter, use the following form to record your responses to Question #1 above. Remember, you no longer differentiate *bullying* and *harassment* but simply use B≈H to refer to all the unacceptable behaviors. Again, be as specific as possible (especially in describing the behavior) and indicate: (1) What was the specific behavior? (2) Who was the perpetrator? (3) Who was the target? (4) How do you know about the B≈H?

The form is on a separate page to enable photocopying for use individually or by groups.

INSTRUCTIONS FOR FORM 2

B≈H Behaviors

B≈H Column: What was the specific behavior? Briefly describe what happened.
Perp. Column: Perpetrator or Offender was (E) an employee/worker, (M) a manager, or (O) someone else (supplier or customer).
Targ. Column: Target or Victim was (E) an employee/worker, (M) manager, or (O) someone else (supplier or customer).
How Column: How you learned about the behavior: from the (P) Perpetrator, (T) the target/victim, (M) a manager, (E) another employee, or (O) a contact outside the company.

CHAPTER 2 CASES

These cases are based on actual situations with identifying names and locations changed or omitted. While anyone would benefit from reading and thinking about these cases, they are best used in a group context where different individual perspectives could be bought forth.

Form 2   *B≈H behaviors*

B≈H BEHAVIORS			
B≈H Behaviors	Perp.	Targ.	How
1.			
2.			
3.			
4.			
5.			
6.			

Case 2.1: Gossiping Co-workers

Ananya is 43 years old. She came to the United States from Mumbai, India when she was just a teenager. Just a year or two later, she found a partner, so she is now married with two teenaged children. Both she and her husband have jobs, but both of their jobs are relatively low-paying. They cannot afford to buy and insure a new car, so they drive an 11-year-old Ford. And the American dream of owning their own home is so far-fetched that they don't even discuss it. Both of their incomes are needed just to meet the expenses of their four-person family. More than anything else, their major desire is for their two children to go to college.

Ananya's husband works as a night janitor in a local bank and sometimes gets an opportunity to work on a cleanup crew after football or baseball games. She has a somewhat better job. Although the pay is about the same, the work is less strenuous. She works in a warehouse for a mid-sized business. She sorts and counts parts to keep an accurate inventory count. The job is not difficult, but it is tedious and boring. Her company has just over 60 employees in three locations. Since each location has relatively few employees, a rather loose managerial atmosphere has developed over time. Perhaps, as a result, the company is known as a great place to work, and employee confidence and enthusiasm are generally quite high.

Recently, however, Ananya's behavior and performance have changed. She had always been a hard worker with good performance evaluations, but in the past few months, she has been late to work several times, her performance has fallen off, and she has requested sick leave a couple of times. Her supervisor has asked her, "What is going on? You have always been a good worker, but lately, you seem to not want your job anymore." She doesn't respond with much information and, indeed, seems evasive about her situation, so he thinks perhaps she is having some personal problems. After several attempts to get her to relax and talk about her problem, he suggests that she might be more comfortable talking with someone in the human resources department, which is located in a different site than the one in which she works.

When Ananya meets with Celia, an HR representative, she blurts out, "I'm being harassed!" She goes on to say, "A couple of my co-workers have begun questioning me about how I handle my work and every decision I make. They interrupt me at work, causing me to be less productive." Ananya finally tells Celia that she believes they criticize her work to her supervisor and that they may be the source of rumors and gossip about her marriage. She breaks down and cries, "I don't know what to do. I'm at my wit's end. I need the job, but those two make it difficult for me."

Celia asks Ananya if she has filed a complaint, to which she shrugs her shoulders and replies, "With whom?" Celia offers her a "complaint form" and suggests that she also talk with some of her co-workers and try to find out why they appear to dislike her. "They won't talk with me, remember?" Ananya says as she glares at Celia. Celia then suggests that Ananya "go through the proper channels"—talk with your supervisor and, if you are not pleased with the results, come back here to HR and "we'll find an acceptable solution." Ananya doesn't bother to tell her about the conversation she has already had with her supervisor. "Another dead end," she thinks as she leaves Celia's office. "So, it is true that HR is for management, not the workers."

1. How would you label the behavior of the various individuals in this case: Ananya? Her co-workers? Her supervisor? Celia? Is there bullying going on? Is harassment involved?
2. What do you think Ananya *should have done* in this situation?
3. What do you think Ananya *should do now*, in her current situation?
4. How might the organization prevent this sort of situation in the future?
5. Should the loose managerial atmosphere be "tightened" and, if so, how?

Case 2.2: Older Worker

I'm Gerald Jackson. I'm 62 years old and have been working in the inventory department for this company for just over 20 years. The company pays well, has an excellent benefits package, and has a nice retirement plan. The latter is particularly important to me given my age.

All the other employees in the department are young women. They are about 35–40 years old and the people with whom we interact are also mostly women. While I can't say it has always been fun working here as the only male in an all-female department, it has not been a bad place to work. That is until recently. A new woman, Olivia, was added to our department a while back. She is a lot younger than me; actually, everyone in the department is younger than me. While I'm the most senior employee, I still have a few years to go before I'm eligible to take advantage of the company's retirement plan.

But as I said, it is recent events that have made this job less than desirable. Here is what has been happening. When there is no third party around to see what she is doing, Olivia blocks the walkways for me. I move to the side; she moves to cut me off. She keeps it up until I'm late getting to work or returning to work. Recently she has gotten others to do the same thing so that if I report it to management, it will appear less believable because it would mean that everyone was out to get me. I need some intervention from management but I'm not sure that I'll get any if I ask.

Blocking me so that I can't meet my production quota seems to be their goal as I have always been one of the top performers in the department. A couple of times as I headed for the restroom, she leaned in front of the door and wouldn't move until I pushed by her to get it. On a couple of other occasions, when I arrived in the parking lot, they even went so far as to box in my car so that I'd either be late for work or barely on time and unable to keep up my good performance. This is driving me crazy! If this keeps up, I don't know what I'll do. But if this keeps up, I think that I should talk to our supervisor about this and see if he can get it stopped.

It wouldn't have surprised me if these had been younger males, as young guys might be prone to "get to" an older worker like me. But I did not expect such behavior from younger women. I tried making Olivia feel more knowledgeable by asking her questions to help me, but she obviously did not want to help me. I have complimented her and others, but thus far the situation has not changed.

1. Is Olivia bullying Gerald or is she harassing him? How would you decide which it is?
2. If you were Gerald, what would you do in this situation?
3. What should he do?
4. Have you ever encountered a situation like this, and, if so, how did you handle it?
5. How might the organization prevent this sort of situation in the future?

NOTE

1. This chapter draws heavily on Van Fleet, White, & Van Fleet (2018).

3.   Types and examples

Recall the definitions that you wrote for bullying and harassment at the beginning of the previous chapter. Now, write down a few examples of each type; and then think about how you would group or categorize them. Note those categories to refer to as you read this chapter.

INTRODUCTION

As discussed in Chapter 2, B≈H has become a problem for individuals and organizations. It can be emotionally, financially, and legally expensive. B≈H in the work environment includes a variety of types of unacceptable behavior.

Although definitions vary, they typically refer to offensive behaviors that are unsolicited and unwelcome. Some research has attempted to identify traits and characteristics of perpetrators and targets (Neuman & Baron, 2003) or organizational influences (Matthiesen, 2004). Other research identifies the influence of external factors (Cowie et al., 2000) or how the organization itself may unintentionally permit or even reinforce B≈H (Parzefall & Salin, 2010). Salin (2003) uses social theory to suggest that the relative powerlessness between members of an organization influences who and why some individuals become targets. In today's organizations, diversity among individuals with different beliefs, values and attitudes may contribute to competitive, stressful situations in which B≈H may occur.

Researchers have identified a great many different kinds of unacceptable workplace behaviors that could constitute B≈H (see, for example, Van Fleet, White, & Van Fleet, 2018; Hollis, 2016; Crothers & Lipinski, 2014; Einarsen et al., 2011). Some of those are based on the perpetrator (e.g., co-worker, manager, customer, supplier), others use ethnicity or gender, others focus on different forms of sexual harassment or bullying, while still others classify by the nature of the B≈H (e.g., intimidation, ridicule, assault, offensive jokes, offensive pictures).

Consider what one person told us about her co-worker Henrietta, when discussing the meaning of bullying.

HURTFUL COMMENTS INTERFERE WITH WORK

My co-worker, Henrietta, frequently makes comments about me, the way I do my hair or my clothes, and her friends egg her on. They laugh about it and say that it is really all a joke, and I shouldn't be so sensitive about it. But I don't think the comments are a joke. They're not funny-funny at all; they hurt. Negative comments about my appearance are the most difficult to hear. Like my makeup and my weight. I would love to slap her face one day and tell her that at least I don't have a crappy *chicken* name like hers – "HEN-ri-etta." Sometimes I have to just walk away, go to the restroom, and cry to recover before I can get back to work. I told my supervisor about this, but he seems only to care about the work, so he just says that he will "speak to them," and nothing gets done. I lose several minutes of worktime, 2–3 times a day, just because I get so upset.

These unacceptable and disruptive behaviors can be sly, quiet, underhanded, manipulative, and direct; hence they may be seen only by the targets. This is especially the case where the perpetrator is a smart, successful individual who has created an impression that the organization would fail without him or her (Sepler, 2015). Also, the perpetrator is probably sufficiently clever to present a totally different personality when others, especially members of upper management, are present or during an investigation of a complaint. But much of this abusive behavior already may be obvious to others. In all these instances, whether observed or not, action should be taken to reduce or hopefully eliminate the behaviors. Consider the actions of Janice.

SHE HELPS HERSELF

Janice helps herself. She takes things. If you have gum or candy at your workplace, she will help herself. If you're away from your workplace, she'll even open drawers and look around and take change, gum, or any little thing that appeals to her. If confronted, she says she didn't take anything; she was just curious and looking around. I'm going to try to set up a trap and see if I can't catch her in her lies and thieving behavior.

What type of B≈H is Janice's behavior? Theft, lying, invasion of one's personal space? B≈H can manifest itself in many different ways. Any classification of the behaviors will lead to categories that tend to overlap, and any such classification is not likely to be all-inclusive. As noted in Chapter 1, numerous classifications have been used (see, for example, Djurkovic et al., 2005;

Rospenda et al., 2005; Schneider et al., 1997); but to aid in understanding B≈H, those many versions can be reduced into the following five types:

- Verbal including psychological;
- Physical including sexual and quid pro quo;
- Personal including discrimination;
- Power (abuse of) including hostile work environments;
- Third-party (e.g., suppliers, customers, investors).

This chapter deals with co-workers and focuses on the first three categories above: verbal, physical and personal types of B≈H. B≈H that can be characterized as "power" almost invariably involves the abuse of power by some member of management. For that reason, examples of the power types of B≈H are presented in Chapter 4, which focuses exclusively on members of management. Similarly, third-party B≈H, which also tends to result from an abuse of the relationship, is covered in that chapter.

VERBAL, INCLUDING PSYCHOLOGICAL

Verbal B≈H can be intermittent or constant; but, in any case, it can threaten the target's health and career. There is a difference between simply complaining about a co-worker or letting off steam and abusive comments that constitute bullying or harassment. However, it is frequently difficult to draw a line between the two.

Verbal B≈H may consist of demeaning remarks, offensive gestures, or unreasonable criticism. It may involve insults, slurs, unwanted "jokes," "yelling," cursing, insulting, or mocking, and hurtful comments. It may be intimidating, threatening or humiliating. It can include sabotaging a person's work to prevent the person from doing what the person is supposed to be doing at work. It is often difficult to recognize as it may be seen as a case of personality conflict rather than harassment or bullying.

HE PUTS ME DOWN

Anytime I make a mistake, Joe lets me know about it. He always says he could have done it with no errors. He puts me down by saying things like, "Let me see if I can put this in simple terms that even a moron could understand."

Peers or co-workers are often the sources of B≈H. They are the perpetrators. Since the verbal forms are the most likely to occur, examples are quite numerous. The following long list consists of a few of the more obvious verbal B≈H behaviors:

- Embarrassing – taunt and tease intentionally to embarrass; humiliate or use other kinds of spoken abuse; ridicule, intimidate; use electronic means (email, Facebook, etc.) to embarrass someone;
- Joking – make someone the brunt of pranks or practical jokes that threaten the personal standing of that person; making sarcastic comments or jokes, followed by "just joking";
- Demeaning – constantly demean someone; belittle, degrade, berate, or patronize someone; personal insults, snide remarks, disparaging remarks;
- Anger – use angry words; act out in anger;
- Gossip and rumors – spread gossip or rumors; spread misinformation or malicious rumors; make unfounded allegations; defame someone;
- Yelling (this could also be thought of as physical) – aggressively yell or shout at the person, constantly yelling;
- Threaten – make a veiled threat of job loss or other negative consequence; make unpleasant or threatening calls; threaten someone, especially in front of others;
- Unwarranted criticism – destructive criticism; overrule, dismiss, or ignore a person's explanations; intentionally put someone on a guilt trip; try to convince someone that management or team members are unhappy with the individual's performance;
- Exclusion – socially exclude someone;
- Trivializing – taking away from your accomplishments, actions, or ideas;
- Discounting – taking away from what you think, say, or do;
- Denial – the perpetrator denies anything and everything;
- Other – retaliate by making accusations or telling lies; regularly target an individual with offensive language, personal remarks, or inappropriate bad language.

PHYSICAL

Words aren't the only way in which perpetrators engage in B≈H. Furthermore, verbal B≈H, if not dealt with, may lead to physical B≈H. Physical B≈H involves using one's body or bodily acts to exert power over the target. It includes hitting, kicking, tripping, pinching, and pushing, damaging property, and other physical attacks. Unlike verbal B≈H, the effects of physical bullying can be easier to spot. Stealing, shoving, hitting, fighting, and destroying property are all types of physical B≈H. Because these types of behavior are easier to spot than verbal behaviors, they are rarely the first type that a target will experience.

TIRED OF HARRY'S PUNCHES

Harry punches me every time he comes by my workstation. He says that he's just being friendly, but his punches sometimes hurt. I've asked him to stop and even try to move away if I see him coming, but he still keeps it up. Recently when I was in line at the canteen, instead of punching me, Harry sort of shoved me out of the way, almost costing me my place in line. Another worker told Harry to be more careful, but Harry just shrugged.

The following are a few of the more obvious physical behaviors:

- Sabotage someone's work to prevent them from doing what they are supposed to be doing or to make them look bad to management;
- Spy on or otherwise invade a person's privacy;
- Physically attack – push, trip, kick, hit;
- Steal someone's personal property;
- Damage someone's work or personal property;
- Make unwanted physical contact.

Sexual B≈H

Perhaps the most devastating type of physical B≈H is sexual in nature. Sexual B≈H is a behavior, physical or non-physical, where sexuality or gender controls or intimidates someone. It may degrade the target, single out the target by using sexual language, gestures, or violence, or victimize the target for his or her appearance. It also includes pressuring the target to act promiscuously and to act in a way that makes others uncomfortable. It consists of unwelcome sexual advances, requests for sexual favors, and other verbal or physical conduct of a sexual nature.

Some of the more obvious sexual B≈H types follow:

- Sharing sexual photos (pornography);
- Posting sexual posters;
- Making sexual comments or jokes;
- Inappropriately touching someone;
- Making inappropriate sexual gestures or signs;
- Making suggestive remarks or sexual innuendos;
- Sending suggestive remarks, innuendos, pictures, or other materials digitally.

Consider Donna's story as just one example of what can and does occur in the workplace.

UNWANTED SEXUAL ATTENTION IN WORKPLACE

I was at a Consumer Show trying to make a pitch to obtain investment capital for my startup company. During a coffee break, a potential investor suddenly grabbed me and tried to make out with me. When I resisted, he became more aggressive. He even tried to follow me to my room. I've asked a male friend to accompany me in the future but feel a bit silly about having to do that.

Quid Pro Quo B≈H

Another particular type of sexual B≈H is when the perpetrator offers or merely suggests that in return for sex, something will be granted to or withheld from the target. It can also occur as part of a threat, specifically a threat to remove a job benefit unless a demand is met. It typically involves a member of management as the perpetrator and an employee as the target.

During a survey to obtain actual examples of bullying and harassment, one respondent reported this incident at her workplace.

QUID PRO QUO?

I overheard our supervisor talking to another worker. He told her that he thought she was sexy and was interested in meeting with her after work. He also said that she could expect better shifts if she cooperated. I was disgusted and talked to her, but she said that she needed the work and that I should mind my own business.

Another woman similarly stated that she was repeatedly asked to go for drinks after work; and if she played her cards right, she could get better performance reviews. Some of the more obvious examples of quid pro quo B≈H are:

- Hinting that a job, promotion, or raise might depend upon the receipt of sexual favors or other sorts of assistance;
- Hinting that to avoid a demotion or termination, sexual favors must be exchanged;
- Explicitly indicating that job opportunities (promotion, raise) depend on the receipt of sexual favors;

- A supervisor giving an employee a trip to the annual convention, with the expectation that the employee will repay the favorable assignment with sexual favors (see one incident in the film *Hearts in Atlantis* for a portrayal of this type).

PERSONAL, INCLUDING DISCRIMINATION

Words and actions are not the only way in which perpetrators engage in B≈H. The B≈H may involve discrimination by making unjustified distinctions between human beings based on their perceived categories. Some forms of discrimination may not be illegal; nevertheless, all forms if unjustified are unacceptable. Many forms are illegal, such as those based on age, race, sex, disability, sexual orientation, religion, national origin, gender reassignment, marriage and civil partnership, pregnancy and maternity, and sexual orienta-tion. However, discrimination may also have to do with the target as a person (e.g., personality, behavior, dress, or the like). While these are not illegal, they can nevertheless be hurtful to individuals and organizations. Consider Julio's situation.

WHEN SHOULD COUNTRY OF ORIGIN MATTER?

Julio notes that his supervisor repeatedly refers to his country of origin in discussing his performance. His supervisor seems to feel that anyone with Julio's background is likely to be a poor performer. Because he feels that way, the supervisor refuses to provide any training to help Julio.

This seems clear. It is most likely discrimination at work.

The following list consists of a few of the more obvious personal acts of discrimination:

- Encourage targets to feel guilty and to believe they're always at fault;
- Torment gay or lesbian workers because of their sexual preferences;
- Dismiss complaints using fabricated charges or flimsy excuses;
- Tease or criticize someone because of religious practices;
- Plagiarize, steal, or copy someone's work or ideas and then present them as their own;
- Provide a bad or misleading reference to prevent someone from getting another job;
- Manager intentionally singling out an individual or a group of people for unequal treatment;

- Imposing lifting requirements for a job that does not actually require lifting (such requirements tend to exclude women or people with certain disabilities);
- Take credit for another's contributions;
- Make insinuations based on someone's physical appearance;
- Telling targets that they can't do the job because they are too old.

Personal may also include appearance and job assignments as reported by one respondent.

DO SKILLS MATTER?

I am actively looking for another job. The reason is that my skills are not being used at my current job. My boss wants me to be a sales representative because I'm attractive and have a friendly disposition. My previous experience and college education are ignored. So, I'm looking for a job that will use my talents rather than hiding them.

Some of these behaviors "overlap" others and differ only in specifics, but all serve to highlight the variability of B≈H that can and does exist in organizations. One type tends to be "quiet" in approach. The perpetrator creates a tense, fearful or abusive environment by spreading misinformation, using nonverbal intimidation, making veiled threats, and sharing information about the target inappropriately. Another type is more obvious. The abuser yells, publicly criticizes, constantly finds fault, publicly humiliates, and even physically threatens targets (Lutgen-Sandvik et al., 2007). Sometimes the behavior is intended not to inflict extensive harm but only to make another person uncomfortable enough – to upset their world enough – to force them to leave. Rose's experience is a typical example.

SHOULD AGE MATTER?

I've been with this organization for years; indeed, I'm the oldest member of my group and might even be the oldest employee of the company. I have always loved and appreciated my job and was willing to give it 100%. I have rarely taken a "sick day" in all these years. I'm still productive and readily pull my weight. I still put in overtime when called upon.

Nevertheless, several of my co-workers keep asking me about my retirement plans. They suggest that early retirement is a good thing and don't know why I haven't elected to do so. This makes me uncomfortable, so I try to avoid group get-togethers and meetings. It also dampens my enthusiasm for the organization and my job.

Even a relatively low level of B≈H behavior can cause significant harm when targets are made to feel that they do not fit well in the work environment. For example, in an organization where almost all employees are male, a female employee may experience problems from being left out of social events or even impromptu conversations in the hall. An older worker may experience similar psychological results from feeling that their presence is not welcome in lunchtime discussions where the conversations center around babies, rock music, auto racing or politics. As you might expect, the misfit problem can easily occur in family-owned businesses when "outsiders" are treated differently than family members.

ARE NON-FAMILY WORKERS TREATED DIFFERENTLY?

I was bullied, sexually harassed, interrogated, and even threatened at one job for years. It was a family-owned business that made up its own rules and made my life hell. Anything a relative did (or failed to do) was overlooked. Unacceptable work was simply handed over to someone else; the family member was not held accountable. Just about any excuse was an acceptable reason for having to arrive late or leave early, whereas we "outsiders" were held to the clock. It almost felt like the company was "us versus them," which made us feel like we had no reason to work hard for the company as we simply did not exist in the minds of the family. So, everyone outside the family left rather soon after they were hired. I was thicker skinned and so I stayed on until I was finally told that they didn't need me anymore. I outlasted them but didn't beat them as I lost that time when I could have been gaining seniority while also being happier somewhere else – and I'm sure the behaviors I experienced are still going on.

If left unchecked, the perpetrator/target conflict results in a variety of personal issues such as antisocial behavior, anxiety, fear, increased irritability, concentration problems, reduced self-confidence, sleeping problems, stress reactions, depression, and post-traumatic stress disorder (PTSD). These, in turn, result in reduced productivity, increased absenteeism and turnover, product or service defects, counseling costs, decreased staff morale, and reduced quality of life.

EARLY SIGNS

It is important to be aware of B≈H behavior before it reaches the point where it damages an individual or the organization. Some possible early warning signs include:

- An individual worker having documents, files, other work-related items, or personal belongings going missing;
- An individual worker always eating lunch alone;
- A manager frequently checking on a particular worker or asking that worker to meet multiple times a week without clear reasons;
- An individual worker being left out of departmental get-togethers;
- Co-workers getting quiet or leaving the area when a particular worker shows up;
- Workers seemingly asked to do work beyond their pay grade or with no training.

There may, of course, be other indicators, but these should alert you or the managers to the type of early warning signs that may exist.

SAFETY ISSUES

Many of these behaviors also can lead to safety issues on the job. Organizations that do little or nothing to reduce B≈H can experience increased rates of accidents. Accidents result from the "four horsemen of safety" (Nichols, 1997, p. 12).

1. Apathy, lack of concern, or indifference. When the organization does nothing to reduce B≈H, employees can become indifferent to their jobs, the company, and its culture. They say, "If the company doesn't care, why should I?"

RACE MATTERS

There are two of us salespersons in our store. I'm a minority, and the other person is not. I was floored when I went to buy something, and he refused to sell it to me. He said that the manager should write up any sales by either of us. At the time that seemed strange to me because he had not raised that issue when he bought something, and I rang it up for him. I looked toward the manager at the back of the store, and he just looked normal – not surprised or wondering what was going on. He came up front to check me out, so I just said "fine, okay," and paid. This is clearly a case of racial discrimination, but our manager seemed to agree with him. Next time he wants to buy something, I'll insist that the manager handle it just like he did.

2. Complacency, content, or lack of vigilance. Employees become out of touch with the hazards and risks around them. Complacency may happen over time, where workers take for granted the conditions or the context around them. Or they may simply feel that the risks to them are worth the possible rewards. Management also may not be vigilant in looking into complaints.

WILL ANYONE LISTEN?

After a year of abuse by my supervisor, I emailed the President of the Organization. I noted that I had documented everything and even recorded conversations with her. I took time off for disability (depression), but then I got a response back that my complaints would be investigated. I now wonder how thorough the investigation will be if it happens while I'm off and not involved. I guess I should be happy that an investigation will take place even though I'm not certain how complete and fair it will be.

3. Distraction, inattention, or absent-mindedness. To try to deal with B≈H, employees may increase their use of smartphones, the Internet, or social media on company time. They tend to "drop by" and gossip or send more emails, all of which distract them and can lead to accidents. This sort of failing to pay attention can lead to accidents that cause physical harm or errors in the work being done.
4. Deviation, taking shortcuts, or willfulness. Employees skip breaks to avoid managers or co-workers who engage in B≈H. They may neglect the proper maintenance of equipment. A loose screw, an unlocked latch, or an unchecked gauge can lead to an accident. Skipping a small step to avoid a confrontation can be disastrous.

In addition to B≈H's costs noted in Chapter 1, one must also expect to experience accidents and their accompanying costs. While accidents at work have generally been decreasing, there were still 2.8 million nonfatal workplace injuries and illnesses reported by private industry employers in 2018 (Bureau of Labor News Release, November 7, 2019). Some of these accidents, particularly those involving slips and falls, may have been the result of some type of

B≈H. However, any kind of sexual assault cannot be considered an accident and could result in legal issues for both the perpetrator and the organization (Wolf, 2015).

The direct costs of such accidents are apparent, but there are indirect costs as well. Those indirect or less obvious costs are usually greater than the more obvious ones. Here are a few of those indirect costs:

- Administrative time by managers and human resource personnel spent on accident-related paperwork and interviews;
- Damage to tools, equipment, and other property;
- Economic loss to the injured worker's family;
- Failure to meet production or complete projects;
- Legal fees;
- Loss of morale and efficiency due to break-up of group or team;
- Lost time by fellow employees;
- Medical expenses;
- Overhead cost (while work was disrupted);
- Spoiled work;
- Time lost for replacing damaged equipment or from work by injured employee(s);
- Training costs for a new worker if necessary;
- Workers' compensation premium.

The long list of B≈H and incidents noted gives rise to the questions as to why they occur, who are likely perpetrators, who are targets, and what can be done about it. Let's try to first understand the nature of B≈H before tackling what can be done about it. Understanding is the first step toward eradicating any B≈H that may exist in your organization.

MINI CASE: FALSIFIES RÉSUMÉ

At my former employer, a guy was hired primarily based on his great résumé. Sometime later a co-worker happened to be on vacation in the small town where the new guy's former employer was. The company was quite small, which aroused the co-worker's curiosity, so he visited the company to see how it operated.

While there, he asked about the person we had just hired. At the mention of his name, there were clear reactions that they remembered him and not favorably. They said that he was incompetent and a blowhard. Our co-worker then asked about specifics from the new guy's résumé. They said, "That's just like him – make up fictitious information when he assumes no one will bother checking." When he was eventually confronted, he said it was all just a misunderstanding.

1. Is falsifying a résumé either bullying or harassment or just some other form of dysfunctional behavior?
2. How does your organization screen résumés for honesty and accuracy?
3. What should organizations do to prevent false résumés?

THINK ABOUT THIS CHAPTER AGAIN

Look at your examples and the categories you thought about at the beginning of this chapter. What changes in your categories would you make after thinking about the material in this chapter?

Then take a few minutes to prepare responses to these questions and actions. In particular, managers and human resource professionals should do this to be better prepared to handle B≈H in their organizations. Make your responses as if you are working in an organization. The responses should then be discussed by all students or participants.

The form is on a separate page to enable photocopying for use individually or by groups.

INSTRUCTIONS FOR FORM 3

Types of B≈H in my Organization

B≈H Column: The behavior that involved the B≈H you carried over from Form 1.
Perp. Column: Sex – M = Male, F = Female.
Targ. Column: Sex – M = Male, F = Female.
Behav. Char. Column: Behavior Characteristics (V) = verbal, (B) = physical but non-sexual, (PS) = physical + sexual, (Q) = quid pro quo.

CHAPTER 3 CASES

These cases are based on actual situations with identifying names and locations changed or omitted. While anyone would benefit from reading and thinking about these cases, they are best used in a group context where different individual perspectives could be bought forth.

Form 3   *Types of B≈H in my organization*

TYPES OF B≈H IN MY ORGANIZATION			
B≈H (behavioral characteristics)	Perp. sex M/F	Targ. sex M/F	Behav. Char.
1.			
2.			
3.			
4.			
5.			
6.			

Case 3.1: Substitute Receptionist

Maria has a bachelor's degree in accounting from a local college. She was active in student organizations, including serving as vice president of ALPFA (Association of Latino Professionals for America). She was named to Beta Alpha Psi, an honor organization for financial information students and professionals. She used that background to obtain a good job with a company in a nearby town. While the company is relatively new and is growing, it involves a lot of documentation work and so has several accountants on its payroll. It is always on the lookout for new customers and works hard to impress and retain existing ones.

Maria is young, attractive, has a pleasing personality, and gets along well with everyone in the company as well as customers. However, it is just those characteristics that have led to her problem.

Recently, her supervisor has asked her to fill in for the receptionist whenever the receptionist is unavailable – on her lunch breaks and even when she is on vacation. Her supervisor tells her that as a relatively new company, the company must always have someone at the front of the office to greet potential customers and make them feel welcome. "There is nothing special to do there so it shouldn't be a difficult thing to do. Besides," he says, "the accounting area is close to the front, so it should be easy for you to get up and move to the receptionist's desk when she isn't there."

Maria doesn't feel she is being treated fairly since she is being singled out for an assignment outside her area of interest and expertise. She feels that such interruptions interfere with her productivity and potentially result in errors, which are intolerable in accounting work. Maria's husband, Carlo, has problems with this arrangement. He argues, "This is entirely inappropriate. Your boss is taking advantage of you just because you are Hispanic. He wouldn't ask one of the other accounting people to fill in in this way."

Maria is not so sure. She suggests, "Carlo, it is my personality, not my background, that my boss notes in his requests. He feels rather strongly that it benefits the company to make good first impressions. And I'm reluctant not to agree since I've only been with the company a few months and don't want to risk getting a reputation for being uncooperative." Carlo, on the other hand, still feels strongly that it is inappropriate to ask an accountant to fill in for a receptionist. However, to keep from arguing with his wife, he says, "Okay, why don't you talk to your co-workers and ask them for advice. If they also feel it is inappropriate, then you should refuse to go along with the boss's requests. If they think it's okay, then I guess you should do it."

1. What types of behavior are evident in this case?
2. What do you think Maria should do?

3. What do you think Maria will do?
4. What might the organization have done to prevent this sort of situation?
5. What should the organization do at this point?

Case 3.2: Quid Pro Quo

Adriana is an attractive, up-and-coming young female who recently graduated with honors in public administration from a major university. She used her college degree to secure a great position in a major state agency. After working there for several years, she has heard that a position will become vacant soon. Getting that position would involve a promotion. She is hoping to get the promotion and the position. She thinks she has a good chance since her work has always been regarded as excellent.

Adriana also knows that her current boss, Sam, will be involved in deciding who will be promoted since the position would involve working closely with him. She tells Sam that she will be applying for the position and that she is very interested in receiving the promotion, particularly since they seem to work quite well together in her current position. Sam says, "We'll see. But remember there will be several others also interested in the position."

A week later, Adriana and Sam travel together on state business that includes an overnight stay in another city. Over dinner, Sam tells Adriana that he hopes he will be able to help promote her because he has always really enjoyed working with her. She says, "The job is really interesting to me, and I know I would be perfect for the job. We will be able to work together to get a lot more accomplished." Sam agrees that she would be a good fit for the job but that some of the other candidates actually "look a bit better on paper." After a few seconds of silence, he adds, "but you are the one I want." He tells her that he can "pull some strings" to get her into the job, and she then asks him if he is okay with putting in a good word for her. He assures her that "it's no trouble – but anyway I think you'd be worth a little trouble, don't you?"

At that point, Adriana thought she could detect a change in his voice and in the eye contact he made. She felt a bit uneasy but remarked that she was really tired and sleepy and needed to rise early the next day for their upcoming strategy meeting. Sam said that he, too, was tired but suggested that they both needed to relax and wind down so they could get a good night's sleep. He suggested that they stop by his hotel room and go over the presentation one more time. "Drinks are on the company, you know." Adriana declined his "offer," but worries about her chances of getting the job.

1. Is this quid pro quo harassment? If not, what is it?
2. Should she accept the new job if offered to her?
3. Should she have accepted Sam's invitation for a drink?

4. How would you rate Adriana's handling of the evening?
5. After tonight, how do you think Adriana should behave at work?

4.   When management is the problem

As indicated in the previous chapter, now your focus should be on bullying and harassment done by managers. Again, write down some examples and think about how you would group or categorize the behaviors that you noted. Note those categories to refer to as you read this chapter.

INTRODUCTION

Unfortunately, many organizations have poor managers or bad bosses – those who are likely to engage in B≈H and those who ignore B≈H by others. Those poor managers or bad bosses may abuse their power, exhibit poor management skills, have poor people skills, or have personality issues or work styles that don't fit their positions in the organization.

Dealing with poor managers or bad bosses is difficult for organizations, but it helps to know the different kinds of managers' behaviors to better correct them. As noted in Chapter 3, it is also important for managers to educate themselves to recognize these behaviors so that they can learn to avoid them or at least not act in some way that will worsen the problem. Even if managers are not the sort who engage in B≈H, they may not be willing to try to solve this problem as they don't perceive it as any of their business. Yet, it is important for all managers to assist their organizations in reducing or eliminating these types of bad managerial behaviors, which are detrimental to the company in many ways.

POOR MANAGERS

Co-worker and third-party issues such as those mentioned in Chapter 3 are almost insignificant when compared to those of management. All too frequently, bad managers are backed by weak/poor upper management (Van Fleet & Van Fleet, 2007). Upper management may ignore their behavior or even uphold it. Worse yet, upper-level managers may contribute to such bad behavior by being bad bosses themselves, unfortunately setting poor examples for others.

Managers Use Fear

These types of poor managers may even threaten employee job security. They know that, when employees feel that layoffs are looming, gossip tends to spread through the workplace. Morale is reduced, and employees will tend to stop trusting and respecting the upper management team. Poor managers also tend to hear only what they want to hear.

DISRUPTIVE COMPLAINTS

My boss called me in and said that my complaints about another worker are disruptive to the work environment and that she was sure he never intended to embarrass me. I asked her why, then, has he continued that behavior after I and a few others had talked with him about it. Her response was not what he and I need to work things out or she might have to let me go. I noted that others have witnessed the situation and would support my version of events. She said that she didn't need to talk to anyone else since she had already talked to him and that she understood the situation. I felt the punch when she said, "It would not be good if we all were timid, dull, and antisocial." A dig on me.

Poor managers may also attempt to instill fear among employees by withholding information or responding to questions in joking or noncommittal ways. They create negative environments by failing to show compassion. These behaviors result in employees feeling anxious and under stress. A boss can be unpredictable and develop inconsistent policies so that no one is sure just where the boss stands on issues. Or they demand personal favors.

BOSS REWARDS FAVORS

My supervisor has indicated that promotions are based solely on his view of us. To assure a positive view, he suggests that we do things to help him – picking up his laundry, taking him to lunch (he never buys), covering for him when his wife calls, and anything else he can come up with. A former employee, a female, quit because his bidding included sex, and also because nobody in management would listen to her.

Upper Management Permits Behavior

While most poor managers are tolerable to many employees, there are others who frequently fly off the handle, purposely intimidate members of their group, and even resort to sexually coercive behavior. Even more confusing to employees is the manager who is a tyrant one day and a nice person the next.

Major problems can occur when upper management permits this kind of bad boss or poor manager behavior. It may be that they don't know about it or don't care about it as long as results keep pouring in "for things that count." Doing something about that employee's behavior may in their minds suggest that they made a poor hiring or promotion decision; and they don't want to admit mistakes or to go to the trouble of recruiting, hiring, and training a replacement. There may be reasons (none good enough to excuse it) for upper management's support or tolerance of such poor managers, but they are always dysfunctional in the long run. For the moment, though, pretending that poor managerial behavior does not exist may seem the easiest way out for upper management. However, the problem does not need to be a costly predicament if management is trained to handle B≈H.

Upper Management Ignores Behavior

Ignoring the bad behavior of a member of management is never a good thing. Ignoring can have the same effect as endorsing it – it worked once, so I'll try it again. In particular, three kinds of bad boss behaviors should never be ignored: bullying, harassment and discrimination. While many companies have made progress in dealing with discrimination, B≈H needs much more attention.

NO PLACE FOR RACIAL BIAS

A white customer in our store started complaining in racist terms about other customers who were black. I told him that the black man was a good customer and a good person, usually pleasant, and never rude. He said, "That's absolutely B-S. Mark my word – black people hanging around your store will cause problems and keep customers from shopping here." I said, quietly but rather sharply, that his comments were uncalled for and that he should shut up. He then complained to management about me, and my manager told me that I should not say things like that to customers! The manager further explained that we needed all the people as our customers; but, naturally, "we try hardest to keep the largest orders." So, I've learned that this is not a good place to work or shop unless maybe you're a bigot.

When upper management ignores the behavior of a poor manager, they are, in effect, telling the poor manager that he or she may continue the behavior. A poor manager whose bad behavior is ignored is not motivated to change that behavior. Poor managers interpret being ignored as a license to continue their ways.

Why do upper-level managers ignore such problems? Maybe they don't want to get involved with what they consider personnel problems. Maybe they feel unprepared to deal with problems of this nature. Or perhaps they have information or habits that make them sympathize with the poor manager. The bad behavior of bosses who are meeting the expectations may escape reprimands or punishment because executives understand the problems the boss is having with employees. Other managers may be aware that upper management is too busy meeting budget constraints or dealing with other issues to bother with replacing a manager who is already in place and trained. It is important to understand why a manager or upper management may be reluctant to act, but it is also too important to be ignored.

Assumes Workers are Easier to Replace

Upper management may assume that losing the worker is better for the organization than losing the manager. Less than satisfactory behavior by managers is sometimes ignored if they are meeting productivity expectations, as it is easier to let the worker's complaints go unheeded than it is to fire or otherwise deal with an angry boss. It is almost always easier to replace a worker than a boss. In some situations, managers may know that they can get by with being a bad boss because their skills are relatively scarce, or they have personal or family contacts, or a good relationship with other customers or suppliers and would not want negative information passed on to those outside contacts.

Upholds Bad Managerial Behavior

When upper management takes the boss's side by choosing not to reprimand him even when they know he is wrong and the employee is right, they are perpetuating the boss's behavior. Similarly, if upper management agrees with the boss and disciplines the worker, they are perpetuating the boss's behavior. When upper management acts so as to perpetuate bad behavior on the part of lower-level managers, the company and its employees are in even greater danger than if they simply ignore the behavior.

WORKPLACE CULTURE IS IMPORTANT

I don't know how much longer I can take this. Every day there are nasty comments, petty remarks, prejudiced and personal innuendos. Sometimes a co-worker will laugh at my speech, make snide comments about my hair or my clothes, ask the supervisor to let them look over my work, or mostly ignore me in a group setting. At the coffee break on Monday mornings, no one seems interested in hearing me. They'll just butt in when I try to participate. I've tried to ignore them by just keeping away from my co-workers, but recently my supervisor suggested that maybe I don't fit in. So rather than trying to help me and improve the working climate here, she seems to be supporting my co-workers. She did not give me any indication that any effort has been or will be made to change the culture. So, I suppose my options are to take it or leave it.

Unfortunately, this sort of action is not uncommon for upper management. When upper management makes excuses for the bad behavior of the lower-level manager and even takes his or her side rather than attempting to remedy the situation, it is like adding fuel to a fire. Lower-level managers and probably others, as well as the workers, know that whatever a boss does, the employees have little or no recourse. Lower-level managers quickly learn that they are part of the management – not the staff – of the organization and that "managers stick together."

Upper management members may uphold the bad behavior of lower-level managers because they think that to do otherwise would be seen as admitting a mistake on their part or that somehow a member of management can be less than perfect. Nevertheless, upper management members need to realize that in taking the lower-level manager's side when the boss is clearly wrong, they are upholding the bad behavior; thus, an improvement in that behavior is not likely to occur.

Contributes to Bad Managerial Behavior

Upholding improper behavior is bad enough; but, in addition, in some cases, upper management contributes to or even creates situations in which bad boss behavior occurs. Upper management members may overlook the negative impact on employees when there is a strong push to increase production or decrease costs. Or they may dismiss employee complaints, particularly if the lower-level managers are achieving their productivity goals. When members of upper management dismiss a complaint without checking the facts, they are, in effect, contributing to bad boss behavior. The bad behavior of lower-level managers is likely to increase because it is, in essence, reinforced by higher management.

WHEN MANAGEMENT WON'T LISTEN

Things got so bad at my former workplace that the police were called. A group of us tried to get the general manager to listen to our grievances but were told that he had left early that day. We said that we would just wait until he got back. Our supervisor said that we were not welcome to wait and that we should vacate the premises immediately. We did not. So, he called the police to have us forcibly removed. That's when things started to get ugly. There was a lot of pushing, shoving, and name-calling before we all left. We contacted the EEOC, but nothing ever really came of it. But word gets around; many local people learned from a newspaper article the next day that this company had become a less desirable place to work.

Upper Management Caused the Problem

As discussed, upper management may ignore the bad behavior of lower-level managers. It is much worse, though, when upper management "causes" or contributes to unacceptable behavior. For example, upper management may make poor hiring or promotion decisions. Furthermore, if upper management members criticize the behavior of the lower-level manager but then fail to prevent its recurrence, they are contributing to continued bad behavior.

MANAGERIAL ABUSE OF WHISTLEBLOWER

Three of my co-workers and I observed a manager abuse a worker. I reported it and the manager was let go. He was well-liked, so my having been seen as the main person in his firing made me unpopular. I was called a whistleblower, a tattletale, a liar, and a cheat. One other manager, in particular, began to talk about me in meetings with other managers. Then she began to call me names and belittle me in front of everyone. If I made the slightest mistake, she made certain that everyone knew about it and, if she could punish me, she would do so to the max – dock my hours or have me work an extra shift. Because she had gotten all the managers on her side, there wasn't much I could do. When I complained, I was told that the company would give me a good reference so that I could find another job. And that is what I did. I've learned to never try to fix a problem if it includes a boss in any way.

Poor Reward System and Managerial Training

Other contributing factors to bad behavior on the part of lower-level managers are a poor reward system and inadequate training for those managers. Lower-level managers may be selected or promoted because upper management wants "strong" supervisors. Unfortunately, "strong" frequently translates to "bully." But even if supervisors are not selected for that reason, the failure of upper management to recognize and correct that bad behavior permits them to continue.

It should be no surprise that many employees wish that their manager would communicate more frequently and provide positive feedback on occasion (https://officevibe.com/state-employee-engagement). When managers distance themselves from employees, those employees may feel unnoticed and unrewarded. Without such communication, morale and productivity may drop. Perhaps that's a major reason why many professionals desire to leave their organizations – to "get away from their boss" (Harper & Adkins, 2015).

The task of human resource personnel in these organizations is especially daunting. Nevertheless, without a strong human resource presence that supports employees, some organizations find themselves slipping into this "bad management" mode. Unfortunately, it is quite difficult for a job applicant to know about management before accepting a job. So, it is important that managers keep in touch with their employees, provide recognition, and be open and honest in dealings with them. Policies must be consistently adhered to, and everyone should be treated fairly and with respect, without regard to their race, religion, sexual preference, or any other identifying personal characteristic.

POOR MANAGER EXAMPLES

The next few pages provide specific examples of many of the more common characteristics of poor managers or bad bosses discussed above (Van Fleet & Van Fleet, 2014b). How many of these problem managers or bad bosses have you seen or experienced in your current organization?

Abuse of Power

All too frequently, bad bosses or managers abuse their power in an effort to be seen as "the boss." In reality, they are "backward bosses"; that is, they are double SOBs (SSOB). Clearly, this sort of behavior is dysfunctional and again can be seen as B≈H. Some of the more common examples of managers abusing power are the following:

- Threaten employees;

- Apply different rules or higher standards for a particular employee;
- Change a particular employee's timecard;
- Coerce an employee into reluctant resignation, enforced redundancy, or early or ill-health retirement;
- Require or allow overtime work in a way that is not equitable for all employees;
- Force someone to work long hours, often without remuneration and under threat of dismissal;
- Accept, allow, and even encourage unacceptable behavior;
- Overload an individual with work to keep him/her busy (with no time to file a complaint) and make it harder to meet objectives;
- Provide ambiguous job instructions and performance feedback consisting of such statements as "Do the best you can" or "If you don't show significant improvement, we'll have to find someone else for that job";
- Purposely mislead about work duties, like incorrect deadlines or unclear directions;
- Record meetings with a particular employee but not with other employees;
- Require mandatory overtime, placing a burden on employees but particularly those with families with small children;
- Set unrealistic goals and deadlines that are unachievable, or that are changed without notice or reason, or whenever the individual gets close to achieving them;
- Set unrealistic production goals, assign forced overtime, or single out those who cannot keep up;
- Subject an individual to unjustified disciplinary action on trivial, specious or patently false charges;
- Use the position of power to exclude or prevent a person who is competent to deal with the unacceptable behavior.

Poor Management Skills

Bad managers frequently have poor management skills. Whether due to a lack of experience or insufficient or improper training, managers with poor management skills contribute to B≈H. These behaviors, then, clearly impede their ability to do their jobs. Some of the more common examples of poor management skills follow:

- Assign blame;
- Assign tasks that are beyond a person's skill level;
- Check on you often or ask you to meet multiple times a week without a clear reason;
- Establish unrealistic timelines or frequently change deadlines;

- Excessively monitor, supervise, micro-manage, record, snoop, etc.;
- Impose unreasonable deadlines;
- Impose unreasonable workloads;
- Inconsistently follow or enforce rules to the detriment of an employee;
- Increase an individual's responsibility but remove the person's authority to get things done;
- Make excessive demands of an employee;
- Micromanage;
- Overload an individual by asking the person to do tasks outside typical duties and without training or help;
- Task a person with work that is below the person's level of competence;
- Use meetings inappropriately or, in other ways, run meetings poorly.

Poor People Skills

Bad managers also frequently have poor people skills. As with poor management skills, this may be a result of either lack of experience or insufficient or improper training. These behaviors, then, impede their ability to do their jobs and can contribute to B≈H. Some of the more common examples of poor people skills are the following:

- Are heavy-handed;
- Exclude an individual from what's happening;
- Forbid employees from talking to one another while at work;
- Give feedback in an insincere or disrespectful manner;
- Give unwarranted or unjustified verbal or written warnings;
- Ignore an employee, or isolate that person from others;
- Invite to "informal chats" or meetings which turn out to be disciplinary hearings;
- Make false accusations (without doing due diligence) about employees to someone higher up in the organization;
- Make unfounded allegations;
- Overrule, ignore, sideline or ostracize;
- Persistently criticize an employee;
- Provide hints or signals that a person should resign or abandon a job;
- Purposefully and inappropriately exclude, isolate or marginalize a person from normal work activities;
- Pressure an employee not to claim entitlements such as annual leave, personal leave or caregiver's leave;
- Raise concerns or express doubts about a person's performance or standard of work, but the concerns lack substance and cannot be quantified or are simply false to begin with;

- Refuse to provide accommodations for workers with disabilities;
- Remove responsibility from a person who has earned it;
- Repeatedly remind someone of past errors or mistakes;
- Ridicule, overrule, dismiss or ignore someone making a complaint;
- Single out and treat differently, e.g., discipline a worker for arriving one minute late when others stroll in late without penalty;
- Subject the individual to nit-picking and trivial fault-finding; the triviality reveals an absence of any serious concern about the individual;
- Take all the person's work away or replace it with inappropriate menial jobs, e.g., photocopying, filing, making coffee;
- Take undue or unfair advantage of an employee;
- Tease an employee;
- Warn employees that the next person who makes a mistake of any kind will be terminated;
- Yell at employees.

Personality Issues

Some individuals are bad managers simply because their personalities are not compatible with their positions in the organization. These personality issues could possibly be overcome with proper training; but without such training, those characteristics, too, impede managers' ability to do their jobs, and they contribute to B≈H. Some of the more common examples of personality issues follow:

- Are insecure and/or incompetent;
- Try to cover up their insecurity or incompetence;
- Make you feel that your work is frequently monitored, to the point where you begin to doubt yourself and have difficulty with your regular tasks;
- Manager/supervisor denies support, so the individual finds himself or herself working in a management vacuum;
- Tell employees to answer manager evaluation surveys favorably.

Work Style

Closely related to personality issues, some individuals are bad managers simply because of their work styles. As with personality issues, these work style issues could possibly be overcome with training. However, without such training, they also impede managers' ability to do their jobs and contribute to

B≈H. Some of the more common examples of work style issues include the following:

- Ask you to do difficult or seemingly pointless tasks and then ridicule or criticize you when you cannot get them done;
- Belittle, demean or degrade employees;
- Display angry outbursts and tantrums;
- Engage in overly harsh or unjust criticism;
- Harass with intimidating memos, notes or emails with no spoken communication, especially immediately before weekends and holidays (e.g., 4 p.m. Friday or Christmas Eve – sometimes hand-delivered);
- Instill fear among the group or team members;
- Intrude on a person's privacy by pestering, spying or stalking;
- Knowingly bump a particular employee to cause the person to stumble or spill whatever is being carried;
- Knowingly embarrass a particular employee through electronic means (email, Facebook, etc.);
- Play practical jokes or pranks on a specific person;
- Proposition a particular employee for sexual favors;
- Shun a particular employee (e.g., refuse to acknowledge when passing in a hall or coming into close contact; give the employee the "silent treatment");
- Use offensive language.

Managerial Inaction

Some managers are "bad" not because of what they do but rather for what they fail to do. Some of the more common failures follow:

- Continually deny an individual's request for time off without providing an appropriate or valid reason for the decision;
- Deny employees' time for restroom breaks without raising their hands to get permission from supervisors. In some cases, such permission is not obtained in time to prevent them from soiling themselves;
- Deny leave (annual, sickness, or especially compassionate);
- Deny or fail to provide information or knowledge necessary for undertaking work and achieving objectives;
- Do not accept criticism;
- Do not control their anger;
- Fail to make certain necessary decisions;
- Fail to provide an individual with necessary work resources while others receive more than they need;

- Fail to provide equitable access to earned time off;
- Fail to take responsibility;
- Ignore a worker's opinion;
- Postpone the manager's own work, knowing that a particular employee must pick up the slack or face reprimands or worse;
- Avoid recognizing people for their efforts;
- Provide poor or no performance appraisal;
- Refuse requests for leave (annual, illness, compassion) or require unacceptable and unnecessary conditions for leave;
- Refuse to provide accommodations for workers with disabilities.

Clearly, managers can engage in many types and forms of unacceptable and B≈H behaviors. Those behaviors must be addressed by organizations. Before attempting to address them, a fuller understanding of B≈H is necessary. As noted in Chapter 3, B≈H can also come from third parties – suppliers, customers or other outside stakeholders. In those cases, the B≈H tends to result from an abuse of the relationship.

THIRD PARTIES

Not all B≈H behaviors are the result of managers. Some are from third parties with whom the organization interacts, including customers, suppliers, repairmen, attorneys, accountants, and the like. A few of the more common behaviors from third parties include the following:

- The client uses foul language when dealing with one of our people;
- The vendor verbally abuses a cashier;
- The supplier threatens a sales associate to get favorable treatment;
- The customer berates a salesperson rather than listening to an explanation.

Not knowing what to do or not to do can be costly to the organization as well as to you, the individual. Is this situation one that you can handle, or is it a case where your boss should handle the problem? Everyone in the organization should understand the right to be free of B≈H. Everyone has a right to feel safe at work.

MINI CASE: ALTER EMPLOYEE RECORDS FOR BOSSES

Alice is a dedicated worker. The problem is that her dedication has led to altering records to help management. Specifically, she helps them commit fraud. She changes dates to ensure that worker compensation insurance premiums are kept low. She alters documents to show that those who actually did hazardous work show up as having done far less risky work. While she is the one who is doing this and her name is signed on all the forms, it is at the behest of management. They give her the information, and she just goes along to protect her job. One of these days, someone will get hurt on the job and then discover that because of her changes, they are not covered for medical care. Then who will receive the blame and the punishment that goes with it?

1. Is falsifying employee records a form of B≈H or just some other form of dysfunctional behavior?
2. What can organizations do to prevent such behaviors?

THINK ABOUT THIS CHAPTER AGAIN

Look at your examples and the categories you thought about when considering how managers engage in bullying or harassing behavior. What changes in your categories would you make after thinking about the material in this chapter?

Then take a few minutes to prepare responses to the following questions and actions. In particular, managers and human resource professionals should do this to be better prepared to handle B≈H in their organizations. Make your responses as if you are working in an organization. The responses should then be discussed by all students or participants.

Problem Management Questions

1. Is management part of the problem in your organization? Why or why not?
2. How may higher levels of management contribute to B≈H? How can they help reduce B≈H?
3. Explain how managerial inaction creates B≈H problems.
4. From the six kinds of bosses below, for which one would you LEAST like to work, and why?
    *   abuses his power
    *   has poor management skills
    *   has poor people skills
    *   has personality issues
    *   has a work style incompatible with yours
    *   fails to act

Problem Management Actions

Use the following two-page form to list ways in which management is a part of the B≈H problem in your organization. Then, using the forms from Chapters 1 and 2, start identifying managerial issues in your organization.

The form is on a separate page to enable photocopying for use individually or by groups.

INSTRUCTIONS FOR FORM 4

Upper-level Managers and B≈H (2 pages)

Explain or give an example of a B≈H behavior that you have observed or might expect from an upper management person in your firm. A few examples from the chapter are listed here.

CHAPTER 4 CASES

These cases are based on actual situations with identifying names and locations changed or omitted. While anyone would benefit from reading and thinking about these cases, they are best used in a group context where different individual perspectives could be bought forth.

Case 4.1: Down's Syndrome

Peyton was born with an extra copy of his 21st chromosome, a condition known as trisomy 21, or more commonly, Down's syndrome. Down's syndrome causes a distinct facial appearance, intellectual disability, and developmental delays, but most of those with the disorder are capable of holding a job.

He is 20 years old and still lives with his caring parents. Despite his learning disability, with encouragement from his parents and the help of a tutor, he has recently finished high school and gotten a job working in an auto parts store. It is a fairly easy job, and he quickly learned the basics of how to do it well. A typical day involves helping customers find the car parts they need or changing windshield wipers, lights or batteries for customers. However, many of the customers are rude and think they know it all, especially when they observe Peyton's distinct facial appearance and that he talks slowly and deliberately.

Nevertheless, Peyton had been enjoying the work and had been getting good weekly feedback from his supervisor. We say "had been" because some things changed about a month ago. The supervisor who had interviewed and then hired Peyton left the company. He was replaced by a man from another store. The new supervisor noting Peyton's difficulties with speech and language has

Form 4   *Upper-level managers and B≈H*

UPPER-LEVEL MANAGERS AND B≈H (2 pages)
Uses fear
Permits behavior
Ignores B≈H behaviors
Upholds B≈H
Avoids replacing B≈H managers
Abuses power

UPPER-LEVEL MANAGERS AND B≈H (2 pages)
Poor management and/or people skills
Assume workers are easier to replace
Contribute to bad managerial behavior
Upper management caused the problem
Poor reward system and managerial training
Insert others here

led him to underestimate both his intelligence and capabilities. He quickly started referring to Peyton as "dumbo" and mocking his mannerisms. Peyton's assignments were also changed, and it seemed that the new assignments were either the more difficult or least desirable ones in the whole store. For example, Peyton was told he would be given responsibility for the bathrooms and the twice-daily trash pickup throughout the store.

Paul, a friend of Peyton, who also works at the auto store, overheard the new supervisor making ugly comments about Peyton. One of the more extreme comments he heard was, "Dumbo is a joke to be around. Anyone could do his work. Why do we pay him minimum wage? I can't believe he was ever hired in the first place, and I'm getting tired of having to put up with his slowly moving around."

Paul says, "Peyton, you should tell the owner about this. You're a good worker, and the new supervisor is a jerk." Peyton isn't so sure about that advice. What if it caused the new supervisor to fire him? His weekly evaluations under the new supervisor are much lower than the ones that the previous supervisor gave him. This makes Peyton anxious and nervous about saying or doing anything. "I love the work and I like coming to this store every day. But I am starting to feel sick at the end of the day. I think maybe Paul is right, that the new supervisor is treating me unfairly. I should talk to my folks and see what they think I should do."

1. How would you label the behavior in this case?
2. What do you think Peyton should do in this situation?
3. What do you think Peyton's parents will say?
4. How might the organization prevent this sort of situation in the future?
5. Does your organization have any policies for dealing with handicapped and disadvantaged employees?

Case 4.2: Embarrassment as Motivation

Sophia is 26 years old. She is short, slender, and seems rather frail. She is also rather plain and dresses quite conservatively. As a student at the local state university, she received very high grades, although she was a bit of a loner and not active in student organizations. After receiving an industrial engineering degree with honors, she got a position at a major corporation in a nearby city. Her job involved analyzing operations, designing workflows and production processes, reducing inefficiency, and ensuring that the final products met the established quality standards. She quickly learned the ins and outs of the job. She still was a loner though, with little interaction with others in her group. So, it came as quite a surprise when she was promoted to head up a new unit. She has been in that new position for only six months and is the youngest supervisor in the organization.

Soon after she assumed her new supervisory position, Sophia began to hold weekly staff meetings. In these meetings, she would go around the room one person at a time and point out each person's flaws, errors and mistakes. She says this is necessary to show them how their performance could be improved. She identifies everything that they have done wrong or could have done better. And she makes sure that everyone's attention is focused on the individual she is calling out. She says, "By embarrassing each of them, I intend to motivate them to do better in the future so that they can avoid being called out in the future. Then, if they don't do better, it will be clear to everyone why they have to be gotten rid of." She feels rather strongly that this will lead to superior performance by her group over the long run, despite an increase in turnover since she took charge.

One of her group members complained, "It isn't just embarrassment; it is intimidation! She is attempting to manage the team by intimidation when she targets individuals the way she does. In addition to identifying what she feels are errors, she gives them the "evil eye"; she glares at them so that they are afraid to ever stand up for themselves." Another group member said, "She often harasses us to the point where we are reduced to tears. It seems almost personal the way she picks on us. She seems to gain satisfaction by making others feel bad. I saw her go so far as to threaten Janice with termination if she didn't perform up to Sophia's performance standards." Still, a third said, "We wonder how long this has to go on. We are afraid to go over her head since the company obviously thought so highly of her when they promoted her so early in her time in the company."

1. Why might upper management have promoted her so quickly?
2. How would you label her behavior in this case?
3. What do you think Sophia's team members should do in this situation?
4. Do you think that embarrassing them will motivate her workers?
5. How might the organization prevent this sort of situation in the future?

5.   Unacceptable workplace behavior in general

For this chapter, consider behaviors that you feel are unacceptable workplace behaviors but that might not be identified as either bullying or harassment. Write down a few examples of each, and then think about how you would group or categorize those behaviors. Make a list of those behaviors and categories to refer to as you read this chapter.

INTRODUCTION

To more fully understand B≈H, all sorts of unacceptable behaviors that may occur in the workplace need to be considered, even if they may not be B≈H. In today's workplace, the widespread acceptance and use of social media and various forms of social and interpersonal networking provide previously unimaginable opportunities for unacceptable behaviors with their own unique social, humanitarian and productivity issues (Sewell & Barker, 2006; Tabak & Smith, 2005).

Less Intensive Behavior

As previously indicated, B≈H occurs in many types and forms. It may involve derogatory jokes, racial slurs, personal insults, expressions of disgust or intolerance toward a particular race, or mocking a worker's accent. Many unacceptable behaviors are simply "milder" or "less intense" and do not rise to the level of B≈H. These workplace behaviors are nevertheless deemed as unacceptable because they erode morale, decrease productivity and increase costs to the organization.

Mislabeled Behaviors

It should also be noted that some kinds of behavior that might be termed B≈H would be incorrectly so classified. People do get upset and angry and react emotionally, but that in and of itself does not constitute B≈H. Consider the employee who, when he or she notes a problem caused by another employee, gets angry and shouts at that other employee using an expletive of some sort.

If it is repeated and especially if no apology follows, this could be B≈H; but if it occurs just this once and especially if an apology is proffered, it clearly would not be B≈H. However, if the nature of the expletive is racial or sexual, training in addition to an apology clearly should follow the action. Consider Joe's comments.

BOSS WITH A SHORT FUSE

My current supervisor tends to have a short fuse – he reacts strongly to any problem but especially any mistakes I make. While his comments sting, at least he apologizes and strives to make things right after one of his outbursts. So, while this may not be the best place to work, we both do try to get along and get the work done.

Behaviors that occur only once or occasionally and generally are followed by apologies may include the following (for a more complete itemization, see Van Fleet, 2018):

1. Criticizing or humiliating (sarcastic or belittling words) someone; talking down to someone;
2. Mis-stating or repeating out of context what someone said;
3. Name-calling;
4. Using "bad" words (e.g., foul words, derogatory, cursing, "dirty," swearing) that are offensive to others;
5. Belittling or being condescending to co-workers;
6. Denying or refusing reasonable requests made by someone; touching another inappropriately;
7. Retaliating;
8. Virtual harassment, which has been brought home by working from home;
9. Simply showing disrespect to other workers.

Isabelle's situation is a case in point. She knows exactly what this means.

SOCIAL MEDIA ATTACKS

I used to just hear comments about me at work, but now I get them via email, Facebook and Twitter. It actually seems to be worse now that I'm working from home. I could stop using social media to avoid seeing the comments, but I need the email to do my work, and I hate to cut off my real friends on Facebook. But I'm saving copies to show to our HR department to see what if anything might be done.

Behaviors Influenced by Environment

Unfortunately, these "little" behaviors may become more frequent and more significant in the changing workplace, especially if the organization's environment is becoming more erratic. If they do become more frequent or hurtful, they could easily rise to the level of B≈H. If so, apologies will not be sufficient to keep them from harming individuals and the organization.

Managers also may be involved through any number of certain behaviors. Direct supervisors, in particular, may show favoritism for one employee versus another. They may employ inappropriate (usually authoritarian) styles of supervision, show little consideration for the problems of their subordinates, or even threaten their subordinates (Ashed, 2012; Human Rights Watch, 2012). Upper management, on the other hand, may ignore the behavior of these supervisors and have even been known to support their bad behavior in order to demonstrate a "solid front" to stave off criticism from outsiders (Human Rights Watch, 2012).

As shown in Figure 5.1, these behaviors likely result from three forces: (1) those outside the organization – economic, social and political, (2) inside influences – inherent characteristics and dispositions of individuals, and (3) the organization's culture and its managers (Van Fleet and Van Fleet, 2014b). Those forces may impact behavior individually or through interplay among them.

Figure 5.1   Behaviors influenced by environment

FORCES OUTSIDE THE ORGANIZATION

Forces or conditions outside the organization can also have an influence on behaviors (Einarsen, 1999; Vartia, 1996). When economic conditions are dire, people may begin to act more aggressively as they compete for jobs or at least better-paying jobs. If the social climate doesn't condemn aggressive behavior or it just ignores such behavior, these behaviors are more likely to morph into B≈H. When the political environment is highly charged and polarized, especially if based on religious ideologies, race or economic positions, these behaviors are more likely to morph into B≈H.

TURNED DOWN BECAUSE OF COLOR

More than once, I have been turned down for a promotion because it might incur social interaction that the company feels would be difficult because of our marriage situation. I'm white but my husband is black, and the company feels it would cause problems. Perhaps it is time to look for another job with a more reasonable company.

Economic Forces

More specifically, when the economy is such that organizations must adapt abruptly, B≈H tends to increase. Any economic environment that fosters high levels of workplace stress – long hours or insecure employment, for example – will increase B≈H. Highly competitive work environments where employees vie against one another can also be a contributing factor. Similarly, competitive environments where workloads are continually high and unevenly spread can contribute to increases in B≈H. And, of course, economic inequality is a major force. The greater the disparity of income and power, the more opportunity there is for those with more to bully and harass those with less.

Eleanor has limited skills but found a company that could use her but only on a day-to-day basis. It wasn't as good an opportunity as she thought.

LYING, DISCRIMINATING BOSS

I'm a day worker. My boss said that during these hard times, we all should be willing to be flexible. I have been told several times that there was no work and so I stayed home and got no pay. However, I recently found out that his buddies at work have never had to stay home and even got overtime on several occasions. When I asked about it, I was told that if I didn't like it, I should look for work elsewhere. So, I guess I'm stuck with this sort of day-by-day harassment until I can find somewhere else to work.

Social and Political Forces

In addition to economic forces, social and political forces may also play a role in increasing B≈H behaviors in the workplace. Studies have shown that the behavior of people is influenced by perceptions of what is socially acceptable or the norm (Matias, 2019). In some social settings, managers and co-workers may not intervene on behalf of targets of disruptive behaviors because they believe that the target needs to toughen up and confront the disruptive behaviors on their own (Neuman & Baron, 2003).

Politics in the workplace can easily cross the line and become workplace B≈H (Cohen & Vigoda, 1999). As was apparent during the 2020 election period in the United States, those with extreme views tended not to calm down or cool off. The B≈H that resulted from conflicting political views harmed social relationships as well as organizational performance (Mutz & Mondak, 2006). However, partisan politics are not the only way in which politics can impact B≈H. Organizational or workplace politics involves attempting to get those in power to get things done for those campaigning to get things done whether these involve hours of work, equipment or even the breakroom. In most organizations, workplace politics rarely results in all-out conflicts, but if it does, the overall goals of the organization suffer (Vigoda & Talmud, 2010).

Elijah had an interesting story about how political expression can result in B≈H.

BOSS RULES ON DRESS CODE

A colleague wore an "All Lives Matter" shirt to the office, so I wore my "Black Lives Matter" shirt. Our manager immediately told me to turn it inside out or go home and change. When I protested and pointed out that another worker was permitted to wear an "All Lives Matter" shirt, she said that his shirt didn't single out a particular group like mine did, so his was acceptable, but mine wasn't. I tried to explain the situation to her, but then she reminded me that she was the boss and that she makes up the rules around here.

INSIDE FORCES

Dress codes are a visual indicator of the culture of an organization (Furnham et al., 2013; Karl et al., 2013; Peluchette et al., 2006). The degree of formality (business formal, business professional, business casual, or casual) helps set the tone for the day-to-day functioning of the organization. Dress codes, in and of themselves, may or may not be a form of protected speech. However, any such code must be enforced consistently, or employees and the courts may assume that the organization supports a particular political religion, philosophy, or even a particular political party reflected by the nature of the clothing being worn by its members.

The characteristics and predispositions of individuals in the organization can lead to unacceptable behaviors.

Antisocial and Dysfunctional Behavior

Importantly, some of these unacceptable behaviors are not "mild." These sorts of unacceptable behavior constitute another kind known as antisocial behavior. Such behavior refers to "any behavior that brings harm or is intended to bring harm, to an organization, its employees or stakeholders" (Giacalone & Greenberg, 1997, vii). Antisocial and dysfunctional or deviant behavior falls within the broader category of antisocial behavior.

Many of the behaviors associated with dysfunctional or antisocial behavior involve violence (Desrumaux et al., 2015; Lopez & Griffin, 2004; Robinson & O'Leary-Kelly, 1998), but not all of them do. Alcohol use; smoking; loud talking; lying; showing disrespect for co-workers, the management, or the organization; cruel or insensitive language toward others; and inappropriate tardiness are all antisocial behaviors that bring some level of harm to others or to the organization. But in and of themselves, they do not constitute B≈H. Human resource professionals can help to distinguish among these to prevent or reduce inappropriate responses.

CONFIDENTIAL COMPLAINT CAUSES RETALIATION

Recently, I filed a complaint against a co-worker based on the racist comments that he had publicly made. My supervisor has changed my work hours to "protect me," but other co-workers now seem to "accidentally" bump or push me and are siding with the one I complained about. So there doesn't seem to be any real protection.

Occupational Deviant Behavior

Occupational deviant behavior (Pino, 2001) involves self-serving deviant acts that occur at the workplace. Occupational deviant behavior may include the following:

- Extramarital relations with a co-worker;
- Consuming alcohol in the workplace;
- Whistleblowing;
- Abuse of sick leave;
- Tardiness;
- Sexual harassment;
- Intimidation and showing open hostility toward co-workers;
- Lying about hours worked.

Occupational crimes vary from theft to espionage (Van Fleet & Van Fleet, 2006; Friedrichs, 2002). They include the theft or unauthorized acquisition of secret or restricted information; kickbacks, payments, or favors given secretly to others in return for selecting the offender's products or services; and fraud of one or more of three broad sorts: asset misappropriation, corruption and fraudulent statements (Greenberg, 1990 & 1998). Other occupational crimes include:

- Embezzlement;
- Pilferage;
- Theft of services;
- Sabotage;
- Robbery;
- Burglary;
- Larceny;
- Crimes involving or using computers;
- Money laundering;
- Altering company records without authorization;
- Committing tax fraud;
- Racketeering;
- Misusing company data or property;
- Committing stock and securities violations.

Violent Behavior and Terrorism

Many unacceptable behaviors involve violence, but not all of them do (e.g., alcohol use, smoking and inappropriate tardiness). Violent behavior, then, is a subset of unacceptable behavior (see, e.g., Lopez & Griffin, 2004). Terrorism within an organization is yet another subset, one that overlaps both the violent behavior set and the non-violent behavior set. Although all internal terrorism is obviously unacceptable, most sorts of unacceptable behavior clearly do not involve terrorism.

Internal terrorism is different from most other sorts of unacceptable behavior in that it always involves the intent to evoke fear or extreme stress for the purpose of bringing about a change that benefits the perpetrator (Van Fleet & Van Fleet, 2006). Internal terrorism is meant to arouse fear in the organization in general or its management in particular in order to achieve the terrorist's goals.

TIPTOE LIGHTY AROUND TIMID BOSSES

Jack is a major problem around here. I tried reporting the situation, but the bosses are afraid. Jack is clearly manipulating the bosses to get his way. He has created a big mess with different people saying different things. I ended up looking like I was crazy because I called him out. But the bosses are so scared of Jack they do nothing. I don't know what he has on them, but I should have tried to "line up my ducks" ahead of time. I'll certainly be more careful in my new job.

Single, isolated incidents of aggressive or violent behavior are unlikely to create a long-lasting climate of fear that would be strong enough to bring about the change in the terrorist's wants. Therefore, internal terrorism generally involves repeated actions that require planning (intentional, premeditated actions) to some degree.

All sorts of antisocial behavior, and especially those that involve violence, must be strongly addressed by organizations. In some instances, outside agencies (e.g., police) may need to be involved.

CULTURE AND MANAGERS

The organization's culture is extremely important. Organizations need to avoid cultures with control-centered managers and those with pessimism, vindictiveness, unclear expectations, lying, open criticism, low morale, favoritism, and an absence of trust.

It is important to realize that a single individual's B≈H can spread throughout the organization. This is especially true if the individual is a manager or a senior co-worker. The negative culture that develops can affect the entire organization as it touches all activities, including recruiting, hiring, productivity and performance. In extreme cases, an affected employee will commit suicide instead of, or in addition to, resigning.

PERSONAL ATTACKS HURT

Susan loves to just continually put me down. I may not be gorgeous, and I don't have designer clothes, but I try to look my best and dress nicely. I also try to be nice and polite to everyone, but she calls me names. She says no man will ever want me unless I get plastic surgery on my face and body and take a course on how to dress for success. It hurts! It hurts to be treated this way and makes it difficult to do my work whenever she is near because I get so tense and can't concentrate on what I'm doing.

The culture should be one in which everyone can feel comfortable and valued, not one that excludes anyone. A positive culture would be one that respects employees while expecting quality work. Such a culture tends to encourage collaboration. Managers trust the experience and decision-making of the employees, allowing them to take on projects without constantly hovering over them or correcting the slightest mistake.

RELIGIOUS CULTURE FUELS DISCRIMINATION

Our organization's culture tends to overemphasize certain holidays. For instance, they go overboard at Christmas and Easter. Since I'm not a Christian, I get a lot of unwanted attention at these times. Co-workers and even managers ask me to go to church with them and to learn carols to sing. I frequently find Christian literature on my desk. One co-worker even said outright that I would be condemned to hell because I'm not a Christian. When I responded that that didn't seem like a very Christian thing to say, she responded that "It's okay to treat heathens badly." As a result, I must admit that I'm not very fond of Christians or their holidays.

There are governmental laws or regulations that forbid discrimination on the basis of individual characteristics such as sex and religion. But to maintain a healthy culture, management must not tolerate even the slightest appearance of discrimination. Management must develop and enforce the rules so that a complaint will never need to be filed by the employee.

Discrimination at the federal level is covered by Title VII of the Civil Rights Act of 1964. There are seven protected classes: race, color, religion, sex, national origin, familial status and handicap (disability in California) (Dover, 2020). A more serious issue would be that of a hostile work environment. Such an environment happens when the behavior is related to one of the protected classes, unwelcome, offensive both to the recipient and to a reasonable person, and severe or pervasive (Henderson, 2019). Recall from Chapter 1 that the focus of this book is on dysfunctional or unacceptable behavior that could impact an organization's reputation and possibly its bottom line and not on what is legal versus illegal.

As noted in Chapter 4, another important kind of unacceptable workplace behavior is abusive supervision. Poorly trained managers or those with aggressive personalities may be abusive in an effort to appear powerful and "in control." If those managers are among the ones at the top of the organization, lower-level managers are likely to follow suit. So, it is particularly important to see that all managers are trained not to discriminate, to be considerate, and to listen to their group members.

FEELING THREATENED BY INCOMPETENT BOSS

Recently, my supervisor has been going to one of my co-workers and asking her about the job I am doing. Then on Friday, right before the end of the day, my supervisor had another supervisor come and ask me to explain about what I had been doing for the last four days. Why didn't my own supervisor ask me? Aren't there records of what I accomplished? I feel threatened. It makes me feel like what I do has no value to the organization.

This sort of behavior on the part of management is clearly abusive; but in many organizations, managers seem to think that they need to yell, scream and use offensive language in order to get anything done. But some managers contribute to behavioral problems by being "too nice." These managers love to joke about everything and form bonds with some workers and ignore others. Workers who are thus ignored, especially if they try to talk to the manager involved, may not only have their performance suffer but may then engage in unacceptable behaviors themselves.

SUMMARY

As can be seen, there are many unacceptable behaviors that may not be considered B≈H. Still, those behaviors must be addressed by organizations as they could easily be associated with B≈H behaviors, could lead to further erosion of the organization's culture, and could damage the organization economically and in terms of its reputation. With this in mind, let's now try to understand B≈H more fully.

MINI CASE: LIES AND RUMORS

Gloria is a liar. She puts on a wonderful front. She is always friendly, cheerful, and smiling. However, behind the scenes, she is vindictive and intent on looking good by making others look bad. She is the source of anonymous notes that have smeared a co-worker. She makes sure that everyone knows if she can find anything negative about someone. When anyone makes a mistake, she broadcasts it far and wide. But of course, to our supervisor, she is all sweet and wonderful.

Not only does she lie and spread rumors, but she also takes credit for the work of others. Sometimes she gets the credit for someone else. When she does that the person now owes her big time. In that way, she develops "friends" who will then cover up for her.

1. Does Gloria's behavior constitute B≈H?
2. How can an organization prevent or at least minimize such behavior?
3. Why do you think a supervisor cannot, or does not, see this type of behavior when it is so obvious to so many?

THINK ABOUT THIS CHAPTER AGAIN

Look at your examples and the categories you thought about before reading this chapter. What changes in your categories would you make after thinking about the material in this chapter?

Then take a few minutes to prepare responses to the following questions and actions. In particular, managers and human resource professionals should do these carefully and completely to be better prepared to handle B≈H in their organizations. Make your responses as if you are working in an organization. The responses should then be discussed by all students or participants.

Unacceptable Behavior Questions

1. What kinds of unacceptable behavior exist in your organization?
2. Is your organization doing anything to deal with these behaviors? If so, what is it doing?
3. Are there any kinds of antisocial behavior evident in your organization?
4. In your organization, what kinds of occupational deviant behavior do you think exist or could develop as a result of your organization's culture?

5.   Is your organization doing anything to deal with these behaviors? If so, what is it doing?

Unacceptable Behavior Actions

Use the following forms to write down and categorize examples of the forces influencing B≈H in your organization. Then consider what you or your organization might do about them.

The form is on a separate page to enable photocopying for use individually or by groups.

INSTRUCTIONS FOR FORMS 5.1 AND 5.2

Forces Influencing B≈H in my Organization

Types of B≈H that Affect my Organization's Culture

Use Form 5.1 to write down at least one example of each of the forces influencing B≈H in your organization. Then use Form 5.2 to categorize the behaviors that you have identified in Form 5.1 as impacting your organization's culture. Then begin considering what you or your organization might do about the behaviors.

CHAPTER 5 CASES

These cases are based on actual situations with identifying names and locations changed or omitted. While anyone would benefit from reading and thinking about these cases, they are best used in a group context where different individual perspectives could be bought forth.

Case 5.1: Male Interests

Caleb is a 32-year-old single male. He recently began to work for a supply company that makes daily deliveries to a store where Waylon is employed as an inventory clerk. Waylon is a nice-looking 22-year-old male who prides himself on being physically fit. During lulls in his work, Waylon keeps in shape by working out doing sit-ups, pushups, running in place, or using heavy boxes as weights. When a delivery is to be made, Waylon must sign for the delivery, put the supplies where they belong, and update the inventory records. Caleb usually waits around while Waylon finishes checking everything and has put the supplies away. When Waylon is finished Caleb engages him in small talk.

Form 5.1   *Forces influencing B≈H in my organization*

FORCES INFLUENCING B≈H IN MY ORGANIZATION
Outside forces (economic, social, political)
Inside influences (individuals)
Inside influences (organization culture and managers)

Form 5.2 *Examples of the five types of B≈H that affect my organization's culture*

EXAMPLES OF THE FIVE TYPES OF B≈H THAT AFFECT MY ORGANIZATION'S CULTURE

Verbal including psychological

Physical (including sexual and quid pro quo)

Personal including discrimination

Power (abuse of) including hostile work environments

Third-party (e.g., suppliers, customers, investors)

Several weeks ago, while making his deliveries, Caleb began complimenting Waylon for his good looks and his physique. He marveled at how Waylon was able to keep in shape doing such mundane work. Occasionally, he makes suggestive comments about how Waylon would look if he weren't wearing the company uniform and instead was in a bathing suit. Waylon noted that Caleb's comments had been increasing in frequency and wondered about how to react. Then, recently Caleb asked Waylon for a date. Waylon was stunned! He told Caleb that he was not interested, noting that he has a girlfriend. To further dissuade Caleb's interest, Waylon stretched his story a bit, characterizing the relationship as serious.

Because the comments have not become less frequent, Waylon has been trying to avoid dealing directly with Caleb, but that's impossible as he is required to sign Caleb's delivery papers. That certainly does narrow his choices! He has thought about talking with his supervisor and maybe asking for another assignment, but he likes this job and would not want to move to another and have to start learning the ropes all over again. Also, he wouldn't want to do something that might affect Caleb's job. He doesn't want to hurt Caleb but instead just wants to force Caleb to learn an important lesson.

One thing is for sure: Waylon has a delicate problem that might either go away if handled correctly (whatever that means!) or otherwise grow into a large, expensive, ugly scene that ends in court and leaves both Waylon and Caleb on the unemployment line. Meanwhile, Waylon will continue making excuses as he signs the delivery papers and immediately trots off to another area to avoid Caleb.

1. What forces seem to be apparent in this case?
2. What should Waylon do in this situation?
3. Should Waylon talk to Caleb's boss?
4. How do you think you would handle a similar case?
5. How might the organization prevent this sort of situation in the future?

Case 5.2: Gay Executive

Will is a 40-year-old male executive who recently married his male partner. He could hardly believe all the good things that had happened recently in his life, including spending his honeymoon in the beautiful Hawaiian islands of Maui and Oahu. When he returned Will brought photographs of the wedding and honeymoon to share with his co-workers. He posted some pictures in his office and carried a few to show individuals at lunch or in their offices.

Later that day, his supervisor, Josh, came to Will's office. Josh saw the photos and exclaimed, "I didn't know you were gay!" Josh soon left Will's office. The next day when Will arrived at work, he saw that his wedding photos had been drawn on with offensive markings and a sign was posted on his door that read: "Marriage is Between a Man and a Woman." The writer had obviously attempted to disguise his handwriting, but it was definitely Josh's. Will was very upset and left work, telling his employer he didn't feel well.

Will came back to work the next day, intent on "staying the course." But there was another sign on his door with quotes about marriage being sacred and not between two men. That was a major attack, he thought; but he was determined to "stay the course." Then later, from his office, he could hear Josh making derogatory remarks about him to other workers. The other workers didn't have an opportunity to say much, and their few interjections were subdued. Did they agree or disagree with Josh? Whether they agreed or disagreed, so what? Josh was the boss.

Will put into his desk drawer all the photos he had carried in his pocket and all but four of the ones he had displayed in his office. He arranged two of the four remaining photos on his desk, two on the shelf behind him. Most of the men in his company kept a few pictures of family or boats or something, some larger than Will's unframed 4x6s. He decided he would go by Walgreen's after work and have at least two of his four shots enlarged to 5x7s and framed tastefully for his office.

He also would cease mentioning anything about his spouse, the wedding, and the honeymoon. He would do his company work as usual, and talk with individuals who seemed to be willing or needing to have a conversation. He would speak and give his usual smile to everyone. Lunchtime would be awkward, he thought, so he would like to brown-bag it. But that would be spineless, if not cowardly.

So, he would try to act normal in the company cafeteria. In other words, he would give everybody an opportunity "to inspect their souls" and then he would make his decision as to whether to stay or to go. His life, he decided, was going too well for him to let others mess it up. Meanwhile, he would begin a job search – a process that is usually quite long. And he should probably (maybe?) not mention this problem to his mate.

1. What forces are evident in this case?
2. How should the wedding photos problem have been handled, and by whom?
3. Do you believe the problem between Josh and Will can be resolved? If so, how? What must be done and by whom?
4. How might the organization prevent this sort of situation in the future?

6.   Workplace violence

Think about behaviors that you feel are not only unacceptable workplace behaviors but also go far beyond the usual concepts of bullying or harassment. Think about behaviors that would be thought of as workplace violence. Write down a few examples, and then think about how you would group or categorize those behaviors. Finally, write down your list of those categories to refer to as you read this chapter.

INTRODUCTION

When B≈H becomes widespread and common in an organization, it may evolve into acts of violence, or it may trigger some individuals inside or outside the organization to react violently. Workplace violence, as used here, refers to any substantial threat, injury, or attack on an organization's physical, human, informational, tangible or intangible assets (Van Fleet, 2017). If not addressed, workplace violence can lead to disastrous consequences both economically and in terms of personal tragedy.

Workplace Violence: Widespread and Growing

Violence in the workplace has been increasing rapidly since the late 1990s (Haynes, 2013; Morgan, 2013). Violence is one of the major causes of death at the workplace, accounting for about 9% of fatalities in 2015 and 17% in 2016 (AlertFind, 2021). Almost two-thirds of all workplace homicides in 1998 occurred in retail trade and services (Sygnatur & Toscano, 2000); and over half of the homicides at work happened in food and beverage establishments (U.S. Bureau of Labor Statistics, 2017).

Unfortunately, violence in the workplace was initially considered an aberration – an uncommon occurrence that did not capture the attention of either managers in organizations or the general public. Now it is clearly an important issue. "According to the U.S. Occupational Safety and Health Administration (OSHA), approximately two million workers are victims of workplace violence every year, and this number is increasing" (Stephenson-Laws, 2018). Some of the more alarming statistics are listed below:

- About two million people become victims of workplace violence every year;
- Workplace violence costs businesses nearly $130 billion per year;
- One in seven employees feels unsafe at work;
- Seventy-five percent of acts of workplace violence cases are classified as assaults;
- Most victims of recent workplace violence incidents are between 25 and 54 years of age;
- Seven percent of fatal assaults involve acts of hitting, kicking, beating, and/ or shoving;
- Twenty-eight percent of sexual violence incidents occur in accommodation, food and retail businesses;
- About 25% of workplace violence incidents go unreported.

There have been an alarming number of violent events since April 2010. You may remember some of the examples listed below, and be aware of others since this chapter was written (Statista, 2021).

Recent Examples of Workplace Violence

- Atlanta, Georgia: 2021, mass shooting at three massage parlors owned by Asian Americans – 9 dead.
- San Jose, California: 2021, mass shooting at a Santa Clara Valley Transportation Authority facility – 10 dead including the gunman.
- Indianapolis, Indiana: 2021, shooting at a FedEx facility – 9 dead, 7 injured.
- Bryan, Texas: 2021, shooting at a cabinet manufacturer – 5 dead, 6 injured.
- Boulder, Colorado: 2021, mass shooting at King Soopers Supermarket – 10 dead.
- Springfield, Missouri: 2020, shooting at Springfield convenience store – 4 dead.
- Milwaukee, Wisconsin: 2020, mass shooting at Molson Coors beverage company – 6 dead.
- Aurora, Illinois: 2019, mass shooting at Henry Pratt valve manufacturer – 6 dead, 7 injured.
- Aurora, Illinois: 2019, Henry Pratt Co. warehouse – 5 dead, 5 policemen wounded.
- Bakersfield, California: 2018, shooting at T&T Trucking – 5 dead.

- El Paso, Texas: 2019, mass shooting at Walmart department store – 22 dead, 26 injured.
- Virginia Beach, Virginia: 2019, mass shooting at Virginia Beach municipal building – 12 dead, 4 injured.
- Sebring, Florida: 2019, shooting at SunTrust Bank – 5 dead.
- Thousand Oaks, California: 2018, mass shooting at Borderline Bar and Grill – 20 dead, including the gunman.
- Manchester, Connecticut: 2018, mass shooting at Hartford beer distributors – 9 dead, 2 injured.
- Pittsburgh, Pennsylvania: 2018, shooting at Tree of Life synagogue – 18 dead and 18 + 5 policemen wounded.
- Chicago, Illinois: 2018, Mercy Hospital shooting – 3 dead.
- Yountville, California: 2018, shooting at Yountville veterans home – 3 dead.
- Annapolis, Maryland: 2018, shooting at *Capital Gazette* newspaper – 5 dead, 2 injured.
- Perryman, Maryland: 2018, shooting at a Rite-Aid warehouse – 3 dead, 6 injured.
- San Francisco, California: 2017, shooting at a UPS location – 3 dead, 5 injured.
- Orlando, Florida: 2017, shooting at Florida awning manufacturer – 5 dead.
- Tunkhannock, Pennsylvania: 2017, shooting at a Pennsylvania supermarket – 3 dead.
- Kirkersville, Ohio: 2017, shooting at a rural Ohio nursing home – 3 dead, 2 injured.
- Edgewood, Maryland: 2017, Edgewood business park shooting – 3 dead, 6 injured.
- Hesston, Kansas: 2016, mass shooting – 3 dead, 14 injured.
- Colorado Springs, Colorado: 2015, mass shooting at Planned Parenthood – 3 dead, 9 injured.
- San Bernardino, California: 2015, mass shooting at Inland Regional Center, Social Services training event for Public Health – 14 dead, 22 with gunshot wounds.
- Minneapolis, Minnesota: 2012, shooting at Accent Signage Systems – 7 dead, 1 injured.

In 2021, as this was being written, there had been at least 247 mass shootings in the U.S.A., with 45 occurring in just one month (Holcombe, 2021; Wikipedia. org, 2021). While most of these are not workplace violence incidents, they do indicate a dangerous tendency for individuals to resort to violence when they feel injured or unfairly treated in some way.

TYPICAL WORKPLACE?

My office is a typical workplace, or so I thought. Everybody did what they were assigned and seemed pleasant with each other. If one of us needed help meeting a deadline or whatever, someone pitched in. Just like it's supposed to be. Then about 3:00 one day Louis suddenly threw a pen across the room, followed by the three-ring binder full of papers on which he had been working. Everyone froze for an instant, then one guy got up from his desk, intending to calm Louis and try to help. Louis needed help all right. He began hitting the wall, kicking, yelling, accusing the boss of overloading him and the rest of us for doing lousy work that he had to re-do. He grabbed his car keys off the desk, stalked out of the building. None of us knew whether we should call the police, call his wife, lock our doors, or what. At that time, our company had not assessed its vulnerability or conducted training classes and established written directions about what to do. Before our management and PR did these things, some of us were scared that Louis would return. According to the last unofficial information we heard, Louis had taken another job but left there after about six months, then found still another job but had left there in a huff after just a few weeks and may have gone to Idaho.

RELATION OF B≈H BEHAVIOR TO VIOLENCE

Of course, not all B≈H evolves into acts of violence, and not all acts of violence begin as B≈H incidents. But some do. Hence, it is suggested that organizations formulate a policy that takes into account words and behaviors that adversely affect a particular individual's mental health. To understand this, consider the following:

> Worker A claims to the boss that Worker B is engaged in B≈H and that while it has not impacted Worker A's job performance, it is making Worker A anxious, distraught and fearful. If the policy is in place, the boss will talk with both workers, investigate the situation, and take appropriate action. Worker A will then be satisfied with the response and stay or, if unsatisfied, will leave.
>
> But what if there is no policy? If the boss is a caring individual, he or she will talk with both workers, investigate the situation, and take action such as recommending counseling and separating the workers. The result will be essentially the same as if a policy were in place.
>
> But if the boss is uncaring, he or she might essentially tell Worker A, "If you can't take the heat, get out of the kitchen." Whereupon Worker A may

be so upset that the next day he comes to work with a gun, shoots Worker B, shoots the boss who didn't care, shoots anyone else who interferes, and possibly even shoots himself.

Clearly, it is in the organization's best interest to have a policy that might prevent such a scenario.

If you are aware of this sort of situation, you may be able to work with the person or steer them to proper authorities who can interrupt their downward spiral. "Going violent" is not generally something that happens quickly and without notice. Rather, the actor – and hence the behavior – evolve, leading to violence. It will not rise initially to the levels of violence discussed earlier. Instead, it might begin with behaviors that are more nuisances than violent. Individuals might start with behaviors such as clogging executive toilets so they'll have to use workers' bathrooms; stealing hotel guests belongings; "parking" housecleaning carts in one location while the maids loaf elsewhere; intentionally damaging a part on an assembly line; or intentionally dropping a washer inside a car door on the assembly line so that it rattles when the car moves, driving the new owner crazy (Mantell & Albrecht, 1994, p. ix).

These examples involve company equipment or facilities being damaged or destroyed, but what about personal impacts also? Consider the mental anguish inflicted by a psychologically battering supervisor or sexual harasser whose actions prohibit the employee who is a victim from being productive and affect their home lives as well. Is that not violence? Or think about the employee or manager who contaminates computer files in an attempt to sabotage the company or to ruin the reputation of an individual or a company. Again, more violence? Words in the form of vicious lies, innuendoes, and ugly rumors can be more damaging to productivity and morale than physical violence (Van Fleet & Van Fleet, 2010).

Fear of violence at work has become yet another threat faced by members of all organizations. The prospect of such violence leads to increased anxiety and uncertainty. Employees are not only expected to perform well in a changing competitive environment but also, they fear death or injury on their jobs not even related to the nature of their work (Van Fleet & Van Fleet, 2010).

Organizations are legally responsible for providing their employees with a safe workplace. The legal liability for workplace violence can be established through a variety of concepts. Those include negligent hiring, retention or supervision. Negligent hiring is where the organization failed to carefully screen out potential violent employees. Negligent retention is where the organization failed to get rid of violent employees. Negligent supervision is where supervisors in the organization fail to identify violent employees. So, organizations have legal responsibilities, but they also have moral and ethical responsibilities to provide their employees with safe, healthy work environments.

CONTRIBUTORS TO VIOLENCE

The contributors to workplace violence are complex so that it is difficult to differentiate between those that originate at work and those that arise from personal or environmental factors. The contributor may be the result of conditions external to the organization, or it may come from conditions internal to the organization, or even just from personal, psychological characteristics of an individual.

There may be a relationship between the depiction of violence on TV and in movies and the news. Social institutions such as family, church and community no longer provide as much support in times of trouble as they once did. Drug use and the existence of gangs may also contribute to general social unrest that can be carried to the workplace. While any weapon can be used in workplace violence, guns seem to be the weapon of choice because people have guns and have experience with guns. More to the point: guns are made to kill. Now, guns seem to be a means of resolving conflicts or disputes at work.

Economic Conditions

Changing economic conditions can lead organizations to make sometimes drastic changes in their workforces. Downsizing, restructuring and re-engineering, as well as increasing diversity in the workforce, are examples of how the external environment can impact conditions at workplaces. These sorts of managerial actions clearly increase stress for those who might find their jobs ending, but they also impact those who survive the process. The survivors frequently find themselves expected to accomplish more or work longer hours to make up for the reduced number of workers. Longer hours and increased stress can also place additional pressure on families. And, of course, economic changes that decrease the worker's take-home pay or take away the job itself are among the highest stressors. Clearly, economic and social environments add to the stress that can result in violence at work.

An Organization's Internal Environment

But, changes in an organization's internal environment can create stress. Those internal changes are most likely even more important. B≈H such as shunning, ostracizing and banishing employees who do not "fit" in with other employees can decrease an individual's sense of dignity and self-worth. When that happens, the individual may resort to violence as a way of showing that they are of value – or showing that they have the power to control their environment. This may be more likely to occur when the individual is a minority in the workforce (women in traditionally male jobs) or has religious or sexual preferences that cause them to be isolated at work.

Changing Nature of Jobs

As society has changed so that sales and services are expected to be available around the clock, more and more jobs involve night work, which has usually been more dangerous. Labor is a variable cost, not a fixed cost. With this in mind, some managers treat workers as parts of the organization that can be easily replaced. Clearly, when this happens, the workers have little loyalty to the organization and may react violently when provoked.

The very nature of the organization can make it more vulnerable to workplace violence. Police departments could be targets for those who feel that the police discriminate or target them. Abortion clinics would be targets for those who oppose abortions. Theaters could be targeted for showing X-rated movies. So, the internal organizational environment is also a source or causal factor in workplace violence.

TYPES OF WORKPLACE VIOLENCE

Workplace violence can be visual, oral or physical and can result in harm to a person or property, an individual's acceptance by peers, or an individual's psychological health (Van Fleet & Van Fleet, 2010, pp. 46–7). Visual types would include graffiti, threatening or obscene gestures or notes, shunning, passive aggression, eye-rolling, or reading someone's personal mail or email. Oral examples would include taunting or laughing at someone, spreading rumors, gossiping, insults, threats, harassing phone calls, name-calling or swearing. Physical examples include defacing property, pushing or shoving someone, blocking aisles, stealing, fighting, sabotage, physical attacks or even arson.

Knowing about the various types and their impacts on individuals and organizations can assist in realizing how such violence occurs, what the consequences of that violence would be, and what might be done about it.

SIX STAGES OF VIOLENCE

Workplace violence rarely just spurts out of nowhere. Generally, there are signs of impending trouble. It likely goes through six stages: reaction, rejection, expression, escalation, intensification – finally ending with eruption (Van Fleet & Van Fleet, 2007; this section is based on Van Fleet & Van Fleet, 2010).

Reaction

Changing conditions cause pressure on the individual to increase. At first, an individual may experience one or more "conditions" or annoyances that frustrate and aggravate them. Those conditions could be such things as physical pain, emotional hurt by a friend or family member, or fear of losing a job or home. In any event, the conditions did not exist before or, if so, were so mild as to be essentially ignored. If the conditions are not alleviated, the next stage may occur.

Rejection

As the conditions continue or even increase, the individual generally begins to react in a relatively quiet way. Focusing on those who are believed to be the cause of the troubles, the individual may simply try to annoy them. The individual may refuse to do what is needed or expected, but by suggesting that they did not know what was wanted or that it was not part of their job. They may also just take their time and say they are working on it when, in fact, they really are not. Then if things do not improve, the individual may begin to express themselves more overtly.

Expression

At this stage, violence begins to appear. The individual begins to express their anger and frustration verbally or behaviorally. They may spread rumors and gossip in an attempt to harm the ones that they feel are causing them problems. Or they may make unwanted sexual comments, initiate arguments with co-workers and customers, or even management. And, of course, they will start to engage in B≈H. If nothing changes in their environment or something is not done, they will move to the next stage.

Escalation

Because the individual is not getting what they want or perhaps need, their behavior will escalate. Now their B≈H behavior is readily seen by anyone. In a sense, they are crying out for something to be done either to correct perceived inequities or to alleviate the concerns that they have. Now they wonder, "How long before somebody does something?"

Intensification

As they ponder why nothing seems to be happening, the pressure intensifies. The individual also begins to "lose it." Their B≈H behavior becomes increasingly dysfunctional. And, of course, if nothing is done, they are likely to see violence as the only recourse.

Eruption

At this point, the individual goes ballistic or berserk and seeks revenge on those who have caused their problems. They act or react forcefully, by sabotaging equipment or stealing property. And, of course, in extreme situations, they use weapons to harm or even kill others.

INTERNAL TERRORISM

A unique form of workplace violence is that of internal terrorism. It is different in that it involves the intent to evoke fear or extreme stress in order to accomplish the perpetrator's views. Its purpose is to arouse fear in the organization in general or its management in particular. It generally involves repeated actions that require planning (intentional, premeditated actions) to some degree (Van Fleet & Van Fleet, 2006). It may involve violent behavior, but not always.

COMPANY TERRORIST

I work in a company where the work is done in workgroups that interface with several other groups. Unfortunately, my workgroup also has a backstabbing, gossiping, lying bully. We interface with legal, payroll, training, and benefits personnel; and not one person in these groups can understand why this bully was not fired years ago. She is constantly trying to shoot down her co-workers. Now she has turned her attention to me – probably because I am new. She has sent emails to my group coordinator filled with lies about me and my performance. Fortunately, I have been able to refute these relatively easily, but that has taken otherwise productive time and has been disruptive to my thinking. She has tried to poison my relations with others in the department with vicious gossip, and this worried me more than anything because it's harder to prove yourself innocent than it is for someone to say you're guilty of something. What's worse, you can never know when she has spread lies or inaccuracies about you unless the person who heard them decides to tell you. Fortunately, her reputation has prevented her from succeeding. I have tried to report it through the channels, but my group coordinator tells me that it is a "personality clash" and not the company's business. It's certainly not a clash on my part – I was fine with all my relationships in the division. So, if she tends to clash with personalities (which, apparently, she has always done), the supervisors need to see that she improves before she runs off the best workers.

Those who engage in internal terrorism are sometimes referred to as "organizational terrorists" (McCurley and Vineyard, 1998). They are current or former members of the organization. They usually employ gossip, harassment, intimidation and threats to create a climate of fear to get their way (Kinney, 1995, p. 96). Internal terrorism then is different from employee or occupational crime, which is generally regarded as a subset of white-collar crime, which in turn is different from corporate crime (Holtfreter, 2005). The impact of internal terrorism, however, is essentially the same as that of workplace violence.

CONSEQUENCES

There are many consequences resulting from workplace violence. Some are borne by the organization, others impact the individuals involved, and still others impact bystanders or society as a whole (Asamani, 2016; Hughes, 2001). Perhaps the most obvious of those consequences are the costs associated with workplace violence.

Many of those costs are clearly identifiable. Those would include the cost of cleanup, repair, and replacement of damaged equipment or facilities and perhaps medical treatment for employees. Costs may also be incurred as a result of increased insurance premiums, security and litigation. Employees who take "early retirement" or "buyouts" as a result of violence should be considered as costs as well. It is more difficult to put dollar values on injuries or death, decreased productivity, and increased absenteeism or turnover, but those are costs as well. It is even more difficult to assign specific values to such things as the cost of interruptions to your business, damage to your organization's reputation and the impact of fear on your personnel.

There are other costs that are virtually non-quantifiable. These tend to be more social costs than economic costs. Nevertheless, they are important and must be considered. They include damage to the mental health of those involved. When the mental health of employees is impacted, the results may not be immediate or apparent. The results may be turnover, absenteeism, conflicts with co-workers, decreased job satisfaction and morale, post-traumatic stress disorder, depression, anxiety, fear and even suicide. Some costs, of course, are simply not capable of being estimated. "What is the real cost to a family when a member is murdered? What happens to the productivity of an employee when he or she is fearful of a co-worker?" (Van Fleet & Van Fleet, 2010, p. 37).

PREVENTION

Clearly, a healthy internal environment free from B≈H is the strongest deterrent to workplace violence. Organizations cannot simply wait until something happens before taking action. Upper management must understand the importance of being proactive in developing and communicating a violence prevention program that goes beyond any B≈H prevention efforts. Furthermore, there may well be legal issues also to consider in violence prevention. Some sort of anti-violence policy would be the first step, but organizations should go beyond that. Plans need to be developed regarding how to respond should a violent event occur, and training of all personnel should be conducted.

SHOULD CO-WORKERS' THREATS BE TAKEN SERIOUSLY?

I work at a non-profit that includes paid employees but also volunteers, donors and clients. The paid workers are very devoted to the mission of our agency and aware of the importance of the other individuals who play major roles in our success. Every now and then, though, one employee (Jolene) gets bent out of shape about something and threatens some kind of physical harm or legal action against someone or the organization. She will scream, "I'll get you for this!" or "You'll hear from my lawyer about this!" or "You'll all pay for this if you don't help me straighten this out by tomorrow morning. And don't you think I won't do it!" We have been instructed to write down who said something, what they said when they said it, and the context or why they said it. Most of the time nothing ever comes of it; because we keep such careful notes, the few times when a lawyer has followed up, once he sees our notes that's the end of it. For them, maybe – not for us. Every time we hear about someone somewhere going ballistic at work, we all wonder if this will someday happen to us. Maybe that's why management hasn't fired these people already – maybe they're afraid they will come back and take out all of us. Or maybe they assume that nothing will ever happen with Jolene because she is a female and women don't express anger like that. "Look at all the shootings," they seem to think. "Are any of them women?" Maybe our bosses are right – or maybe Jolene will be the first or will find another violent way to tell us what she thinks.

Larger organizations may establish a Crisis Management Team that will develop written plans, including who or what units will be responsible for specific actions should an emergency arise. That team may also conduct a needs assessment or hazards assessment to determine any areas that need special attention. It may also be charged with assuring that the security system is adequate and up to date, including sophisticated cameras, alarms and key-card access systems. However, even the best such systems can be bypassed by a determined, violent person.

Security measures do not have to be elaborate or expensive to have an impact. Some rather straightforward measures could include such steps as seeing that no one ever works alone and that anyone who must work after normal hours will be accompanied by a guard or someone else to the parking structure or lot.

Additionally, passwords should be changed often, and specially coded ID badges should be furnished to all employees.

The U.S. OSHA (Occupational Safety and Health Administration) has recommended a list of engineering and administrative controls that organizations should put in place (www.osha.gov/archive/oshinfo/priorities/violence.html):

- Create physical barriers such as bullet-resistant enclosures or shields, pass-through windows, or deep service counters;
- Install alarm systems, panic buttons, global positioning systems (GPS), and radios ("open mike switch");
- Put up convex mirrors, and have elevated vantage points and clear visibility of service and cash register areas;
- Ensure bright and effective lighting;
- Provide adequate staffing;
- Arrange furniture to prevent entrapment;
- Develop cash-handling controls, use of drop safes;
- Have height markers on exit doors to help in the identification of perpetrators;
- Have emergency procedures to use in case of robbery;
- Provide training in identifying hazardous situations and appropriate responses in emergencies;
- Install video surveillance equipment, in-car surveillance cameras and closed-circuit TV;
- Establish liaison with local police.

In addition, organizations should use pre-employment psychological screening as a method to avoid hiring potentially violent employees. However, once hired, the behavior of certain individuals should be monitored to identify issues before it is too late. "Remember, though, that any itemization of personal characteristics, while useful in focusing attention on the early detection and prevention of workplace violence, must also be used very carefully since such lists contain only very general guidance and the lists also change over time as new information is obtained. The presence of one or more of these factors does not guarantee that a person will commit an act of violence in the future" (Van Fleet & Van Fleet, 2010, p. 122).

Individuals to be monitored include those who have recently been disciplined or who have a history of violence; also, those whose job history is suspect, a history of substance abuse, or have unfavorable military records. But the list could also include a fascination with guns and those with extremist views. For a more complete list, see Van Fleet and Van Fleet (2010, chapter 9).

CULTURE

An organization's culture is critically important. The culture can lead to or deter workplace violence. So-called "sick" organizational cultures typically have higher-than-average levels of turnover, grievances and injury claims. There will be noticeable levels of B≈H as well as other indications of over-stressed personnel. A "sick" culture will then nurture conditions that will eventually lead to workplace violence. So, it is imperative to create conditions that will eliminate or prevent your organization from being "sick."

Avoiding a "sick" culture must begin at the top of the organization. Upper management must understand the importance of being proactive in developing and communicating a culture that prevents workplace violence. A culture of that sort not only reduces the chance that violence will occur but also enhances organizational effectiveness and performance. That sort of culture also satisfies the legal, moral and ethical obligations of the organization. Being forced to adopt health and safety regulations is clearly not sufficient, but also mere voluntary compliance isn't either. Upper management should go over and beyond to assure all organizational stakeholders that the health and safety of everyone is vital to the organization.

The culture that should be sought is one that truly values human assets. Accomplishing that culture will necessitate that owners and managers are truly committed to the health and safety of everyone in the organization. They must establish goals for the organization and its members that support this view. And they must be vigilant in their efforts to maintain those goals. When upper management accepts that it has the final responsibility for health and safety in the workplace, employees will genuinely feel that the organization has their interests at heart.

AFTERMATH

Individuals who have been the target of a violent event may experience shock, rage, fear or psychological numbness. They may even be in denial, telling themselves that it wasn't really an attack. But among the worse results may be panic attacks, flashbacks and sleep disturbances, including nightmares. Because of these sorts of impacts on individuals, organizations should provide some sort of stress debriefing and trauma counseling after a violent event. Larger organizations may have employee assistance programs that can provide assistance to victims.

It is also important for managers to understand that things will not quickly return to normal. Management needs to understand that those directly involved, as well as bystanders, will take time to recover. Those who were directly involved will clearly take considerable time to recover, but even those who were not directly involved will have some issues to deal with before "normal" occurs again. To aid the recovery process, managers need to communicate with everyone involved. They need to conduct a thorough review of events and take control of the story by ensuring that a correct version of events is made public.

Once things begin to settle back down, managers and workers need to consider why it happened and what could be done to prevent a recurrence. The next chapters explore what could be done in more detail.

MINI CASE: SECURITY EMPLOYMENT

In order to obtain employment in the highly secure government installation where I work, prospective employees must sign a document affirming their loyalty to our country and pledge to keep everything secret. This is true for even the most mundane jobs. It has recently come to light that a recently hired clerk was either not truthful when he signed the document or has changed since.

It was determined that he held a deep commitment to his former country and that he talked about our work with his friends "back home." He was warned that this was unacceptable, but when he is with his former countrymen, he seems not to be able to keep his mouth shut.

As you might suspect, his co-workers dislike him and want nothing to do with any project he is working on. We are afraid that at some point he will do worse than just talk. He may damage the installation or harm one of us.

1.   While his behavior is dangerous, is it B≈H?
2.   How do you think you would handle this problem if you were the boss?
3.   Is the boss or any employee obligated to report this behavior? Would you report it?

THINK ABOUT THIS CHAPTER AGAIN

Look at your examples of workplace violence and the categories you thought about at the beginning of this chapter. What changes in your categories would you make after thinking about the material in this chapter?

Then take a few minutes to prepare responses to these questions and actions. In particular, managers and human resource professionals should do this to be better prepared to prevent B≈H from evolving into violence in their organizations. Make your responses as if you are working in an organization. The responses should then be discussed by all students or participants.

Violence Questions

1. Have you seen any B≈H behaviors that you feel are evolving toward workplace violence?
2. What security measures has your organization taken to prevent workplace violence?
3. What sort of security measures exist in your organization?
4. Are those measures effective? Why or why not?

Violence Actions

In a way similar to what you did in Chapter 5, use the following form to note the forces that could lead to workplace violence in your organization. Indicate whether they are economic, social, political, individual, the organization's culture, or managers themselves.

The form is on a separate page to enable photocopying for use individually or by groups.

INSTRUCTIONS FOR FORM 6

Workplace Violence Forces in my Organization

In a way similar to what you did in the previous chapter, use this form to make a note of the forces that could lead to workplace violence in your organization. For forces outside the organization, indicate whether they are economic, social, or political. For inside forces note whether they are individuals, the organization's culture, or managers themselves.

Form 6   *Workplace violence forces in my organization*

WORKPLACE VIOLENCE FORCES IN MY ORGANIZATION
Outside Forces:
Economic
Social
Political
Inside Influences:
Individuals
Organization's culture
Managers

CHAPTER 6 CASES

These cases are based on actual situations with identifying names and locations changed or omitted. While anyone would benefit from reading and thinking about these cases, they are best used in a group context where different individual perspectives could be bought forth.

Case 6.1: Public Criticism

Jose is an intelligent, attractive young man. He was born and raised in the U.S.A., and other than his complexion or his name, you wouldn't know that he is Hispanic. After finishing high school, Jose got a cashier's position at a local grocery store to help with college expenses. That job involved providing a positive customer experience, scanning items, totaling customers' purchases, bagging purchases if needed, processing return transactions, collecting payments by accepting cash, check, or charge payments from customers and making change for cash customers, and, of course, balancing the cash drawer by counting cash at beginning and end of each work shift. Jose enjoys the work and feels a certain pride in being trusted to deal with so much money.

The other day Jose's new supervisor told him in front of other workers, "Jose, you made some mistakes when you did the final process of closing down your cash register at the end of the day." Jose asked, "What were the mistakes?" She simply replied, "You should be able to figure it out. You just need to pay closer attention to what you're doing and be more accurate in your counts in the future." While making sure that everyone could hear her, she also suggested that if he continues to make mistakes, she will have to reassign him to a position that doesn't pay as much or possibly even have to let him go. Jose angrily says, "She is picking on me specifically. My previous supervisor never criticized me but rather tried to help me do better. This new one doesn't treat others the same way. I tried to get her help in learning how to do the job well, but she simply said, 'If you can't handle it, then we'll just have to find someone who cares enough to do the job right.'"

Nobody had ever criticized Jose's work before that incident, and he cannot defend himself if the manager won't tell him what errors she thinks he made. Later that week Jose talked to some college friends about his concerns. They agreed that he needed more information from his supervisor but could not agree on how to get it. They also agreed that he should update his résumé and start looking. Maybe the supervisor doesn't know that her managerial skills are not acceptable or that she shows favoritism. Jose thinks that if she keeps on his case and won't help, he may just get so angry that he'll punch her lights out. Meanwhile, Jose is getting angrier and angrier as he thinks about how she acts.

He plans to count and recount, check and recheck, at closing and wait to see if the supervisor "rethinks" the problem. If not, he thinks it will be time to act.

1. How would you label the behavior in this case?
2. What should Jose do in this situation?
3. What is likely to happen?
4. Have you ever encountered a situation like this, and, if so, how did you handle it?
5. How might the organization prevent this sort of situation in the future?

Case 6.2: Screaming Supervisor

Lucy is a middle-aged woman who has been working for years to provide a little extra spending money for her family. Recently she took a new job and began to learn the ropes. However, this has not turned out to be the kind of work environment that she has experienced in the past.

When Lucy's supervisor gets angry with her, he yells and calls her names. He will then apologize, but a few days later, the cycle repeats itself. This has been going on for some time, and Lucy has gotten somewhat accustomed to it. But when she mentions the somewhat tense atmosphere in her division, her family and friends who work elsewhere are genuinely surprised. The company has always had an excellent reputation for the treatment of its employees, its excellent compensation and benefits packages, for providing a safe workplace, training its managers, and other aspects of work.

Outsiders don't see what goes on between the walls, of course, but Lucy and others do. Lucy's boss gets angry and yells at other workers, too, but because Lucy is relatively new on the job, she is more concerned than others seem to be. She worries because she knows that the boss can dismiss her easily without worrying about federal or state laws since she has been on the job for such a short time. And this is starting to make her so tense that it interferes with her work performance. Lucy is still young, does not have dependents, and is very well trained so she should feel free with the knowledge that she has the freedom to job-hop.

She confided in three co-workers that she feels afraid when the boss is around. They said just try to ignore his antics, as he has never hurt anyone – physically, they mean. Actually, a few workers in the past have been hurt enough emotionally or mentally to leave the company.

Lucy is becoming upset, moody and depressed. Other people are noticing her personality change. She tries to hide the work problems but the changes in her appearance and actions are too intense to hide. For example, the smiling Lucy rarely smiles; and when she does smile, it is obviously forced. She seems to have lost interest in spending time with her friends and co-workers – no more volleyball, no more kayaking, no more baking brownies to take to work. To make matters worse, she has started yelling at her husband and children. "When it reaches this point," her husband says, "it has gone too far. When it's broken, you gotta fix it."

1. How would you label the behavior in this case?
2. What should Lucy do in this situation?
3. What may happen in this situation?
4. Have you ever encountered a situation like this, and, if so, how did you handle it?
5. How might the organization prevent this sort of situation in the future?

7.   Trying to understand

Up to now, you have been thinking about B≈H in rather specific and pragmatic ways. Now you need to think more deeply about what might be the root or fundamental causes of the behaviors that you have considered in previous chapters. As in previous chapters, write down what you think those root causes might be and then refer to them as you read this chapter.

INTRODUCTION

To better understand B≈H behaviors, it is necessary to examine the underlying causes. So, in this chapter, factors that have been shown to be the basic sources or root causes of B≈H in organizations will be examined. As shown in Figure 7.1, those factors have been identified as stemming from the individual (characteristics, dispositions), the organization (culture, environments) and aspects of power (imbalances, inequities) (Van Fleet, 2017 & 2018).

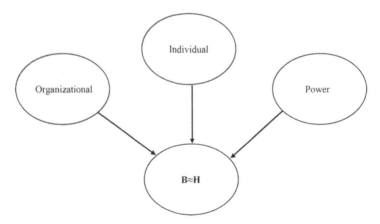

Figure 7.1   Underlying causes of B≈H

Following a discussion of those factors, a unique method for examining how those causes apply to your organization is presented. The method is the V-REEL® framework which, while originally devised to assist in strategic

decision making, provides an excellent and somewhat unusual way of identifying how B≈H might be reduced or even eradicated in your organization.

INDIVIDUAL DISPOSITION

As mentioned in an earlier chapter, some individuals are bad managers or bad
workers simply because their personalities and work styles are not compatible
with their positions in the organization. The individual disposition concept
suggests that personality traits predispose someone to be either a perpetrator or
a target (Nielsen & Knardahl, 2015; Francioli et al., 2015).

Perpetrators

For example, perpetrators may be seen as amiable, amusing or even charis-
matic by individuals who have not been targeted. Furthermore, when a target
finally reports the B≈H behavior and when questioned by authorities, the perpetrator will often charm those in power and convince them that it was a joke
or didn't really happen at all. Perpetrators can also use good looks, impeccable
dressing, and grooming to seduce others. This is known as the halo effect,
where those who look the best are the most trusted and respected by others.

Most perpetrators are male managers who depend on no one talking about
B≈H so they can act with impunity (Namie, 2017). Indicators that a manager is
engaging in B≈H (Gordon, 2021) are that he/she

- impedes your success;
- intimidates you;
- intrudes on your privacy;
- isolates you at work;
- questions your adequacy and your commitment;
- spreads rumors about you;
- undermines your work;
- verbally abuses you.

Perpetrators also are generally convincing liars and actors. They seem to be
able to spread the most compelling rumors and lies. They can persuade others
not to associate with the target so that the target loses support and has no one
to turn to for help or guidance. Targets often react emotionally while the perpetrator remains calm and collected. Charlene is an example.

I'M AN EASY TARGET

My name is Charlene and I know that my personality makes me an easy target in my company. We are on the 20th floor of a major downtown building, where more than 55 workers are occupied with their desktop computers in cubicles. But me? I don't know how to stand up for myself when someone seems to laugh and joke at my expense. I recognize that my problem is magnified by my inability to control my emotions. I cry when I try to deal with this, and many of my co-workers make fun of me behind my back. I simply don't know how to handle all of this. I have been abused for so long; I can't stop the hurt and anger. I don't know what to do.

The emotional responses of Charlene do not deter her tormentors; indeed, they may embolden them. Management and other co-workers will then identify with the perpetrator because of the coolness he or she displays rather than the emotional response of the target. Perpetrators can explain away and rationalize just about any bad behavior. They tell a story so convincingly that others will find it hard not to accept. So, the target gets blamed rather than the perpetrator. In this way, the perpetrator attempts to increase his or her influence in the organization.

Kets De Vries (2018) argues that perpetrators may be seeking attention because that gives them a feeling of importance. Further, he postulates that they may be insecure, moved by envy and resentment as they perceive others as threats. They may use B≈H to boost their self-esteem. They likely had rough upbringings – little positive attention or even abuse as children. Thus, they may be acting as they observed adults acting when they were children. They may have poor social skills and simply don't know how to deal properly with others and their emotions.

Zhang and Leidner (2018) suggest several possible explanations as to how perpetrators legitimize their actions, at least to themselves. They may feel that organizational policies or guidelines are unclear or that the situation leaves them no choice by emphasizing productivity over collegiality. The perpetrators tell themselves and others that there was no harm or injury caused by their actions. Indeed, they may persist because the targets are not defending themselves. Finally, the perpetrator may feel that the target deserves what he or she gets. This, then, minimizes any feelings of shame or guilt for the actions of the perpetrator. Maybe the person just doesn't fit in as in this case.

WHY DOES COLOR NOT FIT IN?

I applied for a greeter's job at a local big box store. I know I met all of their requirements and the interview seemed to go well until it was suggested that I might not "fit in." I did notice that everyone else was white while I was not. I think that was why I didn't fit.

Targets

The example above does appear to show discrimination; however, the discrimination could have been a result of other personal characteristics. Just as perpetrators seem to have common personal dispositions, so do victims. Some individuals may also have dispositions that make them more likely to be targets or victims of B≈H.

While there is not a fixed set of characteristics, there is some evidence to suggest that some individuals are more likely to be victims. Victims tend to be neurotic, less agreeable, and extraverted (Glasø et al., 2007). They also may be aggressive, lack social skills, think negative thoughts, experience difficulties in solving social problems, and be rejected or isolated by their co-workers (Cook et al., 2010).

Kane (2019) suggests a list of personal characteristics of victims. She suggests that victims

- may pose a threat to the perpetrator;
- are vulnerable;
- are less likely to retaliate, confront or report the perpetrator;
- use collaboration, compromise and team building in their work practices;
- have strong morals and integrity;
- are more likely to be women or minorities.

Another set of personal characteristics of targets of bullies has been suggested by Rigglo (2013). He indicates that likely targets

- are *different* (workplace bullies often go after workers who stand out in various ways);
- are *competent* (bullies target those who are skilled or competent, viewing them as competitors);
- are *nice* (bullies pick on those whom they feel won't resist – those who try to get along with everyone);
- are *socially isolated* (bullies target those who have little social support).

ORGANIZATIONAL ENVIRONMENT

The organizational environment and the job design concept suggest that characteristics of the organization or the work itself contribute to B≈H (Li et al., 2019; Hurjui & Stefan, 2016). Jobs that result in high levels of strain have been shown to be associated with both being a target and being a perpetrator of workplace B≈H (Baillien, De Cuyper, & De Witte, 2011).

The idea is that, in work environments where the constraints and norms that create order and predictability are less visible, incivility and negative treatment of co-workers can develop. Bullying can be promoted by poor information flow, an authoritative way of settling differences, a lack of mutual conversations about goals, and insufficient ways to influence an individual's situation. Any kind of disruptive organizational change, lack of procedural justice, and a poor psychosocial safety climate are positively associated with B≈H. Downsizing is particularly problematic as employees become fearful of losing their jobs.

Irregular work schedules lead to higher job demands and hence are also more likely to result in B≈H. Job insecurity promotes a strained climate when employees see colleagues as potential rivals for jobs. The resulting feelings of competition and suspicion may also lead to B≈H. Indeed, the higher the strains, the more likely B≈H will occur. Joe's group is clearly feeling strained as the workforce shrank.

A TIME FOR CAPABLE LEADERS

Our group had people leave because schedules were constantly changing. Because no replacements were hired, the rest of us had to pick up the work that they were doing in addition to our own. Now all of us are overworked, but if we raise questions about this, we are told to "suck it up" or leave. No doubt some of us will leave.

Leadership style is also important. As organizations change to adapt to new conditions, workloads and hours worked may also change – increase or decrease (Astrauskaite et al., 2015). Under these circumstances, managers may become autocratic and dictatorial. These management environments, which may be characterized by fear, seem to encourage B≈H. Perpetrators appear to be emboldened in these conditions. However, passive laissez-faire leadership also increases the probability that B≈H will occur as perpetrators are less likely to be identified or action taken in the event of complaints.

POWER IMBALANCES

Power imbalances contribute to B≈H, especially when the perpetrator perceives a low cost from management for his or her behaviors (Feijó et al., 2019). Indeed, B≈H results from a regular abuse of power (Sharp & Smith, 1994, p. 2). Management members may be guilty of contributing to the problem if they choose to ignore the behavior. Indeed, they are often the cause of the problem as they exhibit the same behavior.

Perpetrators Have More Power than Targets

Because perpetrators use power, they are able to influence and change the behavior and attitudes of others. Perpetrators may be those who are seeking peer group recognition, or they may already have high status in the group. Jane's low power in her firm has resulted in an unexpected consequence.

TOO ATTRACTIVE

I have a college degree, but the owner of our firm insists that I work the front desk because he says it is important to have a good-looking female there. I do think that I am attractive and have always tried to look my best, but it seems to work against me here. What he expects is so beneath what I'm capable of doing. I think maybe I should quit and then dress down in future interviews to prevent this from happening again.

Managers and Older Workers Have More Power

Unskilled workers are far more likely to be subjected to B≈H than are managers or supervisors. Older employees, young employees, and temporary workers in positions with little formal or informal power are also frequent targets. Non-white, multiracial, Asian and black workers are targeted more frequently than are white workers, who are more likely to be the perpetrators. Vulnerable individuals – those with lower educational levels, lower income levels, and hourly workers – are also more likely targets. Females are more apt to be targets than are males but, perhaps surprisingly, the perpetrator is highly likely to be of the same sex (Lutgen-Sandvik et al., 2007). The situation in which Ilene found herself is one of same-sex B≈H.

BOSS DOES NOT UTILIZE HR DEPARTMENT

There is no HR department at my small workplace. I've asked my boss many times to do something about the bullying, but he doesn't do anything. He tells me that he has spoken with her and doesn't expect anything to change. So, I should "put it in a box, put it on a shelf, and get over it." I requested that a formal note should be made in her personnel file, but nothing was done. A rude reply by email just made me feel worse. My only option would appear to be quitting. And when I look for a new job, I'll be sure that the company has an HR department.

Men Have More Power than Women

A 2017 survey showed that just over 60% of American workers are affected by bullying in some fashion. It also showed that 70% of the perpetrators are men, while 60% of the targets are women (www.workplacebullying.org/wbiresearch/wbi-2017-survey). Distressingly, over 70% of organizational reactions to bullying are actually detrimental to the targets, as are 60% of co-worker reactions. It should come as no surprise that 29% of those targeted never reported it, as over 60% of the bullies are bosses, and those in power are not likely to be reported by their workers.

Surveys of harassment, particularly sexual harassment, suggest similar results. A national study conducted in 2019 (www.stopstreetharassment.org/?s=survey) showed that around 71% of women in the U.S.A. had experienced street harassment (e.g., catcalls, wolf whistles, flashing, homophobic or transphobic slurs, persistent requests for the individual's name), as have 28% of men. A 2018 survey of the insurance industry found that 70% had experienced sexual harassment while at work (www.carriermanagement.com/features/2018/08/27/183359.htm). Almost half (49.2%) of the respondents to a survey by the Maine Association of Nonprofits reported experiencing sexual harassment (Hutchins, 2019). Like bullying, the targets of harassment are more likely to be females, and they don't talk about it because the male involved has more power, and the target fears retaliation.

V-REEL®, A NEW WAY OF ANALYZING B≈H

The interaction of the three influences just discussed – organizational, individual and power – are thought to lead some individuals to engage in B≈H. To further develop our understanding, there needs to be a new way of thinking about why B≈H occurs in your organization and what you may be able to do about it. The V-REEL® framework, originally developed for strategic analysis in organizations, provides that new way (Flint, 2018). As used here, it is a framework that provides a unique way of thinking about the causes of B≈H and how to eradicate it in your organization.

The V-REEL® framework consists of five interconnected components – value, rareness, eroding factors, enabling factors and longevity.

Value

Value, as used here, refers to the organization's productivity and its value to customers, clients and employees. Using the concept of V-REEL®, you would try to ascertain how reducing or eliminating B≈H will contribute to the organization's value – the usefulness of the organization's output. Value is the customers', clients' and employees' perceptions "that a product, service, or experience is worth more than the money it costs to create" (Flint, 2018, p. 166).

Every department, indeed every individual in an organization, is engaged in the process of creating value. This goes back to Porter's value chain idea to some degree (Porter, 1985 & 2001; Porter & Kramer, 2011). The human resources department, in particular, is involved in that value creation. The human resources department is given the task of creating more value than it consumes (its budget) relative to the management of human capital inside the organization. Chapter 9 suggests that it can do so by activating the human capital of the organization.

Departments and individual managers strive to develop competencies that inculcate proper behaviors and attitudes in employees by using training, compensation and setting/maintaining the culture. This is the essence of the value-creation process. Spotting an incompetency that is destroying value and eliminating it may not be a means to create new value, but it definitely is a net gain in value creation. Everyone in an organization should strive to increase the organization's value.

Rareness

Rareness refers to the capability of managing the contributing factors to B≈H within the organization. Clearly, some organizations have a greater possibility of managing those factors than do others. It is rare or unique that any organization is able to effectively manage all of the contributing factors at the same time. That rareness is within the context of the organization at large. So, it is important to recognize just how much control the organization has or doesn't have over these factors.

The human resource department has been given the unique responsibility to develop value-creating competencies related to the management of human capital. Human resources personnel should take advantage of those rare responsibilities and their associated resources and capabilities. In a larger view, the human resources department might be able to develop rare competencies in the context of the organization's resources and capabilities that other organizations cannot match. For example, the organization may develop proprietary software for talent acquisition. Talent acquisition is an ongoing strategic approach that focuses on acquiring skilled candidates on a long-term basis.

The social capital inside and around the organization (or other factors) might allow that to happen. If that were the case, the department could become a source of distinctive competency for the organization that allows it to create more unique value as compared to competing organizations. An example might be SouthWest Airline's history regarding its organizational culture that was maintained via human resource policies of selection and compensation plus strong referent leadership (Smith, 2004).

Eroding Factors

Eroding factors are those things that impede your ability to reduce B≈H. They get in the way of achieving productivity. Unconcerned top management is clearly an eroding factor. An organizational culture that supports perpetrators with power would also be an eroding factor. Characteristics of your particular organization will suggest other eroding factors that are at work in your situation. If your organization depends on the talent and skill of a particular person, what will happen if that person suffers a tragic accident or merely leaves the organization? This situation could be particularly relevant in small start-up businesses.

These eroding factors are associated with the way in which an organization treats its basic human resources. These factors feed upward into the erosion of value creation at the organizational level. With enough erosion, the effect will not be localized within the organization and will extend to the shareholders and other stakeholders. So, it is vital that eroding factors be eliminated. Of course, it is probably impossible to eliminate all eroding factors, so you will need to prioritize them and concentrate your efforts on the most impactful ones.

Enabling Factors

Enabling factors are those things that improve your ability to manage B≈H. They help you to achieve productivity. Learning more about the causes of B≈H could well be an enabling factor. Hiring better educated, more capable non-white, multiracial, Asian, and black workers in positions with more formal or informal power could be an enabling factor. Educational and training programs focused on identifying and eliminating B≈H also would be enabling.

Another aspect of enabling factors is to mitigate or eliminate eroding factors. Policies to educate managers about the eroding factors embedded within poor and bad management responses to B≈H activity in the organization would be an important enabling factor. Strong referent power from leadership within the organizational culture would be an enabling factor that works against the eroding factors of lower-level managers' and employees' examples of bad behavior.

The enabling factors feed upward and aggregate into the creation of value at the organization level. They are directed first toward removing any human resource incompetency or increasing any human resource competency; the accumulation of value creation for the organization follows.

Longevity

Finally, longevity suggests how long any given effort to deal with B≈H might be sustained. Will your efforts be short-lived, or will they continue for quite a while? Immediate "fixes" may well be short-lived, but changes to the organization's culture are more likely to last. One could also hope that a combination of strong, supportive enabling factors that work to mitigate or eliminate eroding factors should serve to increase the longevity of a healthy organization that avoids B≈H instances and properly manages any instances that do occur.

At this point, the V-REEL® analysis should help the organization to identify its distinctive competencies. These are the organization's strengths, skills, technologies or resources that differentiate it from competitors and enable it to provide superior and unique customer value. The more difficult it is for competitors to imitate, the greater is the longevity.

The combination of a healthy organizational culture and work environment supporting and enabling strong, distinctive competencies for value creation may also be difficult for competitors to understand and duplicate. Since B≈H is so widespread, the potential to develop rare capabilities related to minimizing the negative effects of B≈H in the organization may exist.

The goal is to remove incompetent behaviors quickly and then to put in place human resource competencies that have strong longevity. Thinking back through issues surrounding value/rareness/eroding/enabling with the goal of maximizing longevity both in terms of minimizing incompetence and maximizing competence might manifest new insights not seen without thinking about the longevity issues.

The V-REEL® framework is not a quick fix, but its use can aid you and your group or team in reducing B≈H and achieving higher productivity. The organization needs to have clear goals and a B≈H policy that is linked to the value of your organization. With the assistance of the organization's human resource personnel, you and your group or team should identify eroding factors and consider how to reduce their impact. Likewise, enabling factors should be identified and efforts made to take advantage of them.

This new way of thinking about managing the factors contributing to B≈H should be useful to both you and your organization. While fully utilizing it will be neither quick nor easy, doing so will result in a strong culture and the achievement of value for the organization.

The use of the V-REEL® framework to prevent or deal with B≈H for individuals and organizations will be described in more detail in the next two chapters. The first (Chapter 8) examines what you as an individual can do in general as well as the specifics identified using the framework. Chapter 9 covers what organizations also can do, again in general and specifically utilizing the framework.

MINI CASE: ANONYMOUS NOTES

Our organization has a peer evaluation system to determine job assignments, travel reimbursements, raises and possible promotions. Clearly, these evaluations are quite important to everyone. However, two co-workers, Al and Claude, seem to suffer in this system. If word gets out that they might be considered for special assignments or promotions, suddenly anonymous notes would appear. The notes might go to a member of management but more frequently are spread to all employees in their unit.

The notes either implicitly or explicitly say that the individual (either Al or Claude) had done something unethical or immoral. One note even suggested that the two of them were lovers. It soon became apparent who the note writer was but no one in management ever examined her computer or specifically asked her about it. In the past, if anyone said anything to her about anything she would holler discrimination and the matter would be dropped. I guess management fears such a charge, so they do nothing.

1. Is the note writer engaging in B≈H?
2. What/who is the real problem in this organization?
3. What should upper management do in such a situation?

THINK ABOUT THIS CHAPTER AGAIN

Look at the causes you thought about. What changes in those would you make after thinking about the material in this chapter? Then take a few minutes to prepare responses to these questions and actions. In particular, managers and human resource professionals should do this to be better prepared to handle B≈H in their organizations.

Understanding Questions

1. Think of several ways that B≈H might be encouraged by the organization.
2. Think of 3–4 ways that power or power imbalances might encourage B≈H.
3. Think about how the three factors (individual, organizational, power) interact in your situation. Does this suggest making any changes in your behavior?
4. What are the eroding factors in your organization? How could they be reduced?
5. What are the enabling factors in your organization? How could they be strengthened? Are there other enabling factors that your upper management might list?

Understanding Actions

Think of an individual whose personality traits suggest to you and probably others that this person is predisposed to be a perpetrator. Describe this individual's appearance and behaviors that lead you to that conclusion. Start by indicating that person's job title and position in the firm. Use the following form to identify enabling and eroding factors in your organization.

The form is on a separate page to enable photocopying for use individually or by groups.

INSTRUCTIONS FOR FORM 7

List five enabling and five eroding factors that exist in your organization.

CHAPTER 7 CASES

These cases are based on actual situations with identifying names and locations changed or omitted. While anyone would benefit from reading and thinking about these cases, they are best used in a group context where different individual perspectives could be bought forth.

Case 7.1: No Help Appeal

Charlotte is a well-educated labor economist. She earned her bachelor's, master's, and doctoral degrees from a well-known university. Upon receipt of her doctorate, she was hired as an Assistant Professor at a major research university. After ten years she was finally awarded tenure and promoted to Associate Professor. She has always gotten good reviews from her students as well as from her Department Chair. She serves as the faculty advisor to the student chapter of the national student organization, United Students Against Sweatshops (USAS). She has secured over $150,000 in grants from the Department of Labor to support her research and has published numerous papers in top journals in her field.

However, all is not well for Charlotte. She has recently begun to be "bothered" by another faculty member. "Bothered" is a bit of an understatement as he has taken to disrupting her experiments, telling his students to avoid taking her classes, and criticizing her work to others in the field. The university does have policies stating that the kind of behaviors that this faculty member was engaged in are unacceptable and that those behaviors would not be tolerated. But unless a complaint is filed, nothing happens.

To make matters worse, Charlotte is pregnant. She says, "I was worried that the stress of dealing with him might somehow harm the baby I was carrying."

Form 7   *Things that improve/reduce the ability to manage B≈H*

ENABLING FACTORS

Things that improve the ability to manage B≈H

ERODING FACTORS IN MY ORGANIZATION

Things that impede the ability to reduce B≈H

So, using those policies to support her, Charlotte reported everything to the Dean of her school. She had taken copious notes about disruptions of her experiments, false statements the other professor had made to students and other faculty, intentionally omitting her name from meetings and committees, and so on. She felt confident that her boss, the Department Chair, would talk to the other professor and stop the bad behaviors instantly.

But her meeting with her Chair was surprising and disappointing. "He has it upside down," she said. "He questioned me about what I do or have done. He actually told me that perhaps I was creating a bad environment! What an accusation!" Charlotte told her husband about the meeting with the Chair: "I couldn't believe what he was saying. It's unreal. Instead of getting some help and support, he suggested that I'm the one causing problems. I should have just left well enough alone. And that's what I would have done except I was concerned about the stress hurting our baby."

1. How would you label the behavior in this case?
2. Are the root causes evident in this case?
3. What should Charlotte do in this situation?
4. Have you ever encountered a situation like this, and, if so, how did you handle it?
5. How might the organization prevent this sort of situation in the future?

Case 7.2: Loss of Job

A few years ago, Ryan moved to Ohio for a job that seemed to be a perfect fit for him and for the company, Azuretta. He says he felt that he had good relationships with co-workers not only in his department but also in other departments. He worked hard and never complained to anyone at work, although at raise time two years ago he did ask his supervisor if he could possibly find a few more dollars since he had had only one raise in eleven years. He got the usual response – we'll try. Nothing else was said.

Seven months ago, Ryan suffered a car accident on the way to work when his 2001 Chevy Cavalier was totaled by a red-light runner. The accident forced him to miss seven months of work. Finally, last week he was able to return to work. Monday morning felt good – he was excited, he had really missed the comradery of co-workers. Staying home had eventually become boring.

He decided to make a quick stop at his workplace and then go by all the other production areas just to say, "I'm back!" But when he slid open the door to the room where he had worked, one of the few women who worked at Azuretta was seated at his previous station. Alicia looked up at Ryan's smiling face in utter shock, then yelled in a loud whisper, "Oh my God! I thought you were dead!!" She then stood up to hug Ryan, tears welling up in her eyes in disbelief. Ryan was surprised, too. Alicia had become so skinny and emaci-ated, weariness from the never-ending abuse written all over her body and face. They laughed heartily as they embraced, and he greeted everyone else in the office.

They didn't have time to say much, though. A "traitor-colleague" at the entrance had already alerted Ryan's supervisor, so Mr. Stanley was already rushing up the corridor to block Ryan from proceeding toward his office and prevent him from greeting anyone else of the 40+ colleagues along the way. He pulled Ryan aside into the meeting office and informed him that he must go home. He said that having been absent so long, Ryan must wait until the company gets him medically approved by the company's own physician. "Don't call us. We'll call you." Ryan called the union worker who had been following his case, and she verified the information. He went home to wait.

Ryan received no word from anyone the following week until late Friday when their legal representative couriered a memo to him and his union representative. The message indicated that Ryan was fired. Ryan and the legal representative were already on their way to a meeting with the union representative, "at which time we are sure we will find a mutually beneficial agreement." He's still waiting.

Ryan calls them The Vipers, because, in Ryan's opinion, "Azuretta bought off all the legal physicians, various key figures in the unions, and all the lawyers I had turned to for help." Ryan also thinks they bought off someone in the "finance and payroll departments as well . . . but no! No corruption in Azuretta! Corruption is non-existent. What a joke!"

A few months later, Ryan got a message from Alicia, saying that Azuretta's treatment of Ryan had given her the courage to say "Enough." She had left Azuretta and found herself another job and also was becoming a life coach on the side. Ryan said that, when he saw her pictures with her eyes sparkling and her face glowing, he knew that she was no longer a defeated, cowering, fearful employee but the captain of her ship – enjoying life and helping others to enjoy theirs. Ryan says he has decided to say goodbye to The Vipers and take control of his life. He's happier already.

1. How are the root causes reflected in this case?
2. What should Azuretta have done promptly when they learned of Ryan's accident and hospitalization?
3. If you had been in Ryan's situation at the time of his accident, what would you have done then? What would you do now?
4. Should Ryan file a lawsuit? Would he have qualified based on his medical condition?
5. How might the organization prevent this sort of situation in the future?

8. Individual actions

Now think about what you personally might do to reduce or eliminate the behaviors that you have identified in previous chapters. Write down specific actions that you think might be useful in this regard. Be reasonable; don't come up with actions that would actually be unrealistic. Developing unrealistic ideas would be a waste of time and lead to frustration.

INTRODUCTION

Since you are reading this book, for whatever the reason, you feel a need or an interest in the problem of unacceptable workplace behavior. Perhaps you or others you know are currently experiencing a problem. What may you, personally, do as an individual to reduce or eliminate the behaviors that you have identified in previous chapters? That is what this chapter is about.

Discover Company Policy

The first thing that you as an individual should do is determine where your organization stands with regard to negative and unacceptable workplace behaviors. Does it already have a policy about bullying, harassment, mistreatment, verbal abuse, or anything similar? If so, then you should follow the guidance provided by that policy or policies. Many small companies do not have a formal policy on B≈H or anything similar. Unfortunately, some individuals in those situations may withdraw or become less involved with their jobs or organizations; and withdrawal is not a good option.

Check with Human Resources

Even if there is no formal policy, you should check with your organization's human resource personnel or employee handbook, or any other document that spells out the organization's values and expectations. Being familiar with this information can strengthen your case if you decide to make a complaint and are able to point to specific language in those documents as the basis for your complaint. You can, of course, try to avoid the perpetrator; but avoidance is not likely to stop the B≈H.

Discuss with Others

If your organization has no policies, no human resource person, no handbook, or anything else that can provide guidance, you must nevertheless strive to act in an ethically and morally sound manner. If others in the organization do not act that way, try to engage them in conversations about what they should be doing. The V-REEL® analysis introduced in the previous chapter should assist you in identifying specific factors for talking with others.

V-REEL® ANALYSIS

Use the V-REEL® framework you developed in that chapter to try to understand better and hence control the B≈H to which you are being subjected. Review the specific eroding and enabling factors that you identified in the form at the end of that chapter.

Identify Eroding Factors

Remember that *eroding factors* are those things that impede your ability to reduce B≈H or things that encourage B≈H in some way. Think of them as negatives; they negate – counteract or neutralize – your efforts to get rid of B≈H. They get in the way of decreasing B≈H and prevent you from being as productive as you might otherwise be.

For example, managers who don't care or are too busy to help are eroding actors, as are co-workers who would rather turn their backs and pretend nothing is happening.

FROM ANXIETY TO WITHDRAWAL

My anxiety makes me feel that there is no way out of the situation that I'm in. I feel insecure. I take things too personally. When my friends don't answer right away, I think that they don't want to talk to me that they are tired of hearing about it. I dread situations where someone might reject me. When I feel rejected, I feel like I'm a non-person – invisible and unimportant. I never invite anyone from work to socialize with me as I would be embarrassed if they turned me down. And no one ever suggests getting together after work, so I just assume they don't want to be around me at work or anywhere else.

There are many possible eroding factors. Interpreting the goals and/or reward system as not caring about the worth of human assets would be eroding. And this would be true even if there do not appear to be any consequences for those who engage in B≈H. A personal lack of empathy or a family history of B≈H behaviors might lead to an individual becoming a perpetrator. Excessive narcissism or feelings of superiority (based on race, gender, religion, etc.) might lead to individuals becoming perpetrators. A history of getting away with B≈H in this or other organizations could also be an eroding factor by encouraging perpetrators.

Without blaming yourself, are you doing something or acting in some way that diminishes your ability to avoid or decrease B≈H? Is there something about your workspace that in some way diminishes your ability to avoid or decrease B≈H? You need to try to eliminate them or reduce their impact through the use of enabling factors.

Identify Enabling Factors

As you will recall, *enabling factors* are those things that improve your ability to manage B≈H. They help you to decrease B≈H and become more productive. Learning more about the causes of B≈H could well be an enabling factor. Developing new skills to improve your standing in the organization could be empowering and help to decrease the B≈H to which you are subjected. Perhaps some sort of change in your workplace would be enabling. Learning about the consequences of B≈H in the lives of workplace violence victims would help you to appreciate both the personal and personnel costs of B≈H.

For example, surrounding oneself with people who will reinforce good behavior might be enabling. Developing empathy through working with others (teams, volunteering with disadvantaged, service projects, etc.) would be enabling, as would exposure to diversity within the organization. Indeed, any sort of relating to others appropriately and developing accountability with others would be enabling. From a theological perspective, if everyone is made in the image of God, then everyone deserves respect and treatment of the highest order. Finding ways to enable that mindset in people could go a long way toward reducing B≈H in organizations.

TALK WITH FAMILY AND FRIENDS

Don't assume that you are alone. Talk with your family and friends, your peers in the organization, or a mentor if you have one. Have them focus on enabling and eroding factors to provide you with more options. They may wish to avoid involvement, but they may also provide helpful advice. Tell them what's going on and what, if anything, you've tried. At the very least, discussing your situation with them may ease the tension and the hurt that you feel.

JOB INSECURITY: AN ERODING FACTOR

I'm afraid of losing my job. My supervisor keeps asking me to have a drink with him after work and implies that if I do, I might be eligible for a promotion, and if I don't, I might have to look for another job since I don't fit here. I didn't know what to do, but my friends have been very supportive and told me to stand up for myself and that if I lose this job, they'll help me get another. But jobs are difficult to find, and my supervisor might give me a bad recommendation.

REHEARSE A SCENARIO

Rather than just talking over things with your family or friends, enlist their assistance in helping you prepare for the next steps. You need not only to think carefully about what you are going to say and do, but it would be best to practice or rehearse each step. In one scenario, have a friend or family member assume the role of the perpetrator. How would you stand up to him or her? What would you say? What would you do?

Then, in another scenario, have them assume the part of your manager or supervisor or someone from human resources. Again, what would you say? What would you do? But in this scenario, the person helping you should ask you questions like: "Tell me what happened? Tell me exactly what occurred. What were you doing? What did you do to provoke this?" Yes, you must be prepared for someone to turn the perpetrator into a victim and accuse you of having caused the incident. Knowing this ahead of time and thinking about how you would respond will enable you to present a more reasonable description of the event.

Do this more than once so that it becomes easier for you to say what you need to say and respond to challenging questions. Then, when you feel you are ready, move on to the next step.

STAND YOUR GROUND

Perpetrators don't like to be called to task. They don't want to be challenged. So, be assertive but not aggressive. Just tell the person that the behavior is unacceptable, ask them to stop, and be firm in doing so. Let him or her know that you are not going to tolerate the behavior. Say things like "This is not funny," "This is not a joke," "Your behavior is not acceptable," or just "Stop it!" Keep your emotions in check, as one thing the perpetrator probably wants is to see you upset. Speak calmly and firmly and walk away to end the incident but be prepared not to be heard – or worse.

TARGET, NOT PERPETRATOR, REPRIMANDED

I confronted the guy who was bullying me and made it clear that his comments and behavior were hurtful. Instead of stopping, he went to our supervisor and suggested that I was making false accusations and needed counseling. He said he was the victim and that I should be reprimanded. Unfortunately, our supervisor listened only to him. So, I got reprimanded and sent to HR for counseling. He didn't listen and neither did HR. In the future, I won't trust a perpetrator, HR, or a supervisor to have adequate training for resolving personnel problems. The solution, I'm afraid, is to find another job.

DOCUMENT PERPETRATOR BEHAVIOR

Document what happened. Gather your evidence. Write down what happened – note what the specific B≈H behavior was – and who did it (full names and, if necessary, titles and positions). Use the Glossary from this book to help you with the proper words to use. Write down the time and date the incident happened and where it occurred (work area, cafeteria, parking lot, etc.). Include the names of any bystanders who were present and may corroborate what occurred. If you think you know why it happened (was there jealousy, retaliation, or something else?), note that as well.

The important thing is to write down every detail as best you can and as soon as you can after the incident. Having a written record is important, particularly if any sort of legal action comes about. A form such as the following one could be used, although your organization may already have a form for you to use. Because not everyone is always truthful in these circumstances or at least doesn't perceive the truth equally, you should attest that what you are stating is the truth as you see it – that it is accurate and correct to the best of your knowledge.

The form (Form 8.1) is on a separate page to enable photocopying for use individually or by groups.

Documenting the B≈H lets you tell your side without being ignored or having your experience belittled by anyone else. It can be therapeutic, in that it lets you express your emotions as you may not otherwise be able to do. It also provides a record of the B≈H that could potentially be used in any legal proceedings.

Form 8.1   *Workplace B≈H report form*

WORKPLACE B≈H REPORT FORM
Important definitions to consider:
• **Unwelcome verbal or physical conduct constitutes B≈H when this conduct explicitly or implicitly adversely affects an individual's employment, unreasonably interferes with an individual's work performance, or creates an intimidating, hostile, or offensive work environment.**
• A **target** is an individual subjected to B≈H by his/her peers, coworkers, supervisor, and/or another manager.
• A **perpetrator** is an individual who initiates or performs the **B≈H.**
Name of person reporting:_____ Name of target:_____   (if different than person reporting) Name of alleged perpetrator:_____ Date(s) of alleged incident(s):_____ Time(s) of alleged incident(s):_____ Location(s) of alleged incident(s):_____ (Include specific location in building)
Description of the alleged incident(s): _____ _____ _____ _____ _____
Any other details that should be considered with regard to this alleged incident(s): _____ _____ _____
I attest that the information here is accurate and correct to the best of my knowledge. Signed: _____ Date submitted:_____
This matter will be handled as confidentially as possible. For administrative use, date submitted:_____

REPORT TO MANAGEMENT

Use your documentation to report the B≈H to management. The above form would be a good one to use, but you should make sure to retain a copy in case something happens to the one you submit. Studies have shown that very few of those who suffer harassment ever file formal complaints (McCann et al., 2018; Feldblum & Lipnic, 2016). Hopefully, using the material and the framework of this book, those of you who are bullied or harassed will have the courage to speak up and address the problem. At the very least, you should have sufficient information to make a reasoned decision as to whether to speak up or leave.

If a manager or supervisor was involved, report it to someone farther up the chain of command. Your organization may have policies that specify how you should go about reporting the incident. Be sure to read the organization's manuals or handbooks or review your employment contract. Your organization may have an employee assistance program where you can obtain confidential support. If there isn't a procedure spelled out, contact your Human Resources office if you have one. If your organization does not have a Human Resources office, you should try to contact a higher level of management in hopes that your request will not be ignored.

If you are a member of a union, be sure to contact your union representatives and fill them in on the details of the B≈H. Check the collective bargaining agreement for a grievance procedure that should be followed. Read the agreement and follow the appropriate procedure. The typical grievance procedure begins with a discussion to see if the matter can be resolved informally. If not, the employer should carry out an investigation by getting statements from everyone concerned.

Then a meeting will be held to discuss possible actions that might be taken. A decision is then made, although such decisions are subject to appeal. Appeals may simply be a review of everything that transpired, or a rehearing may be conducted if there is an indication that the initial hearing was somehow flawed. Note though that in larger organizations, there may be a second or even a third appeal, each to a higher level of management. Be prepared to wait. Investigations can sometimes take weeks and hearings can last for days, so don't expect immediate action or results.

Your report may be oral, written, in person, by phone or hotline, or even anonymous. But no matter what form your report takes, you should keep written notes about the B≈H, how you reported it, and what was done about it. While your incident is being investigated, you may ask for a different work location, a shift change or transfer, or even increased supervision to monitor the situation. If written, a form such as the one shown earlier should be used.

TALK FACTS, NOT FEELINGS

When you make your report, use your documentation, and stick to the facts rather than just your feelings. Remember that you are seeking redress for the situation and not vengeance. Try not to hold a grudge. While your pride, self-esteem or self-confidence may be damaged, a factual account is more likely to be taken seriously. Emphasize how and what the B≈H is costing the organization. Present the facts about the real costs in terms of time wasted, reduced productivity, absenteeism and turnover. Especially if assault and battery occurred, you should get medical attention and note the costs of that as well. Pain and suffering costs should also be noted. Frequently, noting the costs does more than anything else to bring about changes in behavior.

RELIGION IS THE ISSUE

My supervisor has frequently suggested that she feels my Islamic traditions are strange and wonders why I don't convert to Christianity. More recently, she has made some of her comments while others were around. As a result, some of my co-workers are also becoming a bit hostile and standoffish. It's becoming a bad place to work so I've started a notebook documenting everything that's going on.

AWAIT RESULTS

Even if the B≈H can't be officially proven or isn't deemed an official violation, the organization still needs to consider making some changes. After all, when an individual reports an incident, something must have happened. People typically don't report incidents to management until the problem has started to impact their work or the quality of their life. So, organizations and managers need to have plans for getting things back to normal.

Regardless of the outcome, both the victim and the perpetrator need some counseling as to how to behave in the future. The same would also be true for any witnesses. Everyone involved will have suffered psychologically to some degree so informal meetings and possibly even more formal therapy may be needed to return the organization to its usual operating position.

Don't expect a quick return to normality. Be prepared for nothing to happen. All too often, organizations ignore, evade or even cover up complaints. Your complaint about B≈H may well be dismissed as nothing more than the usual sort of grumbling or bellyaching that occurs in any organization. But you should also be prepared to have to "move your complaint" up the chain of command to try to get changes made.

IMMIGRANT

Co-workers constantly refer to me by identifying my home country even though I am now a U.S. citizen. They say things like, "Maria, does everyone in Guatemala work as slow as you do?" or "Do all immigrants do poor work or is it just you?" When I bring this up to the boss, he says that it is just normal business griping, and I shouldn't pay any attention to what they say. Most people consider me to be a hard worker and a nice person to be around, so I know that these people just don't like immigrants. Especially they don't like anyone who speaks English with an accent.

In Maria's case, management may be seemingly unresponsive but actually quite concerned as they try to decide how to keep this complaint out of the Equal Employment Opportunity Commission's (EEOC) hands. They could be quietly "chatting with" a few employees or tossing some positive words or assignments in Maria's direction or doing nothing in the hope that Maria will not pursue the complaint and the problem will go away.

CONSIDER LEGAL ASSISTANCE

If you feel that your organization is not doing enough to stop the B≈H or you are going to quit, you might consider taking legal action.

Find Legal Help

Consider contacting the EEOC (see Appendix B for contact information), a state agency, legal aid society, a nearby law college, or an attorney. EEOC personnel will usually meet with you quickly – they provide knowledgeable advice, and they do not charge for their service. Attorneys are expensive. If you do need one, ask if they will work on contingency so that they only get paid if you win your case. Remember that attorney/client privilege means that anything you share with them will be kept confidential.

Potential Legal Solutions

Any legal action could involve mediation or even arbitration in which a compromise solution is sought. The final result of any litigation will vary with the findings of the investigation. If you are taken seriously, the result at a minimum may be counseling for both parties. If the complaint is found to be accurate, the perpetrator may only be required to make an apology to you or even a public apology. He or she may actually be disciplined, and an injunction may be applied to keep him or her away from you. Hopefully, action will be taken to make sure that no retaliation on the part of the perpetrator takes place.

Sex-related Complaints

If the B≈H involves anything sexual in nature, you may bring a federal, state or even private lawsuit. The process generally involves several steps. First, you file a complaint to which your employer responds. Then each party uses a process called discovery to bring together relevant information about the situation. At this point, mediation or some other kind of negotiation may take place to resolve the complaint. If no agreement is reached, the case goes to trial, during which each party can present their information and call upon witnesses. A judge will then rule on the case and present some method to ensure a remedy.

If your employer is found to be responsible, particularly if the incident involves sexual harassment or quid pro quo harassment, numerous remedies are possible. In the case of a civil lawsuit, as the complainant or plaintiff, you may be entitled to financial redress in terms of damages, even punitive damages from your employer, the defendant. You could be rehired or reinstated at the same pay and seniority or even merit a promotion. If you have been out of your job during the time of the investigation, you may be entitled to backpay, including any lost overtime and benefits. If the job no longer exists for some reason, you may be entitled to front pay, which is like back pay, except it is based on future earnings over some period of time. In addition, the organization could be ordered to adopt, implement and enforce policies and procedures that would be designed to prevent any recurrence of the B≈H.

QUIT

If all else fails or it just seems too much, quit. But if you are considering this option, start a job search as soon as possible. Remember that it is always easier to get a job while you still have a job. Connect with people who can help. Talk with your human resources (HR) or personnel office before finalizing your decision. They may surprise you and actually provide guidance and assistance. But don't be surprised if the HR personnel have a greater loyalty to the organization than to the employees. You may want to delay until you have learned new skills to broaden your possibilities.

Begin your search effort by making a list of your interests, strengths and skills. Then add your education and work experience. Next, develop a list of a few jobs that you think you would like and a brief statement explaining why you would be a good fit for those. Prepare a list of references that you can send if requested.

Consider your online presence. If you use social media, make sure your profiles are up to date and that there is nothing on them that you wouldn't like a future employer to see. While you're at it, develop your online job contacts using job search sites. Update your résumé and be sure to have action verbs and bullets to focus attention on your strengths. Prepare cover letters specific to each position to which you apply.

WHAT YOU CAN DO

Whether you are a manager or a non-manager, you need to carefully consider the five components of V-REEL® introduced in Chapter 7. Specifically, you should examine the list of *eroding* and *enabling* factors that you developed in the last chapter to see if there are some over which you have some control. Next, prioritize those factors, starting with the first *enabling* factor that you want to increase or emphasize. Then, move your focus to the first *eroding* factor and consider how you will try to eliminate it. As you make progress on these two (increasing an enabling factor and decreasing an eroding one), start this process again.

Next, "rinse and repeat" – redoing this process over again should increase your understanding of both B≈H and the V-REEL® framework. It should also lead to more results and move you toward eradicating B≈H in your organization. But there is only so much you as an individual can do. What organizations can do is the subject of the next chapter.

MINI CASE: INTIMIDATE WITH "DIRTY" PICTURES

Recently, I accepted a new position in a small firm. I'm not married despite dating fairly regularly. One or perhaps more of my co-workers have left explicit pictures on my desk, sometimes with phone numbers. I pointed this out to my supervisor, and he told my male co-workers to stop. That hasn't helped.

I complained again to my supervisor and even to the human resources organization the firm uses. The responses have been that since the person or persons doing it are not known, nothing can be done. It was brought up at a staff meeting but other than getting a laugh, nothing happened. I plan to contact the local EEO [Equal Employment Opportunity] office to see if anything can be done. If not, it's back to the job market for me.

1. Is the female in this case being subjected to B≈H?
2. What should the firm do in this case?

3. What should the target have already been doing in preparation for meeting with the appropriate members of the firm?

THINK ABOUT THIS CHAPTER AGAIN

Look at the actions you thought about at the beginning of this chapter. Now after reading this chapter, which of these do you feel you can actually adopt? Take a few minutes to prepare responses to the following set of questions.

Then consider what actions you might take using the form provided. In particular, managers and human resource professionals should do this to be better prepared to handle B≈H in their organizations.

Individual Actions Questions

1. Have you personally experienced B≈H in your organization?
2. Looking back now, can you think what eroding factors may have existed?
3. Try to recall some enabling factors that may have existed in your workplace. Again, looking back, do you think you or your co-workers realized the value of those factors?
4. Name some factors that improve your ability to manage B≈H.
5. What information should be included in your documentation of B≈H behavior?

Individual Actions

1. Re-examine the list of enabling and eroding factors you developed in the previous chapter to see if you need to add to that list.
2. Use the following form to create an action plan for what you should be able to do.

The form is on a separate page to enable photocopying for use individually or by groups.

INSTRUCTIONS FOR FORM 8.2

Identifying Actions for a Target of B≈H

Make a copy of the survey (Appendix A), complete it, and then use the following form to construct an action plan for what you should be able to do.

Form 8.2   *Identify actions for a target of B≈H*

IDENTIFY ACTIONS FOR A TARGET OF B≈H
Tell someone
Document the incident as follows:
What happened?
When (date and time)?
Where (full, specific details)?
Possible reason or cause?
Who was the target?
Who was the perpetrator?
Relation of target and perpetrator?

CHAPTER 8 CASES

These cases are based on actual situations with identifying names and locations changed or omitted. While anyone would benefit from reading and thinking about these cases, they are best used in a group context where different individual perspectives could be bought forth.

Case 8.1: Female Heavy Equipment Operator

Sue is a 36-year-old single mother of two small children. A few years ago, after a contentious divorce, she attended the Operating Engineer Apprenticeship and Training program run by a local chapter of the International Union of Operating Engineers (IUOE). She participated in the heavy equipment operator training school as part of that program. As an apprentice, she spent three years learning the trade by working with skilled, journey-level operating engineers on actual job sites, and attending related classroom instruction and/ or field training. She then earned her license as a heavy equipment operator.

With her experience and her new license, Sue secured a position as a heavy equipment operator for a local construction company. She loves the equipment and the work, but she certainly doesn't love her co-workers. Some of her male co-workers think it is fun to tease her. Sue often hears comments like "Watch out, here she comes – that crazy woman driver!" in a joking manner. Also, someone keeps putting a handmade sign on the only port-a-potty at the work-site that says, "Men only." Recently, however, things have gotten more tense. She senses that rather than jokes, there is real resentment growing among some of her co-workers who feel that the work really is a "man's job" and that she has no place in it.

Sue thinks some of their resentment may be because she has taken advantage of newer classes at the IUOE. Those classes are designed to help members stay on top of technological advances in construction equipment, such as GPS, and other issues. With her knowledge of how to use GPS at work, she quickly learned how to use the information while most of her male co-workers have struggled with it. She also has fewer breakdowns on her equipment because she watches the machines carefully. If there was just a drop of oil coming out of a gear, she would check it and let maintenance know so problems could be fixed before anything major happened. She wasn't picky but she was very thorough. She also keeps her equipment clean, doesn't leave trash in the cabs, and tries to be among the best workers.

But the comments of her male co-workers are starting to take their toll. While her performance is still quite good, her emotions are not. She is becoming depressed and increasingly concerned that she will make a mistake on the job and injure herself or someone else. She wonders if it is time to look for another job.

1. What eroding or enabling factors are present in this situation?
2. What should Sue do in this situation?
3. Have you ever experienced a situation like this and, if so, how did you handle it?
4. What would upper management likely do if Sue reports this?
5. How might the organization prevent this sort of situation in the future?

Case 8.2: Café Assistant Manager

Elizabeth, a 22-year-old college student works in a café within walking distance of her house. She is a hard worker and consistently did very good work. As a result of her performance, she was promoted to assistant manager a few months ago. In her role as an assistant manager, she is responsible for providing premier customer service in a front-of-house barista role. She greets the customers, takes their orders, facilitates the payment process, makes drink orders and delivers food to customers in a counter service restaurant setting. She plays an important role in maintaining a safe, clean, stocked and efficient kitchen and restaurant operation.

Her supervisor, Greg Toomey, often compliments Elizabeth, which she appreciates. She feels that he likes her and that she is doing a good job, given these compliments. Greg is on-site most of the time that the café is open and is respected by all of the employees. He keeps the café looking neat by insisting that the employees be on time and wear the "uniforms" with which they are furnished – white shirts and ironed aprons with the logo of the café on the front. The employees change from their street clothes in a common room of the café and put them in lockers provided.

Several times recently Elizabeth had to look for her work clothes when she arrived for the morning shift. Most recently, she found her apron crumpled in a bin or behind the lockers, which made her late for clocking in. Greg was annoyed and surprised as he had never before seen this behavior by Elizabeth. He told her to get up earlier so she could arrive on time. One day she couldn't find her blouse at all and had to go into the café with her red T-shirt on. Greg got very angry and told her to go home and get a white shirt to wear before coming back.

Elizabeth picked up her purse and walked out the door, but then had second thoughts. Why should she take the blame for this problem? And why did this happen? Did someone take Elizabeth's shirt and apron in an effort to get her in trouble? She went back inside to talk with the supervisor. He told her that he was glad Elizabeth was sharing this information and that she could be confident it would not happen again. He then told her to go on home and take the day off – *with pay* – while he looked into the problem.

1. Can you identify eroding or enabling factors in this situation?
2. Who do you think hid Elizabeth's café uniform? And why?
3. Did Elizabeth handle the problem correctly, or should she have talked to a worker or workers?
4. Did the supervisor handle the problem correctly when he first observed that Elizabeth was not dressed properly?
5. How might the organization prevent this sort of situation in the future?

9. Organizational responsibility

Now that you have considered what you as an individual can do, think about how your organization should respond. As in previous chapters, write down specific actions that you think your organization should adopt in an effort to reduce or eliminate B≈H. Keep your list handy to refer to as you go through this chapter.

INTRODUCTION

As indicated in Chapter 1, the focus of this book is on dysfunctional behavior that could impact an organization's reputation and possibly its bottom line. Our concern is with people in organizations – ensuring that they are treated with dignity and respect for the benefit of all. It is up to lawyers and legislators to wrestle with issues of what is legal versus illegal.

As "agents of the organization," managers are authorized to act on behalf of the organization (within limits). Managers may be legally responsible for dealing with B≈H in the workplace, particularly if it is sexual in nature. "A single sexual harassment claim can dramatically reduce public perceptions of an entire organization's gender equity (i.e., how fair men and women are generally treated, including in terms of hiring and promotion)" (Does et al., 2018).

Managerial responsibility goes beyond simply voluntarily complying with governmental regulations. It includes demonstrating a genuine commitment to the members of the organization to eliminate unwanted, abusive behavior. As such, it is important for all managers to be educated as to the nature and causes of B≈H. Your organization could be liable for a manager's action or inaction and, as noted in Chapter 6, workplace violence could be a consequence. If you are a manager, the EEOC could file a lawsuit against you on behalf of an alleged victim if you mishandle the situation. It is important that you work with your HR professionals to try to reduce and control B≈H in the organization.

In many organizations today, the workplace has become fissured (Weil, 2014). A fissured workplace is where many of those doing the work are "independent contractors" rather than actual employees. The outsourcing of accounting, payroll and HR is frequently followed by janitorial and security activities. But especially as more people work from home, the core activities of the organization may well be part of a fissured workplace. The legal basis of the organization's responsibility in these situations may be unsettled; however, moral and ethical responsibilities remain (Goldman & Weil, 2021).

ERODING AND ENABLING FACTORS

In developing approaches to reduce or eliminate B≈H, organizations should begin at the top of the organization by having the highest-level executives use the V-REEL® framework introduced in Chapter 6. Then the framework and discussions surrounding it should gradually move to lower-level managers until all managerial and non-managerial personnel have been involved.

Each discussion should begin with a general consideration of each of the five components of the V-REEL® framework introduced in Chapters 7 and 8. However, at this point, the primary focus should be on identifying and prioritizing the eroding and enabling factors, as those are the most critical in the short run.

Identify Eroding Factors

Remember that eroding factors are those things that impede your ability to reduce B≈H. They are, therefore, factors that reduce the organization's ability to create value. They get in the way of decreasing B≈H and prevent individuals from being productive members of the organization. One such important eroding factor would be managers who don't care or are too busy to help. As explained by the salesperson below, a manager's brush-off or outright refusal of a target's call for help can have a tremendous effect on workers' attitudes and, hence, their productivity.

NO HR PLUS DO-NOTHING BOSS

There is no HR department at the small company I work for. I've asked my boss many times to do something about the bullying, but he doesn't do anything. He tells me that he has spoken with her and doesn't expect anything to change. So, I should "put it in a box, put it on a shelf, and get over it." I requested that a formal note should be made in her personnel file, but as far as I know, nothing was done. A rude reply by email just made me feel worse. My only option would appear to be quitting.

A corporate history of discrimination is an eroding factor, particularly if there have been few or no efforts to reduce or eliminate that discrimination. A corporate culture that focuses exclusively on profits with little regard for the organization's human resources is an eroding factor. Supervisors who dismiss complaints as "just normal grumbling" would be an eroding factor. Upper management that supports lower management with no regard as to what may be actually happening also would be an eroding factor.

There could be a long list of eroding factors. For international organizations, the erosion might come from the surrounding culture in a particular area. The messages from that culture could infect the organization and individuals. Perceptions of reward for B≈H activity (real or not) would be a factor, particularly if this includes a lack of punishment, which is a type of reward by default. One respondent provided this description.

MANAGING BY PUNISHING IS AN ERODING FACTOR

They isolate you and make it look as if you are the problem. They restrict access to information and then say that if you had gone to them, they would have helped. It's painful to be ostracized and given only partial or incorrect information. HR got involved, but they seemed to not support me. I felt like they were trying to brush everything under the carpet. I asked to be transferred, but that took well over two months, during which I still had to put up with the situation. I went to work and tried to keep quiet. I had been there for ten years, and when I got a new job, I didn't say anything to anybody. People were shocked that I left so abruptly.

An awareness of how other organizations are behaving and managing B≈H could also become an eroding issue in one's own organization. If a company is allowing B≈H behavior with no punishment – which is tantamount to sanctioning or rewarding it by not penalizing – other managers who themselves engage in B≈H behavior may feel empowered. This feeling may be reached more easily when the "guilty" organization is a competitor and is "winning" in the market.

Still other eroding factors might include overly aggressive goals linked exclusively to compensation outcomes that could push B≈H behavior in an effort to meet the goals and gain the compensation. A strict and autocratic hierarchy in the organization may promote B≈H because of the "lesser" and "higher" status positions in the organization. Those of "higher" status may feel justified in their behavior simply because of their status. A board of directors or governing authority that is not adequately overseeing top management could allow those managers to feel free to engage in B≈H. A celebrity CEO or others in the organization could encourage hubris that builds toward B≈H over time. Too much independence in divisions or functional areas could breed toxic subcultures.

Prioritize Eroding Factors

Since there are possibly a great many eroding factors, they need to be prioritized. Following the suggestion of Flint (2018), you should use two scales. For the first scale, estimate the likelihood of each eroding factor from 1 to 10, where 10 is certainty. For the second, estimate the effect size of the eroding factor, if it occurs, from 1 to 10, where 10 is the most devastating. Then multiply the two numbers. A higher result is a higher priority. But in addition to identifying and reducing or eliminating eroding factors, organizations need to identify and increase enabling factors.

Identify Enabling Factors

Enabling factors are those things that improve the organization's ability to manage B≈H. There are numerous opportunities for B≈H to emerge and fester in organizations. But there are also lots of ways to reduce its occurrence through enabling factors. Those factors help to decrease B≈H and enable individuals to become more productive and increase their psychological health and well-being. Training and/or retraining managers at all levels about the costs and causes of B≈H is an enabling factor that has been shown to be effective (Munir & Zafar, 2020). Having an independent agency that would investigate serious B≈H incidents could be an enabling factor. Working to prevent B≈H is an enabling factor.

As noted, strong codes of conduct with periodic and meaningful training/engagement, especially if clearly supported by the leaders in the organization, would be enabling factors. Rewarding the efforts of employees who report and managers who remedy B≈H problems would be enabling, as would a strong board of directors or governing authority. Another enabling factor would be the encouragement of a team (in the original meaning of the word – those with whom I pull together) culture. Drawing strong contrasts between broader problems in the surrounding culture or in other organizations regarding what is acceptable in the organization could be an enabling factor.

Regular "check-ups" with divisions or functional areas about their specific issues and how they are handling B≈H would be enabling. Eliminating compensation goals that reward over-aggressive behaviors or that send mixed signals could be enabling. And, of course, improved communication is a key enabling factor, particularly having conversations when B≈H occurs.

Prioritize Enabling Factors

As with eroding factors, enabling factors need to be prioritized. Again, following the suggestion of Flint (2018), use two scales. For the first scale, estimate the ability to put each enabling factor in place from 1 to 10, where 10 is certainty. For the second scale, estimate the effect size of the enabling factor, if it occurs, from 1 to 10, where 10 completely solves an existential dire eroding factor. Then multiply the two numbers. A higher result is a higher priority.

This analysis, again starting from the top, should be repeated whenever it appears that B≈H is occurring. As the saying goes, "An ounce of prevention is worth a pound of cure."

PREVENTING B≈H

Organizations should first act to prevent B≈H from even occurring. Screening individuals during the hiring process to attempt to screen out potential bullies or harassers would be a first but very difficult step because it is unclear what these individuals "look like" or "act like" (Van Fleet & Van Fleet, 2007). Remember that those who engage in B≈H may be smart, successful, skilled individuals who would look quite good as potential employees. It may be only after they are hired that issues occur. So, managers should be trained to observe – to notice – what's going on with employees, including changes in job performance, moods and relationships.

SCREEN LEGALLY AND WISELY IN HIRING

I applied for a sales position at a national company. The advertised position called for a "native English speaker." Even though I am Mexican, I speak English fluently with almost no trace of an accent. But I guess that wasn't good enough. I didn't even get passed [*sic*] the first step in the hiring process.

Observe and Document Behaviors

Observations should be documented. Managers should write specific, thorough details regarding observable behaviors. They should ensure that any incidents are recorded in appropriate records, such as the OSHA 200 Log, internal assault records, insurance records, worker's compensation records, and medical records. They should then prepare to meet with the employees involved. List the behavioral issues already confirmed in the documented evidence. They should confront those involved with care. The manner in which an individual is approached will either improve his or her chances of getting help or provoke additional anger. Finally, there needs to be follow-up – meetings to check on the emotional response of those involved and to provide clarification if needed (Van Fleet & Van Fleet, 1996).

Maintain Open Communications

As previously indicated, communication is vital. The organization should have an open-door policy that encourages openness and transparency between managers and non-managers in the organization. An open-door policy means that employees are free and even encouraged to raise issues or concerns with managers. Cultures that foster open-door policies also generally are associated with high-performance organizations, as employees are involved in decision-making processes. An open-door policy might be one of the top enabling factors regarding B≈H elimination.

SEXUAL HARASSMENT DEMANDS IMMEDIATE ACTION

One of the workers in my department constantly arranges objects to suggest sexual positions. Other co-workers simply move the objects back, but they really bother me since it usually happens in my workspace. It is getting on my nerves. Thankfully, our company makes it easy to discuss these things with management, and they promised to talk to the person involved. Hopefully, something will be done soon.

As part of its communication efforts, the organization should conduct employee attitude surveys (Schneider et al., 1996; see Appendix A for an example). They also should have periodic meetings to go over the results of those surveys and to be sure that everyone knows what B≈H is and what to do about it. To assure employees that their concerns will be taken seriously, the organization should attempt to provide a way that is independent of the usual "chain of command" to raise concerns, ask questions or file complaints. This would be a special HR contact or even an external agency of some sort.

Provide Training for Managers and Employees

Managerial training should also be accompanied by training for all employees. Everyone should be shown examples of correct behavior as well as examples of incorrect behavior. Discussions as to why particular behaviors are acceptable or unacceptable should be held to open channels of communication within the organization. The training should also include topics such as interpersonal communication skills, developing assertiveness, giving and getting feedback, and how to listen to what is really being said. Training should also include information about what assistance is available to would-be targets and to those who engage in B≈H. Finally, the training should include information as to how to report (for victims) or to handle (for supervisors) incidents of B≈H.

ACTIVATE THE HUMAN CAPITAL OF THE ORGANIZATION

The important point is that the organization needs to create a culture that encourages open, transparent communication. That culture should also ensure that everyone knows that high performance is expected and what their roles are in attaining that. Everyone should understand that high performance is expected but also that everyone is an important asset to the organization and so should be protected. Morrison suggests that activating an organization's human capital produces a way to accomplish this (Morrison, 2017; https://transformationsolutionsgroup.com/). He suggests seeing employees as valuable human capital through the adoption of eight "principles." The adoption of those principles will ensure that everyone in the organization is seen as valuable and that everyone strives for high performance.

The principles are:

1. Make certain that everyone understands the "big picture".
2. Communicate widely.
3. Manage the organization to adapt to social, economic, cultural and other changes.
4. Create a culture of worth so that everyone is seen as a valuable contributor to the organization's purpose.
5. Create a culture of hope whereby employees are trusted, and fear is avoided.
6. Reward performance.
7. Use participation to create a vision that inspires employees.
8. Express gratitude; be sure to say thanks.

While some of these ideas are not new, the principles of creating a culture of worth and hope and expressing gratitude appear novel and important (Van Fleet, 2018). Morrison posits two objectives. One is having managers ask if they are effective in motivating their employees. Another is to manage people, not positions. The intent is to shift the perspectives of managers so that they would see their employees as valuable human capital. By developing the full potential of its employees and helping them become highly motivated, both individuals and the organization benefit.

Following these principles would help to prevent B≈H. But should B≈H occur, action must be taken.

TAKE IMMEDIATE ACTION

When a supervisor becomes aware of B≈H, he or she should take immediate action to deal with the situation. A verbal warning, counseling or coaching may be all that is required to prevent a recurrence of the behavior (Lutgen-Sandvik et al., 2007). The supervisor may also need to contact the organization's personnel or HR department. And the supervisor may need to talk to other employees about what they have observed. This may mean that confidentiality cannot be preserved; but if someone refuses to cooperate, your HR representative will need to be so informed.

Of course, supportive leaders who show consideration for others are less likely to have B≈H incidents in their group or team (Li et al., 2019). Additionally, employees working in jobs that permit more discretion in decision-making or more job autonomy are less likely to experience B≈H. So, supervisors should strive to be supportive leaders and to create cultures that allow more autonomy among their group or team members.

Hopefully, your organization has a culture with a strong ethics component that will reduce B≈H. But in any event, organizations need to be free from bias and have clear policies and procedures for addressing B≈H.

DEVELOP ANTI-DISCRIMINATION POLICIES

Organizations must make it clear that they are serious about eliminating B≈H. The existence of a strong policy statement supported by action is essential. However, reminders such as posting OSHA-type signs throughout the workplace and notes in newsletters or other communications channels are also important.

Organizations should have anti-discrimination and anti-B≈H policies (see Chapter 1). The following is an example of an anti-discrimination policy.

Anti-discrimination Policy

EXAMPLE POLICY

This organization is an equal opportunity employer that will not discriminate in hiring, job assignments, promotions, or other personnel actions. The organization will act affirmatively to ensure against discrimination on the basis of race, creed, color, national origin, or sex.

Anti-B≈H Policy

Expanding on the earlier discussion, any policy dealing with B≈H should be developed through a joint effort of managers and non-managers in the organization. The following draws on suggestions by the Society for Human Resource Management and is just one example of what such a policy might look like.

EXAMPLE POLICY

This organization endeavors to create and maintain an environment in which people are treated with dignity, decency, and respect. That environment shall be characterized by mutual trust and the absence of intimidation, oppression, and exploitation. The organization will not in any instance tolerate bullying, discrimination, harassment, unlawful behavior of any kind, or B≈H. B≈H refers to words and behaviors that comprise inappropriate pressure, coercion, or intimidation. Through enforcement of this policy and by training and educating its employees, the organization will seek to prevent, correct, and discipline behavior that violates this policy.

The organization considers the following as examples of B≈H: [the managers and non-managers who develop the policy then should select examples from their own experiences or ones like those found in this book. These should include mental health as noted in Chapter 6].

All employees, regardless of their positions, must comply with this policy and take appropriate measures to ensure that prohibited conduct does not occur. Appropriate disciplinary action will be taken against any employee who violates this policy. Based on the seriousness of the offense, disciplinary action may include verbal or written reprimand, suspension, or termination of employment.

Managers and supervisors who knowingly allow or tolerate B≈H, or who fail to immediately report such misconduct to human resources (HR), are in violation of this policy and subject to discipline.

This policy does not preclude the victim or the perpetrator from pursuing legal remedies or resolution through local, state, or federal agencies or the courts.

Once a policy is agreed upon, all members of the organization should sign a form such as the one here.

I acknowledge that I have received, read, and understand the B≈H policy of [enter Company Name]. I understand that failure to comply with the policy could result in disciplinary action up to and including termination of employment.

Employee Signature	Date

Employee Name (please print)

DEVELOP B≈H PROCEDURES

Policies alone are insufficient. There need to be clear, concise procedures for dealing with B≈H whenever it occurs. It is important that action be swift. Everyone should always be treated with respect and dignity, particularly if corrective or disciplinary action is called for. Confidentiality must also be assured to protect the rights of all concerned.

The speed, of course, may depend on how quickly an investigation can be performed. Conducting a thorough investigation is important, and, in some cases, it may take considerable time. Due diligence is important in investigations. Due diligence involves enough time and effort to obtain all relevant information in contentious situations while at the same time protecting the rights of everyone involved. All sides must be heard, and unbiased decisions or actions made or taken. If the organization is unable to find an "inside ombudsman" who is trusted by both management and workers, it may be necessary to go outside the organization. Rarely should such an investigation be conducted solely by the organization's HR department as it is likely to side with management, or at least be perceived that way.

DEVELOP BASIC INVESTIGATION PROCEDURES

Specific procedures will vary considerably among organizations, depending on their size and the nature of work performed. The following are basic procedures; but for more detailed suggestions, contact the Society for Human Resource Management (SHRM).

1. Any member of the organization who has experienced B≈H based on sex, race, national origin, ethnic background, or any other protected characteristic should report it to the appropriate supervisor. The report should be made in writing as soon as possible after the incident. If the supervisor is not available, or if the supervisor was the perpetrator, the victim should contact that supervisor's superior or HR.

2. All complaints of unlawful harassment will be handled confidentially to the extent reasonably possible.

3. The recipient of the report will then notify senior management and review it with the company's legal counsel. Once the incident has been reported, the organization will promptly investigate to determine whether there is a reasonable basis for believing that a violation of this policy occurred. Said investigation will involve the target and the perpetrator, and others, as necessary. The severity, frequency, and circumstances of the conduct will all be taken into account.

4. Once the investigation is complete, a report will be submitted to upper management. If the report concludes that the policy was violated, any necessary corrective action will be taken. That action will vary depending on prior complaints and the severity or frequency of the B$\approx$H. If the investigation finds no violation, action may nevertheless be taken to separate the parties involved.

5. If the complaint is found to be true, various actions may be mandated again depending on the severity, frequency and circumstances of the conduct. The person making the complaint may receive an apology, monetary compensation, reinstatement of any time off, training, coaching and/or counseling. For the perpetrator, the consequences may include having to make an apology, receive training, coaching and/or counseling, disciplinary action, up to and including termination.

6. If the complaint is found to be untrue, various actions may be mandated depending on whether the complainant intentionally made false statements, misremembered factual information or overstated the case. In this situation, the consequences are essentially the reverse. The person making the complaint may have to make an apology, receive training, coaching and/or counseling, disciplinary action, up to and including termination. The individual against whom the complaint was made may receive an apology, monetary compensation, reinstatement of any time off, training, coaching and/or counseling.

The investigation is particularly important because perpetrators may well be seen as hard-working, solid members of the organization. Organizations must exercise due diligence to be sure that these sorts of investigations are above reproach. The investigation must be seen by all parties as thorough, complete and fair.

ENFORCE THE POLICY

Additionally, if the complaint is true, it is important that perpetrators be held accountable. All too frequently, organizations are more bark than bite. They have admirable policies and procedures but avoid actually taking any actions against perpetrators. Abby comments on just such a situation.

HARRY'S CONSTANT BOTHER IS HARASSMENT

Harry is really being a jerk. When I indicated that I wasn't interested in a relationship with him, he began a campaign to make me look bad. He posts pictures of me (after altering them) on social media platforms and constantly calls me late at night and very early in the morning. I have reported it to management, and they said they would speak to Harry, but while it may have lessened, it hasn't gone away. Management seems to only be half-heartedly willing to confront the situation.

Managers such as the ones Harry and Abby have don't do much because the perpetrators (Harry in this case) are otherwise good employees. Or it may be because management fears that the perpetrator may initiate legal action that could be long and protracted and, hence, costly to the organization. So, they elect to do as little as possible in hopes that somehow the situation will just go away.

AVOID RETALIATION

Fear of retaliation is a major reason those experiencing B≈H don't speak up, so it is important to take care to avoid it. An employee charging retaliation can be costly. While a typical out of court settlement is only around $40,000, about 10% of wrongful termination and discrimination cases result in $1 million settlements, and "the majority of cases, about 67%, are ruled in the plaintiff's favor when taken to litigation" (Cutting Edge Recruiting Solutions, 2012). So, it clearly is in the interest of an organization to avoid retaliation.

Having policies in place is not sufficient. They must be followed and enforced consistently. The organization should have an open-door policy to encourage employees to share concerns with management. When a complaint is made, managers must avoid taking out their frustrations on the person making the complaint. And, of course, it is important to recognize that punishing or retaliating against employees or even former employees is illegal.

There may be "implicit" or "subconscious" bias on the part of those in the organization. This sort of bias is quite difficult to identify and can be difficult to correct. Training programs using examples such as those in this book should help to contextualize what is meant by this form of bias. That would be an important step in reducing and hopefully eliminating B≈H from your workplace.

Illegal Retaliation Acts by Non-managers

The EEOC (Equal Employment Opportunity Commission, 2016) indicates that it is unlawful to retaliate against those who:

- Participate in a complaint process;
- Communicate with a member of management about discrimination or harassment;
- Respond to questions during an investigation of a complaint;
- Refuse to follow orders that would cause discrimination;
- Resist sexual advances or intervene to help another employee;
- Request accommodation of a disability or for a religious practice;
- Ask co-workers about salary information to identify possible wage discrimination.

Illegal Retaliation Acts by Managers

Further, the EEOC suggests that the following actions by a supervisor or member of management may be considered retaliation:

- Reprimanding the complainant or giving them a performance evaluation lower than merited;
- Transferring the complainant to a less desirable position;
- Verbally or physically abusing the complainant;
- Threatening to make or actually making a report to authorities (e.g., reporting the complainant's immigration status or contacting the police);
- Spreading false rumors, treating a family member negatively (e.g., canceling a contract with the complainant's spouse);
- Making the complainant's work more difficult (e.g., changing their work schedule to conflict with family responsibilities).

Employees who complain to the EEOC are not protected from all discipline or from being terminated. Organizations may discipline or terminate employees if there are non-retaliatory and non-discriminatory reasons. Obviously, preventing B≈H is the best way to avoid complaints, possible retaliation, and any legal actions by employees or management. And it should be noted that pleading ignorance may not be sufficient. "It essentially ratifies a harasser's discriminatory conduct" (Stanciu, 2020).

MINI CASE: UNDUE SYMPATHY

In my organization, we have one older worker who really takes the cake. She constantly pleads her health or that of her mother to get reduced work assignments. She does the same thing with us and will use it to explain why she has to make so many trips to the restroom and has to lie on a couch there. But when she is not assigned to a project, she suddenly seems to feel much better. She has said to our boss and us that our company is unfair for expecting "people in my situation" to perform as well as everyone else. If the boss pushes, she says that her condition is because he's driving her too hard.

What we cannot understand is why our boss hasn't told her to go see a physician for herself and go to the human resources department for help in getting nursing care for her mother. If the boss or the organization won't do anything, we think we will have to arrange our work, so her behavior doesn't jeopardize the group's performance.

1.   Is the older worker engaged in B≈H?
2.   How should this or any organization deal with a worker like this one? Are there actions that cannot be taken for the employee with self-described health problems?
3.   What do you think is the real reason for her behavior?

THINK ABOUT THIS CHAPTER AGAIN

Examine the list of specific actions that you think your organization should adopt in an effort to reduce or eliminate bullying and harassment. What changes might you make after reading this chapter?

Then take a few minutes to prepare responses to these questions and actions. In particular, managers and human resource professionals should do this to be better prepared to handle B≈H in their organizations.

Organizational Questions

1.   Has your organization taken any steps to prevent or respond to B≈H in your organization?
2.   Have you personally experienced or witnessed your organization responding positively to B≈H in your organization?
3.   Name five eroding factors that impede your ability to reduce and/or prevent B≈H within an organization. Prioritize them, and then for the top three, indicate what enabling factors the organization might implement to alleviate them.
4.   Morrison suggests seeing employees as valuable human capital through the adoption of certain "principles." What are those principles?
5.   Write an anti-B≈H policy that includes a definition of B≈H.

Organizational Actions

Use the following form to apply the V-REEL® framework in your organization.
The form is on a separate page to enable photocopying for use individually or by groups.

INSTRUCTIONS FOR FORM 9

A Modified Approach for the V-REEL® Framework

Have your manager or supervisor copy the survey (Appendix A), and then have everyone in your group or team complete it. Use that information and apply the V-REEL® framework (see Chapter 5) to analyze B≈H carefully in your organization. The following form should assist you in this task.

CHAPTER 9 CASES

These cases are based on actual situations with identifying names and locations changed or omitted. While anyone would benefit from reading and thinking about these cases, they are best used in a group context where different individual perspectives could be bought forth.

Case 9.1: Harassing Supervisor

At 21 years old, Maryann is a bright young graduate of a top private university. Even though it was a male-dominated field, she majored in computer science and programming. She got very good grades and was well respected by her fellow students as well as her professors. She even became president of the university's chapter of Upsilon Pi Epsilon, the honor society for computing and information majors. Upon graduation (with honors), she landed a good position as a programmer for a major corporation in a nearby city. The position involved testing and deploying programs and specific applications developed by the company. It also involved troubleshooting, debugging, maintaining and trying to improve the company's existing software. While it was challenging to learn the ropes in the company, it seemed to Maryann to be almost a dream job and she quickly became noted for her skills, but things soon began to change that made it less so.

Maryann noted, "About two months after I began working at the company, my supervisor started to pick on me. For some reason, she singled me out. She gave me coding assignments that seemed trivial and clearly well below my skill level. Or she would give me ones so late in the day that I couldn't finish them on time or could do so only by putting in a bit of overtime. Even

Form 9   *A modified approach for the V-REEL® framework*

A MODIFIED APPROACH FOR THE V-REEL® FRAMEWORK

Value: What is your value to the organization? Your group or team's value? The value of the organization itself?

Rareness: Are there any distinctive competencies that set you, your group or team, or the organization apart from others?

Eroding factors: These are things that impede your ability to reduce B≈H and create value. Reexamine your lists from Chapters 5 and 6 to consider making changes.

Enabling factors: These are things that improve your ability to manage B≈H and create value. Reexamine your lists from Chapters 5 and 6 to consider making changes.

Longevity: How long will any use of one or more enabling factors be sustained? How long will it be necessary to remove eroding factors?

---

so, I have always completed my assignments and done so with no errors." The behavior of her supervisor, however, continued off and on for weeks, and it soon became clear that only Maryann was being treated in this way. Maryann was certain that, for some reason, her supervisor was trying to make her look bad or put her down. Nevertheless, she continued to do her work without complaining about her supervisor. She never had a problem completing any of her assignments. She just tried to ignore the supervisor as best she could.

Then one day a colleague, Lynna, nearby was struggling with a coding problem. Maryann recognized that it was similar to one she had encountered some time ago. She also noted that their supervisor, Dr. Crabtree, had stopped by, apparently on her way to lunch, and was giving them hints but not solutions. She was a well-respected physicist and could have shown all of them in less than a minute, probably, how to solve the problem. Maryann knew that all eight of them must be at a 1:00 meeting, code solution or not. So, she stepped up, pointed her Bic pen toward a line about halfway down the paper that was now filled with wasted ideas and guesses. Then in her sweetest Texas twang, she said, "Right about there's the error. Look for a simple reversal of numbers – you were almost there!"

Dr. Crabtree, their supervisor, quickly jumped from her chair, which just happened to be unlucky enough to be in the wrong place at the right time. This prematurely gray-haired little woman pointed her blue-inked Sharpie at Maryann, flapping her arms like she was about to fly, and yelling, "You should concentrate on your own work and not butt in on the work of others."

At that point, Maryann stormed off, telling anyone who would listen, "After all that I did was help someone." "Apparently, she sees me as a threat and wants to be sure that upper management doesn't see my real value to the company. I don't know what to do."

1. Can you identify eroding factors here?
2. What do you think Maryann should do in this situation?
3. What do you think she will do?
4. Should employees be able to step in and assist one another?
5. How might the organization prevent this sort of situation in the future?

Case 9.2: No Means No

Shizuko is a young woman of Japanese descent. She has a trim figure and is attractive. While she dates occasionally, she has no serious relationship just now. She has been working in an office for a local business for several years and thoroughly enjoys the pleasant although sometimes frantic atmosphere.

One of Shizuko's co-workers, Noah, has just been through a divorce. He drops comments on a few occasions that he is lonely and needs to find a new girlfriend. Shizuko and Noah have been friendly in the past and have had lunch together in local restaurants on many occasions. Recently, Noah asked Shizuko to go on a date with him – dinner and a movie.

Shizuko likes Noah as a friend and accepted the invitation to go out with him. She enjoyed the evening but decided that a relationship is not a good idea. She thanks Noah for a nice time but explains that she does not want to have a relationship with him or anyone else right now. Noah waited two weeks and then started asking Shizuko for more dates. She has refused every time, but Noah does not stop. He keeps pressurizing her to go out with him.

Shizuko is not sure what to do. She almost "lost her cool" a few days ago when she was working on a fixed deadline, and he cornered her in the copy room. "I came so close to picking up my purse and walking out, throwing my badge over my shoulder as I passed through the big glass security door," she told a couple of her friends. She had thought a few times earlier of doing this, but this time the thought of leaving her job – leaving Noah! – was overwhelming!

Her friends immediately reminded her that the rule of success always is to look for a job while you still have a job. And furthermore, finding a job in the current market is harder than ever. She had already thought about that. "Yes but . . ." she reminded them. "Keeping my sanity is also not simple. The only part of NO that this weirdo doesn't understand is EVERY part. I am at my wit's end."

The room got quiet as Shizuko's friends contemplated the situation. "One of us must go," Shizuko said in a calm voice as she searched their faces, "and I just have to make up my mind which one it will be."

1. What are eroding factors in this case?
2. You know what Shizuko is thinking she will do. But what do *you* think she will do?
3. What do you think she *should* do?
4. What would *you* do if you were in her situation?
5. How might an organization prevent this sort of situation in the future?

10. Government regulations

Now that you have considered what you as an individual can do and what your organization also should do, write down what you feel the role of government is or should be. Focus on the federal government but also consider state and local jurisdictions. Then keep your notes handy as you go over the material in this chapter.

INTRODUCTION

This chapter presents a general overview to help you understand the role of government as it pertains to B≈H. The focus in this chapter is on the role of the federal government, but you should also seek information about any state or local legislation that may impact you or your organization.

Your organization's HR professionals can apprise you of pertinent governmental rules and regulations. If your organization does not have an HR person, you should nevertheless be aware of regulations that pertain to all organizations, including small organizations (Lucas, 2019). If there is no HR person or department in your organization, start with your supervisor and if your supervisor is the problem, take it to a higher level. You could also contact the EEOC or another human resource organization (see Appendix B) for information. In any event, there are government regulations that apply to any organization, although those regulations may be different for private as opposed to public organizations. And, of course, dealing with B≈H is the morally and ethically correct thing to do.

Dana Hundley, the co-founder of Career Cooperative, an Oakland, California-based consulting firm, provides suggestions for what to do if there is not an HR department or person at your organization. She also provides a personal example.

PLAN MATERNITY LEAVE CAREFULLY

I was the first person to go on maternity leave at my last company, and I needed to figure out how to take care of myself and my future child while also following my company's policies and tying up any loose ends. With the help of my ally, a seasoned HR professional who also happens to be a close

college friend, I felt empowered to call a maternity leave planning meeting
with my boss and came with a thorough checklist in hand (Hundley, 2020).

She educated herself and took direct action with positive results. Since educating yourself is a crucial first step, this chapter sketches a short history of
workers' rights followed by some specific important legislation pertaining to
bullying or harassment. Your local library or searching the Internet can help
you to get more detailed information should you feel the need for it.

EARLY LEGISLATION RE WORKERS' RIGHTS

Workers, employees, and members of organizations generally have long
sought fair treatment and rights in the workplace (the following several para-
graphs are based on Dubofsky & McCartin, 2017; Dray, 2010; and Skurzynski,
2009). Isolated incidents of civil unrest occurred during the Industrial
Revolution in the seventeenth and eighteenth centuries. Many of these early
incidents were about taxes of one sort or another. Such civil unrest increased
in frequency during the nineteenth century, predominantly in the form of riots
such as the Cincinnati riots of 1829 and 1836. Those protests began by competition for jobs between Irish immigrants and African Americans and former
slaves (https://en.wikipedia.org/wiki/List_of_incidents_of_civil_unrest_in_the
_United_States).

The earliest recorded strike occurred in 1619 in the Jamestown Colony of
what would later become the United States. Polish workers who had been
denied the right to vote because they were not of English descent struck to
obtain voting rights for continental workers. But a more important strike
occurred in 1768 when New York journeymen tailors refused to work as
a protest against a wage reduction. (A journeyman is someone who has completed an apprenticeship and is now certified to work under the supervision
of a master in that trade.) Following this, in Philadelphia in 1794, a group of
shoemakers formed the Federal Society of Journeymen Cordwainers (the name
derived from the cordovan leather that they used). This organizing of a trade
group is generally seen as the beginning of a sustained trade union movement
among American workers (History.com Editors, 2022).

Then, during the latter part of the nineteenth century, other organized
labor groups began to appear, including what would become the American
Federation of Labor. The Department of Labor (DOL) was created in 1913 "to
foster, promote and develop the welfare of working people, to improve their
working conditions, and to enhance their opportunities for profitable employment" (MacLaury, n.d.). The DOL focuses on worker protection, unemploy-

ment compensation and training, and provides statistics and analyses regarding the economy in general and the labor market in particular.

In 1916 the federal government passed the Adamson Act, which standardized the eight-hour workday for railroad workers and most private-sector employees. Businesses, however, used the Sherman Antitrust Act (1890) to limit the power of organized labor. The Clayton Act (1914) was intended to strengthen the Sherman Act, but it was not until the passage of the Norris–La Guardia Act (1932) that employers were prohibited from interfering against workers who were trying to join a union. The National Industrial Recovery Act was passed in 1933. It protected collective bargaining rights and attempted to establish fair working conditions such as minimum wages and maximum hours. In addition, the National Labor Relations Act (Wagner Act) was passed in 1935 to guarantee the rights of employees to form unions and bargain collectively. Around this same time, state governments began to take action to help employees in one form or another.

The early 1930s was also the time of the Dust Bowl and the start of the migrant worker movement. The Dust Bowl was created when vegetation was lost in years of drought; the soil was reduced to dust and eroded. The result was that it was no longer suitable for farming. So, farm families from Kansas, Colorado, Oklahoma and Texas headed to California in the hope of better lives, only to find that it was not necessarily so (Bennett, 2014).

Then in 1939, women went to work while their men went to war. Now we had the ingredients for B≈H! They would later fight for equal rights and equal pay, but for some, it has been a long time coming. In 1947, the Labor Management Relations Act (Taft–Hartley Act) was passed to limit the power of unions. As union membership declined, mergers among unions occurred, and restrictions on union activities increased. The Landrum–Griffin Act (1959) required the reporting and disclosure of financial transactions and administrative practices of labor organizations and to provide election standards for officers of labor organizations. Soon after, federal workers were granted the right to bargain, although this was later restricted. Then came the Equal Pay Act of 1963, which aimed at abolishing gender-based wage disparity for performing the same job. It was followed by the Equal Pay Act of 2010, which requires equal pay in the same workplace. Other federal legislation, such as the Civil Rights Acts of 1964 and 1968, has extended the protection of individuals outside the workplace.

ANTI-B≈H LEGISLATION

These Acts did not specifically address B≈H at work, and the federal government has not passed any comprehensive workplace bullying legislation. But governments have not entirely ignored B≈H.

Bullying

There is no federal law that specifically applies to bullying as commonly defined. However, when bullying is based on race or another protected class, it overlaps with discrimination and harassment, so the organization is legally obligated to address the bullying (www.stopbullying.gov/resources/laws).

However, regulations regarding bullying have been enacted at the state and local levels, focusing primarily on bullying in schools. The laws, policies and regulations vary considerably, having no common, agreed-upon definition. Most require schools and/or school districts to develop their own policies and procedures, and some require the establishment of prevention programs. Consequences are rarely specified and few, if any, of those laws regard bullying as criminal.

Despite the at-will doctrine (an employee can be terminated for good cause, bad cause or no cause at all) being recognized by most states, most state laws allow employees to sue their organizations for creating hostile or abusive work environments. The legal actions are made through discrimination, harassment, safety and union protection regulations. These are based on protected characteristics, such as race, color, national origin, religion, sex, age or disability.

In 2010 the U.S. Department of Education found that all states and territories required school districts to have anti-bullying policies. Almost all had definitions, reporting and investigating procedures, and consequences. Most also called for prevention education, staff training, ways to communicate the policies, engagement of parents, review procedures and safeguards. However, fewer than half identified which groups were protected. There is little evidence that the government is focused on workplaces other than schools.

Eldercare centers is one area that needs more attention. Consider the following situation.

RACIAL B≈H BY ELDERLY AND SENILE NOT OK

I work at a senior center helping to care for the elderly residents who can't look after themselves. I'm also the only one of my race there. The residents make comments to or about me all the time. They insult me and have even used racial epitaphs to refer to me. My supervisor says they are old and getting senile and so don't know any better and that I shouldn't take it personally. How can I help but take it personally? My self-image and, as a result, my job performance suffers from this abuse.

Is senility really at fault, or are the residents committing discriminatory B≈H? A closer examination would be required to answer that question; but either way, some "training" of the residents would still be required.

Harassment

Harassment, on the other hand, has received considerable attention at the federal level, with new legislation coming as definitions are expanded or clarified. Currently, the EEOC specifies that harassment is a form of employment discrimination. As such, it is covered by three different statutes: Title VII of the Civil Rights Act of 1964, the Age Discrimination in Employment Act (ADEA) of 1967, and the Americans with Disabilities Act (ADA) of 1990 (https://www.eeoc.gov/harassment).

In addition, the EEOC enforces numerous other laws, including The Pregnancy Discrimination Act, The Equal Pay Act of 1963, Sections 102 and 103 of the Civil Rights Act of 1991, Sections 501 and 505 of the Rehabilitation Act of 1973, and The Genetic Information Nondiscrimination Act of 2008. In enforcing these, reasonable accommodation is required, and retaliation is forbidden.

Absent specific workplace bullying legislation facing varied, complex harassment legislation, it is difficult for organizations, especially small ones, to be assured that they are in compliance with regulations. Of course, just "being in compliance" is insufficient. Organizations need to have cultures and managers such that they are acting well above any sort of minimum required by law. Morals and ethics demand behavior that is above reproach. Unfortunately, that is not always what workers find, regardless of their age, sex or other characteristics.

Small businesses may or may not be covered by federal legislation, depending on their size. Equal pay for equal work for male and female employees pertains to all businesses with at least one employee. As the organization grows to 15 to 19 employees, laws that prohibit discrimination apply. With more than 20 employees, all of the legislation is applicable. But state and/or local legislation may also apply to your business even if it is small. Small business owners need to make sure that they are up to date with state regulations, as incorrectly identifying workers as independent contractors when they should have been classified as employees could result in substantial fines.

B≈H OF MINORS NOT OK IN SMALL BUSINESSES

My minor son works in a small restaurant as a busboy and dishwasher. He has had all sorts of derogatory comments made to him because of his race.

> I have asked the owner to deal with this but have gotten nowhere. I even spoke with a lawyer but was told that little could really be done since the business has fewer than eight employees. He suggested that my son should try to find another job.

The U.S. EEOC has identified five core principles that seem important to curtailing B≈H:

- Committed and engaged leadership;
- Consistent and demonstrated accountability;
- Strong and comprehensive harassment policies;
- Trusted and accessible complaint procedures;
- Regular, interactive training tailored to the audience and the organization (https://www.eeoc.gov/laws/guidance/promising-practices-preventing-harassment).

OSHA

The Occupational Safety and Health Administration (OSHA) was created in 1970 as part of the United States DOL. OSHA has as its mission, "To ensure safe and healthful working conditions for working men and women by setting and enforcing standards and by providing training, outreach, education and assistance" (https://www.osha.gov/aboutosha).

OSHA has numerous programs, procedures, rules, plans and regulations that address B≈H (https://www.osha.gov/laws-regs/regulations/standardnumber). In addition to safety issues, they cover such things as retaliation complaints, privacy and, of course, discrimination. Some states require that certain notices be shared or posted in the workplace (e.g., no alcohol; wash your hands). If you use union employees, you may need to file reports and handle personnel matters in specified ways. You may also need to verify that your employees are citizens or have permission to work legally in the United States.

SPECIFIC LEGISLATION

With this general background in mind, consider some of the specifics of laws related to employee rights that may impact incidents of B≈H or how they are handled, including but not limited to the following.

The Immigration Act of 1924

This limited the number of immigrants allowed entry into the United States. A quota based on the 1890 census was established as 2% of each nationality.

Norris–LaGuardia Act of 1932

This outlawed so-called yellow-dog contracts that forced workers to say they would not join a union. It declared that union members should have freedom of association unimpeded by employers.

National Labor Relations (Wagner) Act of 1935

This act guaranteed the right of private-sector employees (except agricultural and domestic workers) to organize unions, engage in collective bargaining, and strike. The National Labor Relations Board (NLRB) was created that year to administer the Act. Even if your company doesn't employ unionized workers, you are still subject to the requirements of the Act.

The Fair Labor Standard Act of 1938

This Act and its updates set the standards for wages and overtime pay. Most employers must pay the federal minimum wage and overtime pay at one-and-one-half-times the regular rate of pay. It also limited the use of child labor. Note that on January 1, 2020, overtime pay rules were changed to grant higher levels of compensation for overtime work. At that same time, states increased their minimum wage levels. Employers need to ensure that child workers do not work for more than the legal number of hours.

The Labor Management Relations (Taft–Hartley) Act of 1947

This law restricted the activities and power of unions. It gave workers the right to decline union membership and outlawed closed shops (businesses that hired only union members). It also requires disclosure of a union's financial and political activities.

The Immigration Act (McCarran–Walter Act) of 1952

This upheld the national origins quota system established by the Immigration Act of 1924. However, it ended the exclusion of Asians and introduced preferences based on family reunification.

Labor-management Reporting and Disclosure Act (1959)

Also known as the Landrum–Griffin Act, this act is intended to prevent improper practices by labor organizations and employers. It protects union funds and requires labor organizations to file annual financial reports. It created standards for the election of officers of labor organizations. Further, if the NLRB declined to hear a case, this act provided that state courts could have jurisdiction.

The Equal Pay Act of 1963

This amended the Fair Labor Standards Act by making discrimination based on sex illegal. Thus, it makes it illegal to pay different wages to men and women if they perform equal work in the same workplace. This was a major step toward eliminating gender discrimination in organizations.

Title VII of the Civil Rights Act of 1964

This act pertains to all employers with at least 15 employees. Title VII makes it illegal to discriminate against someone based on race, color, religion, national origin or sex.

However, the EEOC uses a reasonable person standard to determine whether harassment is sufficient to create a hostile environment. This means that the perpetrator's conduct is evaluated from the standpoint of a "reasonable person." Petty slights or those suffered by the hypersensitive would not qualify.

Section 615 Harassment

This section of the EEOC Compliance Manual discusses workplace harassment based on discrimination on the basis of sex, sexual harassment, and harassment, which is based on sex, but which does not constitute sexual harassment. It imposes strict liability on the employer for sexual harassment committed by the employer, its agents, or supervisory employees but does not impose strict liability on the employer if the sexual harassment was done by a co-worker.

Immigration and Nationality Act (1965)

Also known as the Hart–Celler Act, it abolished the National Origins Formula, which had been around since the 1920s. It requires employers who want to use foreign temporary workers on H-2A visas (agricultural workers) to get a labor certificate from the Employment and Training Administration certifying that there are no able, willing and qualified U.S. workers available to do the work. Similar to the H-2A program, recently the Department of Labor created the H-2B program that allows employers to hire non-immigrants on a temporary, seasonal basis for certain non-agricultural jobs.

The Age Discrimination in Employment Act of 1967

This act makes it illegal to discriminate against those people who are 40 years of age or older. Thus, it prohibits organizations from using age in hiring, firing or promotion decisions. Despite the fact that it refers to "age discrimination," it does not apply to younger workers.

Consumer Credit Protection Act (1969)

Title I of the Act, known as the Truth in Lending Act, was meant to provide consumers full disclosure of the terms and conditions of finance charges in credit transactions. Among other issues, this act regulates the garnishment of employee wages by employers which were identified as a predatory extension of credit.

Occupational Safety and Health Act (OSHA) of 1970

Safe and healthful working conditions for working men and women were established by this Act. Employers must provide a workplace free from recognized, serious hazards such as excessive noise levels, exposure to toxic chemicals, mechanical dangers, heat or cold stress, or unsanitary conditions. Workers have rights as regards safety, including to be trained in their language, to have the necessary equipment to do their work safely, and to report or voice concerns about unsafe situations without fear of retaliation.

Sections 501, 503, 504 and 505 of the Rehabilitation Act of 1973

These laws make it illegal to discriminate against disabled people in the public sector including the post office and employers with federal contracts or subcontracts that exceed $10,000. It also prohibits discrimination based on disabilities in public service organizations and telecommunications.

Employee Retirement Income Security Act, ERISA (1974)

Minimum standards for most voluntarily established retirement and health plans in private industry are established to provide protection for individuals in these plans. It also has rules regarding the federal income tax effects associated with employee benefit plans.

The Pregnancy Discrimination Act (1978)

This amendment to Title VII makes it illegal to discriminate against a woman because of pregnancy, childbirth, or a medical condition related to pregnancy or childbirth.

Longshore and Harbor Workers Act (1984)

This act provides medical and other benefits to longshoremen, harbor workers and other maritime employees. It was originally passed in 1927 and amended in 1972. This Act amends it again.

Worker Adjustment and Retraining Notification (WARN) Act (1988)

This Act requires most employers to provide 60 calendar-day advance notification of plant closings and mass layoffs. Those impacted are organizations with 100 or more employees and employees who work fewer than 20 hours per week.

Employee Polygraph Protection Act (1988)

Although certain exemptions are recognized, employers are prevented from using polygraph (lie detector) tests either for pre-employment screening or during the course of employment. Employers also cannot discharge, discipline or discriminate against an employee for refusing to take a test.

Title I of the Americans with Disabilities Act of 1990

This makes it illegal to discriminate against disabled people in both the private sector and in state and local governments. It applies to job application procedures, hiring, firing, advancement, compensation and job training.

Sections 102 and 103 of the Civil Rights Act of 1991

These sections amend Title VII and the Age Discrimination in Employment Act to permit jury trials and compensatory and punitive damage awards in intentional discrimination cases.

Family and Medical Leave Act (1993)

Granted employees the right to take time off from work in order to care for a newborn (or recently adopted) child or to look after an ill family member or themselves with no fear of losing their jobs.

The Genetic Information Nondiscrimination Act of 2008

This act makes it illegal to discriminate against employees or applicants because of genetic information, including information about someone's genetic tests and the genetic tests of an individual's family members, as well as information about an individual's family medical history.

Lilly Ledbetter Fair Pay Act (2009)

This Act strengthened worker protections against pay discrimination by extending the time in which an employee can bring a lawsuit and allowing individuals to seek rectification under federal antidiscrimination laws. To be sure to meet the requirements, employers should carefully examine their pay policies and practices.

Don't Ask, Don't Tell Repeal Act (2010)

Established under the Clinton Administration in 1993, the military was instructed that they cannot ask applicants about their sexual orientation. This is known as "Don't Ask, Don't Tell." The 2010 Act established a process for ending the Don't Ask, Don't Tell policy, thus allowing gay, lesbian and bisexual people to serve openly in the United States Armed Forces.

Section 503 of the Rehabilitation Act (2013)

This prohibits federal contractors from discriminating in employment against individuals with disabilities. It also requires them to act affirmatively to recruit, hire, promote and retain these individuals.

OSHA's Whistleblower Protection Program

OSHA's Whistleblower Protection Program is intended to enforce the provisions of numerous federal safety regulations designed to protect employees from retaliation. Retaliation is a harmful action against an employee protected by one of the whistleblower laws. Retaliation includes such actions as:

- Firing or laying off;
- Blacklisting;
- Demoting;
- Denying overtime or promotion;
- Disciplining;
- Denying benefits;
- Failing to hire or rehire;
- Intimidation;
- Reassignment affecting promotion prospects;
- Reducing pay or hours;
- Making threats.

(OSHA Fact Sheet; available at: https://www.osha.gov/sites/default/files/publications/OSHA3638.pdf).

Ending Forced Arbitration of Sexual Assault and Harassment Act (2022)

This act ends forced arbitration in workplace sexual assault and harassment cases, allowing survivors to file lawsuits in court against perpetrators.

Yet, despite all of these efforts, Executive Orders and court decisions can change the rights of employees. This is especially the case whenever the political party controlling the government changes. You should be aware that legislation can always be enacted; so, check with your HR department to keep up. As noted at the beginning of this chapter, if you do not have an HR department, you may need to monitor government activity on your own or with the help of others.

It is important for you to become familiar with current regulations, but it is even more important for you and your organization to go above and beyond in the proper treatment of the organization's human capital (in this regard, see Morrison, 2017). As just one example, your organization may need to update its policy regarding the use of cannabis as many states have legalized the use of marijuana.

As noted earlier, if your organization is small, you may be exempt from many of these federal or state labor laws. Nevertheless, following them is morally and ethically the thing to do. Following them also demonstrates good faith to your employees and your customers. Abiding by labor and employment laws – even when you are exempt from them – may enable your organization to be more successful in recruiting loyal and productive employees and gaining respect as a good corporate citizen with suppliers and customers.

MINI CASE: HIGH-SECURITY FAILURES

Security is our business. Our organization is responsible for the safety and security of all state agencies and offices in our state. One step in achieving that end is to hold workshops for employees. Another is to inspect their offices for security flaws. Security issues arose in a neighboring state and, as a result, our director called for checking the files of all state employees. An external human resource-auditing firm was hired to do the job. Wow! That audit found several high-level officials had bogus master's degrees while others had degrees from "diploma mills." In another case, an individual was found to have never worked at several companies he had listed on his résumé. Two security officers had failed to indicate that they had served prison time in other states. There were others with inflated job titles and lengthened experience on their records.

These were the people handling security in our state government. Most of them had repeatedly lied or misrepresented their credentials.

1. Is this sort of behavior B≈H?
2. Now that the company has discovered this information, how do you think they should proceed?
3. What should organizations do to prevent this sort of behavior?

THINK ABOUT THIS CHAPTER AGAIN

After reading this chapter, are you satisfied with the current role of government? Is it too much, or do you feel more needs to be done?

Then take a few minutes to prepare responses to the following questions and actions. In particular, managers and human resource professionals should do this to be better prepared to handle B≈H in their organizations.

Government Questions

1. Has your state or local government taken any steps to prevent or respond to B≈H in organizations? If so, what were those steps?
2. Have you personally had any experience with a governmental organization in connection with B≈H in your or another organization?
3. Discuss/summarize how federal regulations have changed since the Industrial Revolution.
4. What was the purpose of most federal acts that were enacted in the 1930s? The 1960s? The 1970s? The 1990s?
5. How have governmental regulations regarding labor and labor unions changed or evolved since the late 1800s?

Government Actions

Identify governmental organizations you would need to contact when/if you personally witness or experience B≈H at work and what you would specifically say.

Use the following form to note any legislation that you feel has impacted your organization.

The form is on a separate page to enable photocopying for use individually or by groups.

INSTRUCTIONS FOR FORM 10

Ways in Which Your Organization May Have Been Impacted by Selected Legislation

For each of the selected legislative actions in the following two-page form, try to identify at least two ways in which they have benefitted or should benefit management and/or workers. Try to be specific, as those benefits might apply to your organization.

CHAPTER 10 CASES

These cases are based on actual situations with identifying names and locations changed or omitted. While anyone would benefit from reading and thinking about these cases, they are best used in a group context where different individual perspectives could be bought forth.

Case 10.1: Unwanted Advances

Aya is a petite woman whose marriage had ended following a situation that involved extreme domestic violence. She had been hospitalized on several occasions and, in one instance, thought she would lose her sight in one eye. Finally, a few years ago she got a divorce and ended that horrible situation. As a result, after the divorce, she left not only the marriage but also her country. She and her four children emigrated from Japan to the United States. The failure of her marriage and relocating to the United States had left her traumatized and quite vulnerable psychologically. Aya has had difficulty finding work because although she can read English quite well, she speaks little of it. She has sole financial responsibility for her four children, so it was important for her to find a job and keep working. She has had to take whatever work she could find.

Form 10   *Identify ways in which your organization may have been impacted by selected legislation*

IDENTIFY WAYS IN WHICH YOUR ORGANIZATION MAY HAVE BEEN IMPACTED BY
SELECTED LEGISLATION

National Labor Relations (Wagner) Act of 1935

The Equal Pay Act of 1963

Title VII of the Civil Rights Act of 1964

Occupational Safety and Health Act (OSHA) of 1970

Title I of the Americans with Disabilities Act of 1990

IDENTIFY WAYS IN WHICH YOUR ORGANIZATION MAY HAVE BEEN IMPACTED BY SELECTED LEGISLATION

Family and Medical Leave Act (1993)

Sections 102 and 103 of the Civil Rights Act of 1991

OSHA's Whistleblower Protection Program

The Genetic Information Nondiscrimination Act of 2008

Lilly Ledbetter Fair Pay Act (2009)

Don't Ask, Don't Tell Repeal Act (2010)

After some searching and a lot of going from place to place, she finally found an opening for work in a mailroom for a small company. The position involved reading but little speaking so she was comfortable with it. It was low-paid, and there were no benefits, but it was a start. Even with her limited knowledge of working conditions in the U.S.A., she understood that she could easily be replaced as there was no security in the job. Her lack of language skills and the tenuous nature of the job made her very nervous and insecure. The job itself was not a highly desirable one either. It involved long hours working Monday through Saturday with some Sundays and even holidays. The specifics of the job consisted of accepting incoming mail and packages, sorting the items, and then delivering them to the proper recipients. Keeping track of the inventory of materials used in shipping and mailing was also involved, although that was a minor part of the job.

After a few weeks on the job, she found herself in a difficult situation. Increasingly she has been subjected to unwanted advances from a co-worker, who is much older than she is. He touches her legs, or her bottom, has pushed himself against her so that she could feel his genitals, and more recently has explicitly asked her for sexual favors. She explained to her supervisor, "He seems like a nice man but touches me where I don't want." The supervisor asked the co-worker about it, but he said, "She has it backwards. She pushes herself against me, not the other way around. The messages were jokes, but I guess she hasn't been in the U.S. long enough to appreciate our sense of humor."

1. From what you think you know about the personalities of Aya and the older co-worker, how do you think she could have – maybe – solved this problem when it first began?
2. What federal laws may be involved?
3. What do you think Aya should do *now* in this situation? Can she "forgive and forget" enough to give her the staying power that she will need?
4. How might the organization prevent this sort of situation in the future?
5. How would you label the behavior in this case?

Case 10.2: Boss Coming On

Brett and Charlotte met in a biology lab class when they were first-semester freshmen at RTU (Raleigh Tech University). Both had outgoing personalities, especially Charlotte. In their sophomore year, their paths crossed frequently as they enrolled in four of the same required courses and labs for "computer majors." In their third year, they progressed from studying together to serious dating and were married soon after graduating from RTU. Since both had lived all their life in the Northeast, they decided to seek jobs in the West since that would offer many outdoor adventures, maybe water-, snow- and cross-country skiing, plus hiking. They made a conscious decision not to seek jobs in the same company, so they were pleased when Charlotte was offered an interesting IT job at a state agency in the same western state where Brett had been recruited by a private tech business nearby.

Five years and loving every minute of it ... their fifth anniversary and they were still loving living "out West." The couple was talking about maybe they should think seriously about starting a family soon. Charlotte admitted she was not real keen on the idea of giving up her job for a few years or not being able to give a job enough attention and effort to build her career like single women could do. They decided to begin asking other couples how they had resolved the dual-career issue.

Then one day the **it hit the fan, as Charlotte told Brett that her boss had been coming onto her through text messages. Brett was upset but managed to keep his composure, mostly. They discussed the boss's behavior thoroughly, but Charlotte did not show Brett any examples of the text messages. He asked if she would like for him to talk with the boss, but she said that she didn't think it was serious. Brett agreed. He thought that Charlotte was probably over-reacting. "Just because a man tells you that you look good," he snapped, "doesn't mean he is trying to get in your pants." Charlotte gave him a slightly disgusted look and countered with "Brett, darling, I'm 27 years old and I think I can judge a man's stare better than you can."

"Here's where I could kick myself," Brett later told investigators. "That I didn't do more at the time to put a stop to this nonsense." But Charlotte had been hoping and working toward a promotion that could come soon and she had told Brett she didn't want anything to jeopardize that. So, after several discussions, they both felt that she would be able to handle it herself. They agreed that, above all, she would say "no" in clear, perspicuous, unambiguous words of rejection. "Like what part of NO ...," Charlotte mumbled the words. She would also keep a log of everything the boss says and does, and how and when and where; and what she says and does.

Now, three months later, and Brett has seen an email on Charlotte's phone. She admitted that at some point she stopped logging the messages and started deleting the messages to prevent Brett from knowing. Actually, she started flirting with her boss, responding to his compliments – basically engaging in an emotional affair. And that's when the **it really hit the fan. The whole thing started five years ago, and it had not ever stopped.

Charlotte admitted the affair, as did her boss, who also admitted that he had been the instigator. Brett also talked with the boss's wife on the phone because he felt that she should know that her husband had failed his family and might try it again someday.

Brett felt like the boss was getting away with terrible behavior. And of course, he wanted the boss gone from that job ASAP. As for Charlotte, she should have never been put in this situation in the first place, but she failed to shut her boss down and then went on to encourage it. She does not want to go to HR. She was promoted to a managerial position the previous year. Brett is not sure whether his talks with the boss and his wife will ensure an end to the problem.

1. What is the problem (or problems) from the viewpoint of (a) the company and (b) the individuals?
2. What federal laws may they be breaking?
3. Should any of these individuals report the problem? If so, who and to whom?
4. In your opinion, if upper management learns about the affair now, after it is already broken, will they take action and what will they do?
5. How should organizations handle these sorts of situations?

11. What's next?

In this final chapter, you should reflect on all of the material that has been presented. Again, write down what you feel should be done by you, your organization, the government, or other organizations such as educational institutions to reduce or eliminate B≈H in work organizations. So, you should have at least four sets of notes to keep handy as you consider the points made in this concluding chapter.

INTRODUCTION

In addressing B≈H, you would all do well to remember Franklin Roosevelt's Four Freedoms speech: freedom of speech and expression, freedom to worship God in your own way, freedom from want, and freedom from fear (Olson, 1983). He added "anywhere in the world" to each of these (Crowell, 1955); instead, add "everywhere in the organization." But as we have been learning, from the standpoint of organizations, there are some limitations to freedom of speech and perhaps freedom from want. However, religious freedom must be maintained and, most importantly, freedom from fear must exist for everyone in the organization. No one should ever experience fear while at work. Now expand this list of four freedoms by adding freedom of assembly and freedom from discrimination, as those are important to all members of organizations.

FREE SPEECH

Members of private sector organizations typically do not have a constitutional right to free speech at work; however, federal and state laws may protect their speech in certain situations. For example, as noted in Chapter 10, the National Labor Relations Act (NLRA) protects members of organizations if they discuss their wages with each other, decide if they are not being paid enough, and seek raises from their employer, including collective action. Organizational members may also have the right to discuss possible unlawful conduct in the workplace. Generally, they may complain about harassment, discrimination, workplace safety violations and other issues; but under no circumstances are they free to express racist, sexist or other discriminatory comments. Employees can also lose their right to free speech when they denigrate or speak falsely of their employer or the company's products or services.

Posts on social media (e.g., SocialBee, TikTok, Trello, Reddit, LinkedIn, Twitch, Instagram, Facebook) may be a different matter. Such posts may be "protected concerted activity" if the discussion involves working conditions and other labor relations matters, but they still may not express racist, sexist or other discriminatory comments. However, organizations can have policies designed to create the sort of culture preferred by the owners or top management, and the organization may be able to terminate an employee for violating policies even if his or her speech is protected. So long as they do not illegally discriminate, organizations can elect to get rid of employees who do not fit the organization's culture.

Employers have fired employees who post statements outside of the workplace, especially on social media (the following is from Moskowitz, 2018). An individual lost his job when Twitter users posted both his photo and place of employment after he was identified as having participated in a white nationalist rally. A dean at a major university was fired after he referred to people as "white trash" in Yelp reviews. And the former chief executive of Mozilla was forced to resign after it became public that he supported a ban on gay marriage. In the following situation, the manager would fire the employee if gun sales drop. But if the employee is fired, would it be because of the comments or the decreased sales?

GUN CONTROL

I work for a small retail company that sells, among other things, guns. But I am a firm supporter of gun regulations and have spoken out on Facebook about that. The manager has suggested that if my views get in the way of his business, I'll be fired. Shouldn't I have the right to say what I want on social media?

If, however, you work for the federal government, there are still limits but, generally, you have greater freedom of speech than if you work in the private sector. If what you are saying or writing is part of your official job duties, you are likely protected. If what's being said is a legitimate news topic and is being said not as an employee but as a regular citizen, then it is likely to be protected. If what you are saying or writing is a matter of public concern, you are likely protected. Subjects of public concern are such things as corruption, elections, pending legislation, public health and safety, and racial discrimination. Internal organizational policies, on the other hand, are normally not protected.

FREEDOM FROM WANT

Freedom from want at work does not mean that employees get paid whatever they want. It does mean that the organization should provide competitive compensation and benefits that help employees improve their health, reduce stress, balance their careers and personal lives, and increase their financial security. The complete "package" should ensure that the organization can obtain and retain productive employees who will grow with the organization.

A truly complete compensation package would include the following (Heathfield, 2019):

1. Health insurance
2. Paid time off (PTO)
3. Short-term disability insurance
4. Long-term disability insurance
5. Dental insurance
6. Vision insurance
7. Life insurance
8. 401(k) or other retirement plan
9. Healthcare Flexible Spending Account (FSA) plans.

Employer-paid time off from work is an important component of any comprehensive employee benefits package.

Compensation packages in smaller organizations may not have all these benefits; on the other hand, there may be no benefits at all. In those situations, employees are on their own. However, a well-managed small organization may offer some limited benefits and, as the organization grows, so, too, will the compensation package. Some inexpensive benefits that are easy to stop might include a company T-shirt or an employee pizza party. Far more costly are medical insurance and health savings plans. In a small business, it is important to start slowly in offering these more costly benefits as it is almost impossible to go back, once you start.

The level of compensation may not be the primary reason individuals leave their jobs, but it is certainly one of the main ones. Unfortunately, many people assume that they are being paid less than market conditions. As a result, they may leave when they shouldn't. If the organization would provide compensation information from an independent source, that information would form the basis for more accurate and realistic reactions from employees. If the organization's pay rates are below the market, employees deserve to know why. It is not uncommon for newer businesses to pay below the market while they are getting started or for particular employees to be paid lower until they receive more training, but whatever the reason, an explanation is in order. Open, transparent communication is the key.

FREEDOM OF RELIGION

Title VII of the Civil Rights Act of 1964 prohibits private employers from discriminating on several bases, including religion. Indeed, courts have recognized various kinds of prohibited discrimination, including not only disparate treatment (intentionally discriminatory) but also disparate impact (unintentionally discriminatory, as when a seemingly neutral policy or practice has a disproportional impact on a particular protected group).

In other words, organizations have legal obligations regarding religious freedom. So long as job performance is acceptable, it might seem as though there would be no issues; but with increasing diversity in the workplace, religious freedom is not always that simple. It can be quite complicated, as religion may involve more than beliefs. It may involve attire, hairstyle, diet, prayer practices, following or avoiding certain language or behavior, and, of course, religious holidays.

Accommodating all these differences in a highly diverse workplace can place an unreasonable burden on an organization. In such circumstances, open communication can be helpful in seeking some sort of reasonable accommodation that avoids litigation. If organizations make sure that people feel respected, potentially bad situations can be prevented from escalating. Consider a simple thing like an organization's dress code – could it restrict the freedom of religion?

DRESS CODES AND RELIGION

My boss says that wearing a hijab is against the company's dress code. I don't think so and I can't find anything in writing about it. And a co-worker has joined me by wearing a yarmulke! If we can get along, the company should respect us. If the company's code won't permit us to follow our religious practices, it's time to change the code!

Organizations should practice the following to help ensure that religious freedom is protected:

- Encourage diversity;
- Promote tolerance;
- Promote nondenominational "values" and ethics;
- Establish a mechanism to review and consider requests for accommodation;

- Encourage employees to report any discrimination or harassment;
- Train managers and human resource professionals on religious discrimination, harassment and accommodation issues;
- Offer employees the opportunity to promote voluntary participation in religious and non-religious activities outside work hours;
- Be wary of workplace proselytizing; respect employee beliefs, privacy and dignity;
- Follow best practices, like any other EEO category (Homans & Johnson, 2008, pp. 16–17).

To protect religious freedom, organizations should *not do* the following:

- Don't mandate attendance at religious services;
- Don't discriminate at work based on religion or non-religion;
- Don't base accommodation decisions on the religion at issue;
- Don't allow employees to condemn as "evil" or to vilify others who believe differently;
- Don't rely on the literature of only one religion to promote values or company ethos;
- Don't give overly generous or solicitous accommodations to employees of one religion unless it is done for all;
- Don't accommodate individual conduct, speech or religious observance that creates a harassing environment for others or otherwise impinges on other employees' rights (Homans & Johnson, 2008, pp. 17–18).

FREEDOM FROM FEAR

No one should be afraid at work – afraid of being singled out, called names or overworked. And, certainly, no one should fear B≈H at work. Particularly in difficult economic and social conditions, managers may create conditions in which individuals work in constant fear (Keegan, 2015). But no one should fear retaliation for filing a claim or complaint against an employer; they should be able to exercise their "whistleblower" rights as protected by law. Employees should trust their organization and their colleagues rather than fear them. Some of the signs that serve to identify fear-based workplaces include the following (Ryan, 2017):

- An intense focus on short-term goals where everyone is focused on daily goals because, if a goal is missed, they could lose their jobs;
- Human resource personnel focus on measuring results, punishing infractions and maintaining order rather than listening to workers;
- People won't tell the truth about conditions at work;
- A strong rumor mill exists about who's in and who's out;

- Everyone is unsure about whether or not they will have a job next week;
- Following rules is more important than innovation, but most of all, "Don't screw up";
- Management talks about thinking out of the box, but no one takes it seriously;
- Occasionally, someone just is no longer there, and no one talks about what happened to them;
- Promotions go to those who embrace the fear-based culture rather than to those who are the best performers;
- Humor and warmth are missing and, if displayed, are labeled as "unprofessional." The place is too quiet!

Unfortunately, as long as organizations such as the Ku Klux Klan, The Proud Boys, American First Committee, Advanced White Society, Black Separatist, and American Patriot Brigade exist – and as long as concepts such as "man cave" and "she shed" exist – and as long as offensive terms such as "kike," "nigger" and "Paki" are employed by certain individuals – discrimination of one sort or another will continue to exist, and some employees will remain fearful at work (Balleck, 2019). Meanwhile, what can be done?

AFRAID OF LOSING JOB

Because there have been layoffs at my company over the last couple of years, I live in constant fear of losing my job. I'm a good worker but a bit of a loner so I think the company wouldn't hesitate to get rid of me. I want to talk to my coordinator about this but don't know how to begin.

Freedom from fear extends to safety as well. The workplace should be free of dangerous conditions like weapons, toxic substances and other potential safety hazards. According to OSHA, the Occupational Health and Safety Act ensures everyone in an organization has three fundamental rights:

1. *The right to know* about health and safety matters.[1]
2. *The right to participate* in decisions that could affect their health and safety.[2]
3. *The right to refuse* work that could affect their health and safety and that of others (OSHguide, 2020).[3]

FREEDOM OF ASSEMBLY

Members of organizations should also be free to assemble, to form groups, and have unions. Their freedom of assembly or association refers to their right to come together and collectively express, promote, pursue and defend their collective or shared ideas. Of course, that freedom does not mean that they can use the facilities or property of the organization for purposes of assembly. Nor does it mean that they can assemble on company time.

As noted in Chapter 10, members of organizations have legal protections regarding assembly and association. Organizations cannot prevent unions from seeking members from among their employees, and they cannot punish employees for supporting a union. On the other hand, organizations can express their disapproval of labor unions to their employees as a way of preventing a union from gaining support among the organization's employees. However, organizations may cooperate with groups and provide both time and resources to facilitate the meeting(s) of a group. But they are not legally bound to provide unions access unless the organization provides such access to other (non-union) organizations (McGurie & O'Keefe, 2014).

Of course, a union can be perhaps too powerful and become perceived as a threat, as in this situation (although, hopefully, this is not typical).

SCARED BOSS

My boss is scared of our union because the company has lost several big cases involving the union. I have noticed this and taken advantage of him by humming "The union is behind us. We shall not be moved" any time he is around. It's kind of fun having a bit of an upper hand for once.

Freedom of assembly can be limited. Local legislative authorities may limit it through the legitimate use of its police powers. It is obviously limited if violence occurs or if the gathering poses an immediate threat to public safety. There may also be ordinances that prohibit the blocking of sidewalks or pathways. Private organizations may also prohibit individuals from entering or remaining on their property (Stricker, 2006).

FREEDOM FROM DISCRIMINATION

Members of organizations should feel free from discrimination with respect to employment and occupation. Discrimination by organizations on the basis of race, color, religion, sex, political opinion, national or social origin, and other grounds is detrimental to the effectiveness and efficiency of those organizations and so should not exist. This also means that there should be "equal pay for equal work" and reasonable accommodation for individuals with special medical conditions or religious beliefs. There should also be an expectation that medical and physical information shared with an organization should be kept confidential.

PAST ASSOCIATIONS

I just moved into a new apartment building. I'm in my early 20s, try to dress nicely, and have a college degree. That being said, other tenants try to avoid me probably because I have visible gang tattoos. I long ago gave up that side of my life but it apparently still haunts me.

While it is never ethical to discriminate in the workplace, at least one form of legal but unethical discrimination has recently been noted. Weight discrimination has been documented as a widespread phenomenon that is having a negative impact on the lives of individuals as well as depriving organizations of potentially highly productive individuals. While it is legal to do so, it is not ethical to do so. "Fair-minded organizations need to be vigilant in recognizing the ethical issues associated with the disparate treatment of overweight employees" (Roehling, 2002).

Two more complicated issues involve discrimination based on the use of cannabis and on the LGBTQ community. As more jurisdictions ease the regulations on the use of marijuana, what to do with those who test positive for its use becomes a complicated legal and ethical issue (Lytle, 2019). In June 2020, the U.S. Supreme Court ruled that the 1964 Civil Rights Act protects gay, lesbian and transgender employees from discrimination based on sex (Totenberg, 2020). Organizations need to work with HR professionals and legal counsel to determine what needs to be done with regard to these difficult issues.

RECOMMENDATIONS

So, given all that has been covered, what is recommended?

- The single most important recommendation for any organization is to understand B≈H. Policies and plans cannot be developed unless the organization has a comprehensive view of what B≈H really is.
- A second recommendation is to have a group (e.g., committee, task force) comprised of managers and non-managers develop a single policy to prohibit B≈H.
- A third recommendation is to develop training programs focused on the use of the V-REEL® framework to identify and prioritize eroding and enabling factors in the organization.

Develop a Positive Workplace Culture

As part of a single policy or multiple policies and plans, organizations need to develop a positive workplace culture with a zero-tolerance environment. As noted in the suggested policy in Chapter 9, organizations should strive to create and maintain cultures in which people are treated with dignity, decency and respect. Such cultures should be characterized by mutual trust and the absence of intimidation, oppression and exploitation. An open-door policy that encourages and empowers employees to speak up in a safe, supportive environment without judgment or penalty would be a significant part of that environment. All policies and plans should, of course, be periodically reviewed and revised as necessary to keep them up to date. The changing regulatory environment necessitates such revisions.

Identify Eroding and Enabling Factors

All managers, but especially supervisors, should learn to use the V-REEL® framework. In doing so, suggestions and comments from all employees should be used to examine each of the components: V (value), R (rareness), E (eroding factors), E (enabling factors), and L (longevity). The emphasis, however, should be on identifying and prioritizing the eroding and enabling factors. Remember that *eroding factors* are those things that impede your ability to reduce B≈H or that encourage B≈H in some way. As noted earlier, an organizational culture that supports perpetrators with power would also be an eroding factor. These and other eroding factors should be eliminated or at least reduced. *Enabling factors* are those things that improve your ability to manage B≈H. Hiring a better educated, more capable, diverse workforce could be an enabling factor. This and other enabling factors should be fostered and expanded where possible. By focusing everyone's attention on the two Es (eroding and enabling factors) and with open communication, substantial reductions in B≈H may be achieved.

Maintain Open Communications

Open communication entails all managers but especially supervisors, talking the talk and walking the walk. They must "keep their ears to the ground" and closely monitor the workplace for any signs of B≈H. They must listen attentively and take all complaints seriously, especially if the complaint is of a sexual nature. When they do perceive a problem or hear a complaint, they should carefully investigate the situation before taking any action.

Develop Training Objectives and Programs

Our primary recommendation, however, is that working with HR professionals, your organization should develop training programs using the concepts covered in this book. The first step would be to assess how much (several hours or several days) and/or what level (all managers, supervisors or other employees) of training is needed. Then SMART (specific, measurable, achievable, relevant, time-bound) learning objectives must be developed:

- Specific: The training program should identify which specific enabling and eroding factors will be the focus.
- Measurable: The organization should determine how progress toward achieving objectives related to each of these will be determined.
- Achievable: The training goals must be evaluated to ensure that they are actually achievable.
- Relevant: The training goals also must be evaluated to ensure that they are relevant to the individuals and the organization.
- Time: Finally, there should be a timetable indicating when those results of that training would be expected.

The organization's training objectives also should identify the ABCDs:

A for actors (those being trained);
B for behaviors (that the actors should exhibit);
C for conditions (under which the behaviors should occur);
D for the degree to which the actors must perform the behaviors.

Behaviors discussed in the book should be used to create specific training action plans and materials. Then the training should be implemented, following these guidelines:

- Adopt our definition for organizations (not academics, researchers, or lawyers) (Chapter 1);
- Develop a policy (Chapter 1);
- Provide examples (Chapters 2–5);
- Educate everyone in the use of V-REEL® (Chapters 6 & 7);
- Take steps to prevent B≈H from happening (Chapters 7–9);
- Conduct biannual attitude surveys (Chapter 8);
- Develop procedures based on the policy (Chapter 8);
- Develop enforcement for violations of the policy (Chapter 8);
- Recognize the role of government (Chapter 9);
- Periodically review the whole process to keep it current;
- Evaluate and revise your training programs, as necessary.

Will following these recommendations totally eradicate B≈H in your organization? Maybe not, but they should drastically reduce any such incidents.

TAKE RESPONSIBILITY

But regardless of what your organization does, what should you as an individual do? First and foremost, you should support your organization's efforts to reduce and eliminate B≈H. However, should you personally become the victim of B≈H, you should do the following:

- Talk with your family and friends, your peers in the organization, or a mentor if you have one. These individuals may provide helpful advice and will be part of your support group to help you deal with the situation.
- Rehearse what you plan to do. You need not only to think carefully about what you are going to say and do, but it would be best to practice or rehearse each step. This should enable you to anticipate the reactions of others and how you might respond to them.
- Determine if your organization has someone to whom you can turn (e.g., EEOC person) or, if not, is there a local office of the U.S. Equal Employment Commission that you could contact. A list of EEOC offices may be found in Appendix B.
- Make the person committing the B≈H aware that you recognize that the behavior is unwanted and that they are the person who did it. Be assertive but not aggressive. Tell the person that the behavior is unacceptable, ask them to stop, and be firm in doing so. You should also note where and when you have done so and provide a witness to the exchange if possible.
- Follow up on telling the person that their behavior is unacceptable, as soon as you experience the B≈H, write down exactly what happened. Be as specific as possible, noting when and where it occurred and anyone who may have seen the incident.
- Report the incident and be sure to also document to whom you reported it and when you reported it. If your organization has a policy for reporting B≈H, be sure to follow it as closely as possible. Do this in writing, but if a meeting was involved, make a written summary of that meeting and be sure to indicate the date and time. Be sure to hang on to a copy of any written materials that you make or your organization's responses.
- See if there are any witnesses who would support your version of the incident or who have seen other such incidents. Try to find an ally who would be supportive and help you through these steps. Here's where peers are especially helpful.
- While looking for support, see what you may find on social media about the perpetrator. There may be comments on Facebook, Twitter, or some

other social network that would indicate what kind of person he or she is, and that could be used to bolster your case.

- If need be, get medical or therapy attention to keep yourself going while this process works its way through the organizational channels.
- While this is going on and you are waiting for some sort of resolution, be sure to keep up your job performance. If the organization doesn't have ongoing performance records, keep your own daily log of how well you did.
- If you are initially unsatisfied with the organization's response, seek legal assistance. The EEOC doesn't charge for their advice, but lawyers do. However, you may find one that would work on a contingency basis so that they don't get paid until you get a settlement.
- Finally, of course, you need to decide if you are going to stay or leave. Quitting may not end your involvement, particularly if an attorney or outside agency is involved. Nevertheless, you need to consider your options and the difficulties associated with locating a new position where you will feel more secure.

MINI CASE: RELIGIOUS PRESSURE

I have a co-worker, Faith, who is constantly going on and on about religion. Shortly after she was hired, she invited everyone to her home for a get-acquainted party. However, it quickly became apparent that it was not for us getting to know one another better but rather it was a recruiting meeting for her church. That was just the beginning. She sends us emails and pamphlets about her religion and can't seem to talk about anything else. Whenever she gets a chance, she pushes her religion and how we would benefit by becoming members. She has even called some of us at home.

Several of us recently met with our manager about her behavior. We were in for a big surprise. She goes to the same church as Faith! She suggested that Faith just cares for her co-workers and that maybe we should try to understand her better. So, instead of alleviating the situation, we may well have made things worse!

1. Is Faith engaging in B≈H?
2. What can an organization do in such a situation?

THINK ABOUT THIS CHAPTER AGAIN

Examine what you wrote at the beginning of this chapter. Do you want to make any changes after reading the chapter?

Then take a few minutes to prepare responses to these questions and actions. In particular, managers, human resource professionals and legal counsel should do this to be better prepared to handle B≈H in their organizations.

What's Next Questions

1. Do the four freedoms exist in your organization? Why or why not?
2. Does your organization have a clear policy dealing with B≈H and training for everyone based on that policy?
3. What are some things that your organization can do to help ensure religious freedom?
4. Explain what is meant by disparate treatment and disparate impact?
5. How do you think that you would respond to Faith if she approached you? Why do you think your idea would work?

What's Next Actions

Use the following form to make sure you have a clear plan for dealing with B≈H in your organization.

INSTRUCTIONS FOR FORM 11

Action Plan Steps

Now is the time to develop an educational program based on the concepts presented in this book. You can prepare yourself by reading the books and articles in the references. Your organization can prepare by using the steps indicated in the following form (the first two steps may have been done previously in Chapters 3 and 7).

The form is on a separate page to enable photocopying for use individually or by groups.

CHAPTER 11 CASES

These cases are based on actual situations with identifying names and locations changed or omitted. While anyone would benefit from reading and thinking about these cases, they are best used in a group context where different individual perspectives could be bought forth.

Form 11   *Action plan steps*

ACTION PLAN STEPS

(The first two steps may have been done previously in Chapters 3 and 7)

---

1. Has someone or some unit in your organization conducted a survey like the one in Appendix A?

---

2. Use the V-REEL® framework to develop a list of eroding and enabling factors.

---

3. Consider those factors along with the four freedoms and incorporate those into an action plan.

---

4. Prepare policies and reporting documents, including who or what department receives complaints and how such complaints would be investigated.

---

5. Develop training programs for managers and workers.

---

6. Periodically redo your analysis using the V-REEL® framework.

Case 11.1: Co-workers' Plot

Dewayne is 26 years old and single. After two years at a nearby community college, he began full-time employment as a picker for a packaging company that had opened up a few years ago. The facility is huge – one could easily get lost in it – and the work is physically demanding. Working ten-hour shifts, a picker reads a digital or printed request for a product, pulls the requested item or items from shelves, and places them in the correct box or loading container for the order packers. To keep the information accurate and up to date, the picker must then make a note on the inventory system that the items have been removed from the shelves. A robot could handle the job easily.

The performance of a picker is measured by units per hour and the amount of time it takes to process an item. The performance information is maintained digitally and updated every hour so there is intense pressure on pickers to do good work. Because Dewayne was a rapid learner and a good worker, his times are fast, and his units per hour are high. As a result, he rarely interacts with anyone in management. Management's practice is to leave workers alone so long as their performance meets or exceeds standards.

Like many single young men, Dewayne likes to party and has been known to enjoy more than a few drinks when he does. However, he never drinks while at work, nor does he ever show up at work under the influence. Indeed, he is one of the highest performing workers in his unit and quite successful. Therein lies the problem.

A couple of his co-workers feel that because of his race, his performance ratings have been inflated. They began to conspire about a way to "put him down." The idea is to make sure that he gets plenty to drink; and when he seems clearly drunk and seemingly out of control, they snap a few pics with their phones. Then just post copies of the pics on the company bulletin board and maybe Facebook or Twitter as well. Captions can be added, like "A drunk in action," or "Would you trust this man with your daughter?"

Dewayne's co-workers decide that to make the situation seem even clearer, the location where Dewayne-the-pretending-boss is supposedly misbehaving must be easily identifiable. Where better than the company premises? And just to be sure, more than one instance of his partying should be caught on camera. When the pictures get posted, the plotters feel sure the company will pay attention. Since the company takes great pride in its excellent reputation and its standing in the community, they are sure that when his supervisor and upper management see the pictures, Dewayne will be in big trouble despite his overall good performance at the company in the past.

1.   How would you label the behavior in this case?
2.   Do the four freedoms exist in this organization?

3. Does your organization have any drinking guidelines?
4. What do you think Dewayne should do in this situation?
5. How might the organization prevent this sort of situation in the future?

Case 11.2: Isolation

Elijah Mohammad is a bright young man. He was born and raised in a mid-size college town in the heart of the United States. He is a Muslim, which is not common in the town. He is known as a hard-working individual where he is employed in the supply room of a local business. The job involves using SAP inventory management software to maintain, count and report all material, parts and supplies. The job is relatively routine since the program helps keep everything going smoothly.

Among his friends, Elijah is known to be friendly with everyone even though he is not very talkative. He is especially uncomfortable with people he doesn't know. Fortunately, his job does not require him to interact very much with people outside the company, so that part of his work doesn't cause him any discomfort.

Elijah likes his work, but he is thinking about quitting his job because of the breaks. It is normal for the employees to spend the breaks together in a common area, known as the breakroom. He would like to participate, but he feels like the others ignore him. He has tried to start conversations with his colleagues, but he says that his colleagues pretend that he said nothing. He usually sits alone at a table near the television, pretending to be interested in whatever program happens to be airing at that time.

Elijah's job does require him to work with some of the other employees individually, as when they are requesting supplies or preparing a shipment. But he almost never has an opportunity to act as a team member. He thinks that he would feel more comfortable with others if he had a job that required him to intermingle with a few people. Working with a group, he told his father, would give others an opportunity to see how intelligent he is, and they would perhaps respect him and want to associate with him.

Elijah's parents disagree. They have always taught him that, if he limits his association with others, they have fewer opportunities to render negative judgments of him or his work. Elijah feels that he is probably smarter than most of his co-workers because his parents have always pushed him to be a high achiever as a means of showing people that immigrants are good people. Elijah has reached the point where he feels almost brave enough to rely on his own assessments and decision-making ability. He wants things to change.

1. Do the four freedoms exist in this organization?
2. What's next for Elijah at this point?

3. What would be the pluses and the minuses of Elijah's going versus staying, including both work and family?

4. Assuming Elijah stays at his current company, prepare an action plan to show him what changes he must make in order to achieve his personal and professional goals. Include suggestions and examples (e.g., try not to sit alone at the TV at lunch. When you arrive at lunch, ask persons at one table, "May I join you?" as you place your hand on top of the chair. Listen intently and try to toss in a good idea, or joke. At the end of lunch, compliment one or two persons ("really interesting")).

5. How might the organization help new hires get acquainted with company personnel? What are some departments or offices that the new hires would most likely need on their first day at work? Their first week?

NOTES

1. https://ohsguide.worksafenb.ca/topic/rights.html#know.
2. https://ohsguide.worksafenb.ca/topic/rights.html#participate.
3. https://ohsguide.worksafenb.ca/topic/rights.html#refuse.

Appendix A: Employee attitude survey

This survey is anonymous. Please answer the following questions honestly.

Unwelcome verbal or physical conduct constitutes B≈H when this conduct explicitly or implicitly adversely affects an individual's physical or mental health, negatively impacts their employment, unreasonably interferes with an individual's work performance, or creates an intimidating, hostile or offensive work environment.

Please indicate how you feel about each statement by indicating your level of agreement or disagreement or answering yes or no.

PART 1: B≈H FOCUSED ITEMS

1.   I am familiar with the organization's policy with regard to B≈H.

Strongly agree   Mostly agree   Neutral   Mostly disagree   Strongly disagree

2.   B≈H is largely in the eye of the beholder.

Strongly agree   Mostly agree   Neutral   Mostly disagree   Strongly disagree

3.   B≈H and intimidation are stressful.

Strongly agree   Mostly agree   Neutral   Mostly disagree   Strongly disagree

4.   I have observed or experienced B≈H from a member of management.

Strongly agree   Mostly agree   Neutral   Mostly disagree   Strongly disagree

5.   B≈H is tolerated within my workplace.

Strongly agree   Mostly agree   Neutral   Mostly disagree   Strongly disagree

6.   B≈H has been an important issue for me in the past three months.

Strongly agree   Mostly agree   Neutral   Mostly disagree   Strongly disagree

7.   I saw or have been involved in incidents involving B≈H.

Strongly agree   Mostly agree   Neutral   Mostly disagree   Strongly disagree

8. B≈H incidents impact my general health, well-being, or ability to do normal work-related duties.

Strongly agree   Mostly agree   Neutral   Mostly disagree   Strongly disagree

9. I have observed or experienced B≈H from a customer or supplier.

Strongly agree   Mostly agree   Neutral   Mostly disagree   Strongly disagree

10. Reporting B≈H is supported by our human resources personnel.

Strongly agree   Mostly agree   Neutral   Mostly disagree   Strongly disagree

11. Reporting B≈H is supported by my manager/supervisor.

Strongly agree   Mostly agree   Neutral   Mostly disagree   Strongly disagree

12. I have experienced B≈H that was unwanted pressure for sexual favors.

Strongly agree   Mostly agree   Neutral   Mostly disagree   Strongly disagree

13. I have experienced B≈H that was unwanted emails or calls of a sexual nature.

Strongly agree   Mostly agree   Neutral   Mostly disagree   Strongly disagree

14. I have experienced B≈H that was pressure for dates.

Strongly agree   Mostly agree   Neutral   Mostly disagree   Strongly disagree

15. I have experienced B≈H that was sexual teasing, jokes, remarks or questions.

Strongly agree   Mostly agree   Neutral   Mostly disagree   Strongly disagree

16. Have you talked with your family or friends regarding B≈H you have experienced at work?

    Yes   No

17. Have you talked with your family or friends regarding B≈H of a sexual attention?

    Yes   No

18. Have you consulted someone from the EEOC or an attorney regarding B≈H you have experienced at work?

    Yes   No

19. If you experienced or witnessed B≈H, did you have time off work using sick leave or workers compensation leave?

   Yes   No

20. If you did do something about it, was there a favorable outcome (the B≈H stopped)?

   Yes   No

PART 2: GENERAL QUESTIONS

21. I am respected by the people I work with.

Strongly agree   Mostly agree   Neutral   Mostly disagree   Strongly disagree

22. I trust my colleagues.

Strongly agree   Mostly agree   Neutral   Mostly disagree   Strongly disagree

23. In general, I like working here.

Strongly agree   Mostly agree   Neutral   Mostly disagree   Strongly disagree

24. I work hard at my job.

Strongly agree   Mostly agree   Neutral   Mostly disagree   Strongly disagree

25. My work is generally interesting.

Strongly agree   Mostly agree   Neutral   Mostly disagree   Strongly disagree

26. I understand how performance is evaluated.

Strongly agree   Mostly agree   Neutral   Mostly disagree   Strongly disagree

27. My manager/supervisor and I agree on what good job performance means.

Strongly agree   Mostly agree   Neutral   Mostly disagree   Strongly disagree

28. The evaluations of my performance by my manager/supervisor are fair and objective.

Strongly agree   Mostly agree   Neutral   Mostly disagree   Strongly disagree

29. I receive feedback that helps improve my job performance.

Strongly agree   Mostly agree   Neutral   Mostly disagree   Strongly disagree

30. High standards of performance are demanded by my manager/supervisor.

Strongly agree   Mostly agree   Neutral   Mostly disagree   Strongly disagree

31. How do you rate the effectiveness of your manager/supervisor?

Ineffective   1   2   Somewhat effective   3   4   5   Very effective   6   7

32. How satisfied are you with your manager/supervisor?

Dissatisfied   1   2   Neutral   3   4   5   Satisfied   6   7

33. I'm encouraged to express my ideas and opinions about important aspects of my job.

Strongly agree   Mostly agree   Neutral   Mostly disagree   Strongly disagree

34. My job duties are clearly defined by my manager/supervisor.

Strongly agree   Mostly agree   Neutral   Mostly disagree   Strongly disagree

35. I receive recognition for the work I do.

Strongly agree   Mostly agree   Neutral   Mostly disagree   Strongly disagree

36. Hard work gains me respect from my co-workers.

Strongly agree   Mostly agree   Neutral   Mostly disagree   Strongly disagree

37. I will be rebuked if I perform poorly.

Strongly agree   Mostly agree   Neutral   Mostly disagree   Strongly disagree

38. People have reported minor thefts from their workplaces.

Strongly agree   Mostly agree   Neutral   Mostly disagree   Strongly disagree

39. There is adequate lighting to make me feel safe at night.

Strongly agree   Mostly agree   Neutral   Mostly disagree   Strongly disagree

40. People have reported physical assaults here at work.

Strongly agree   Mostly agree   Neutral   Mostly disagree   Strongly disagree

41. I generally feel safe while working.

Strongly agree   Mostly agree   Neutral   Mostly disagree   Strongly disagree

42. Younger employees, as compared to older employees, are treated the same.

Strongly agree   Mostly agree   Neutral   Mostly disagree   Strongly disagree

43. Female employees, as compared to male employees, are treated the same.

Strongly agree   Mostly agree   Neutral   Mostly disagree   Strongly disagree

44. Employees of color as compared to white employees are treated the same.

Strongly agree   Mostly agree   Neutral   Mostly disagree   Strongly disagree

45. LGBTQ employees as compared to other employees are treated the same.

Strongly agree   Mostly agree   Neutral   Mostly disagree   Strongly disagree

46. My organization values diversity.

Strongly agree   Mostly agree   Neutral   Mostly disagree   Strongly disagree

47. My organization has high standards for ethics.

Strongly agree   Mostly agree   Neutral   Mostly disagree   Strongly disagree

48. Promotions are fair and equitable.

Strongly agree   Mostly agree   Neutral   Mostly disagree   Strongly disagree

49. Pay raises are fair and equitable.

Strongly agree   Mostly agree   Neutral   Mostly disagree   Strongly disagree

50. People in my area/unit/department participate in deciding how the work gets done.

Strongly agree   Mostly agree   Neutral   Mostly disagree   Strongly disagree

51. I can contact the senior management if needed.

Strongly agree   Mostly agree   Neutral   Mostly disagree   Strongly disagree

52. My work environment allows me to be highly productive.

Strongly agree   Mostly agree   Neutral   Mostly disagree   Strongly disagree

53. My supervisor listens to comments and suggestions.

Strongly agree   Mostly agree   Neutral   Mostly disagree   Strongly disagree

54. My co-workers work well together to accomplish our goals.

Strongly agree   Mostly agree   Neutral   Mostly disagree   Strongly disagree

55. Considering workplace safety at your organization, how likely are you to recommend the organization to your family/friends?

Don't recommend   1   2   Neutral   3   4   5   Highly recommend   6   7

PART 3: CLASSIFICATION INFORMATION

Please indicate your gender.

Male   Female   Other   Prefer not to say

Please indicate your age.

Less than 30   31–50   51 or older   Prefer not to say

Please indicate your ethnicity.

Black   Caucasian   Chinese   Filipino   Hmong   Indian
Japanese   Korean   Latino   Native American   Other

Appendix B: Addresses or contact information for helpful organizations

EQUAL EMPLOYMENT OPPORTUNITY COMMISSION OFFICES

Data as of 2022.

EEOC Headquarters
U.S. Equal Employment Opportunity Commission
131 M Street, NE
Washington, DC 20507
202-921-3191

District, Area and Local Offices
(Phone number for all of these is 1-800-669-4000)

Alabama
Birmingham District Office
Ridge Park Place
1130 22nd Street South, Suite 2000
Birmingham, AL 35205

Mobile Local Office
63 South Royal Street, Suite 504
Mobile, AL 36602

Arizona
Phoenix District Office
3300 North Central Avenue, Suite 690
Phoenix, AZ 85012-2504

Arkansas
Little Rock Area Office
820 Louisiana Street, Suite 200
Little Rock, AR 72201

California
Los Angeles District Office
Roybal Federal Building
255 East Temple St., 4th Floor
Los Angeles, CA 90012

San Francisco District Office
450 Golden Gate Avenue
5 West, P.O Box 36025
San Francisco, CA 94102-3661

Fresno Local Office
Robert E. Coyle Federal Courthouse
2500 Tulare Street, Suite 2601
Fresno, CA 93721

Oakland Local Office
1301 Clay Street, Suite 680-N
Oakland, CA 94612-5217

San Diego Local Office
555 West Beech Street, Suite 504
San Diego, CA 92101

San Jose Local Office
96 N. Third St., Suite 250
San Jose, CA 95112

Colorado
Denver Field Office
950 17th Street, Suite 300
Denver, CO 80202

Florida
Miami District Office
Miami Tower
100 SE 2nd Street, Suite 1500
Miami, FL 33131

Tampa Field Office
501 East Polk Street, Suite 1000
Tampa, FL 33602

Georgia
Atlanta District Office

Sam Nunn Atlanta Federal Center
100 Alabama Street, SW, Suite 4R30
Atlanta, GA 30303

Savannah Local Office
7391 Hodgson Memorial Drive, Suite 200
Savannah, GA 31406-2579

Hawaii
Honolulu Local Office
Prince Jonah Kuhio Kalanianaole Federal Building
300 Ala Moana Boulevard, Room 4-257
Honolulu, HI 96850

Illinois
Chicago District Office
JCK Federal Building
230 S Dearborn Street
Chicago, IL 60604

Indiana
Indianapolis District Office
101 West Ohio St, Ste 1900
Indianapolis, IN 46204

Kansas
Kansas City Area Office
Gateway Tower II
400 State Ave., Suite 905
Kansas City, KS 66101

Kentucky
Louisville Area Office
600 Dr. Martin Luther King, Jr. Place, Suite 268
Louisville, KY 40202

Louisiana
New Orleans Field Office
Hale Boggs Federal Building
500 Poydras Street, Suite 809
New Orleans, LA 70130

Maryland
Baltimore Field Office
GH Fallon Federal Building

31 Hopkins Plaza, Suite 1432
Baltimore, MD 21201

Massachusetts
Boston Area Office
JFK Federal Building
15 New Sudbury Street, Room 475
Boston, MA 02203-0506

Michigan
Detroit Field Office
Patrick V. McNamara Building
477 Michigan Avenue, Room 865
Detroit, MI 48226

Minnesota
Minneapolis Area Office
Towle Building
330 South Second Avenue, Suite 720
Minneapolis, MN 55401-2224

Mississippi
Jackson Area Office
Dr. A. H. McCoy Federal Building
100 West Capitol Street, Suite 338
Jackson, MS 39269

Missouri
St. Louis District Office
Robert A. Young Federal Building
1222 Spruce St., Rm 8.100
St. Louis, MO 63103

Nevada
Las Vegas Local Office
333 Las Vegas Blvd South, Suite 5560
Las Vegas, NV 89101

New Jersey
Newark Area Office
Two Gateway Center
283–299 Market Street, Suite 1703
Newark, NJ 07102

New Mexico
Albuquerque Area Office
505 Marquette Avenue, NW
Suite 900 – 9th Floor
Albuquerque, NM 87102

New York
New York District Office
33 Whitehall Street, 5th Floor
New York, NY 10004

Buffalo Local Office
Olympic Towers
300 Pearl Street, Suite 450
Buffalo, NY 14202

North Carolina
Charlotte District Office
129 West Trade Street, Suite 400
Charlotte, NC 28202

Raleigh Area Office
434 Fayetteville Street, Suite 700
Raleigh, NC 27601

Greensboro Local Office
Asheville Building
1500 Pinecroft Road, Suite 212
Greensboro, NC 27407

Oklahoma
Oklahoma City Area Office
215 Dean A McGee Avenue, Suite 524
Oklahoma City, OK 73102

Ohio
Cincinnati Area Office
John W. Peck Federal Office Building
550 Main Street, Suite 10-191
Cincinnati, OH 45202

Cleveland Field Office
Anthony J. Celebrezze Federal Building
1240 E. 9th Street, Suite 3001
Cleveland, OH 44199

Pennsylvania
Philadelphia District Office
801 Market Street, Suite 1300
Philadelphia, PA 19107-3127

Pittsburgh Area Office
William S. Moorhead Federal Building
1000 Liberty Avenue, Suite 1112
Pittsburgh, PA 15222

Puerto Rico
San Juan Local Office
525 F.D. Roosevelt Ave.
Plaza Las Americas, Suite 1202
San Juan, PR 00918-8001

South Carolina
Greenville Local Office
301 N. Main Street, Suite 1402
Greenville, SC 29601-9916

Tennessee
Memphis District Office
1407 Union Avenue, 9th floor
Memphis, TN 38104

Nashville Area Office
220 Athens Way, Suite 350
Nashville, TN 37228-9940

Texas
Dallas District Office
207 S. Houston Street, 3rd Floor
Dallas, TX 75202

San Antonio Field Office
Legacy Oaks, Building A
5410 Fredericksburg Road, Suite 200
San Antonio, TX 78229

El Paso Area Office
100 Stanton Towers
100 N. Stanton Street, Suite 600
El Paso, TX 79901-1433

Houston District Office
Mickey Leland Building
1919 Smith Street, 6th Floor
Houston, TX 77002

Virginia
Norfolk Local Office
Federal Building
200 Granby Street, Suite 739
Norfolk, VA 23510

Richmond Local Office
400 N. Eight Street, Suite 350
Richmond, VA 23219

Wisconsin
Milwaukee Area Office
Reuss Federal Plaza
310 West Wisconsin Avenue, Suite 500
Milwaukee, WI 53203

Washington
Seattle Field Office
Federal Office Building
909 First Avenue, Suite 400
Seattle, WA 98104-1061

Washington, DC
Washington Field Office
131 M Street, NE
Fourth Floor, Suite 4NWO2F
Washington, DC 20507-0100

HEALTH AND HUMAN SERVICES OFFICES

Data as of 2022.

HHS Headquarters
U.S. Department of Health & Human Services
200 Independence Avenue, S.W.
Washington, D.C. 20201
Toll-Free Call Center: 1-877-696-6775

Region 1
John F. Kennedy Federal Building
Government Center – Room 2100
Boston, MA 02203
(617)-565-1500

Region 2
26 Federal Plaza Suite 3835
New York, NY 10278
(212)-264-4600

Region 3
801 Market Street, Suite 8000
Philadelphia, PA 19107
(215)-861-4633

Region 4
61 Forsyth St. SW, Suite 5B95
Atlanta, GA 30303
(404)-562-7888

Region 5
233 North Michigan Avenue, Suite 1300
Chicago, IL 60601
(312)-353-5160

Region 6
1301 Young Street, Suite 106-1124
Dallas, TX 75202
(214)-767-3301

Region 7
601 East 12th Street, Room S1801
Kansas City, MO 64106
(816)-426-2821

Region 8
1961 Stout Street, Room 08-148
Denver, CO 80294
(303)-844-3372

Region 9
90 Seventh Street
San Francisco, CA 94103
(415)-437-8500

Region 10
701 5th Avenue, Suite 1600 MS-01
Seattle, WA 98104
(206)-615-2010

RELATED OFFICES FOR TRIBAL AFFAIRS

Office of Intergovernmental and External Affairs (IEA)
U.S. Department of Health and Human Services
Hubert Humphrey Building, 620E
200 Independence Avenue, SW
Washington, DC 20201
(202)-690-6060

Secretary's Tribal Advisory Committee (STAC)
Office of Intergovernmental Affairs
US Department of Health and Human Services
200 Independence Ave SW Room 630-F
Washington, DC 20201

HUMAN RIGHTS WATCH U.S. CONTACTS

New York
Address: 350 Fifth Avenue, 34th floor
New York, NY 10118-3299 USA
Tel: +1-212-290-4700
Fax: +1-212-736-1300

Chicago
Address: 314 West Superior, Suite 300
Chicago, IL 60654
Tel: +1-312-828-9100
Email: chicago@hrw.org

Los Angeles
Address: 11500 W. Olympic Blvd., Suite 608
Los Angeles, CA 90064 USA
Tel: +1-310-477-5540
Fax: +1-310-477-4622

San Francisco
Address: 350 Sansome St., Suite 1000
San Francisco, CA 94104 USA

Tel: +1-415-362-3250
Fax: +1-415-362-3255

Silicon Valley
Address: 855 El Camino Real, Suite 333
Palo Alto, California, 94301 USA
Tel: +1-(650)-656-8314

Washington, DC
Address: 1275 K Street, NW
Suite 1100
Washington, DC 20005 USA
Tel: +1-202-612-4321
Fax: +1-202-612-4333

Glossary

Everyone, especially managers, should be familiar with these terms.

AA	Affirmative Action
Abjection	The separating of an individual from the group through statements of disgust
Absenteeism	Intentional or habitual absence from work
Abuse	Any action that intentionally harms or injures another person
Acceptable Use Policy (AUP)	A policy that defines the responsibilities and appropriate behavior of computer and network users
Accommodation	The process of adapting or adjusting to someone or something
Accountability	Answerability for actions, decisions and performance
Activate	To make active; cause to function or act
ADA	Americans with Disabilities Act
ADD	Administration on Developmental Disabilities
ADEA	Age Discrimination in Employment Act
AFAB and AMAB	Acronyms meaning "assigned female/male at birth" (also designated female/male at birth or female/male assigned at birth)
AFDC	Aid to Families with Dependent Children
Affect	An emotion that changes or influences what you do or think
Affirmative action	Plans of action undertaken by organizations to comply with human rights legislation by actively striving to recruit, hire, train, develop, and promote women and members of minority groups
Affirmed gender	The gender by which one wishes to be known
Age discrimination	Discrimination based on age
Agent	A person who acts for or in the place of another person
Aggravation	A source or cause of annoyance or exasperation
Aggressive	Pursuing one's aims and interests forcefully, sometimes unduly so
Aggressor	A person who says or does hurtful things
Aggrieved person	Someone who has been discriminated against in some way
Agreeableness	The tendency to get along with other people
AIDS	Acquired Immune Deficiency Syndrome
Ally	A person who helps or stands up for someone who is being bullied or is the target of prejudice

Ambiguous information	Information that can be interpreted in multiple and often conflicting ways
Antibias	A commitment to avoid prejudice, stereotyping, and all forms of discrimination
Antisocial	Not sociable; not wanting the company of others
Anxiety	A feeling of worry, nervousness or unease, typically about an imminent event or something with an uncertain outcome
Apology	A regretful acknowledgment of an offense
Arbitrator	A labor law specialist paid jointly by the union and the organization to listen to both sides of a labor dispute and then decide how the dispute should be settled
Assault	Intentionally putting someone in reasonable apprehension of an imminent harmful or offensive contact; physical injury is not required
Assault and battery	Assault and battery are related but distinct crimes. An assault is when a person commits an act that puts a "victim" in reasonable apprehension of harmful or offensive contact (threat of violence). Battery, on the other hand, is when someone commits an act that actually inflicts harmful or offensive contact on the victim (actual physical violence)
Assessment center	An employee selection technique that allows human resource managers to observe and evaluate a prospective employee's performance on simulated tasks such as decision-making and time management
Assets	Items of value owned by the company
Attitudes	Predispositions to respond favorably or unfavorably to something
Attorney/client privilege	Communication made in confidence between a client and counsel for the purpose of seeking or providing legal counsel or advice
At-Will	An employee can be fired for any reason or for no reason at all
Avoidance	Actions a person takes to escape from difficult thoughts and feelings
Backpay	Money which an employer owes an employee for work that he or she did in the past
Basis	A basis is the "reason" being alleged for discrimination
Battery	The actual act that causes physical harm
Benchmarking	Comparing performance on specific dimensions with the performance of high-performing organizations
Benefits (fringe)	Indirect compensation paid to employees, such as healthcare, life insurance, vacations, sick leave
BFOQ	Bona Fide Occupational Qualification
Bias	A tendency to believe that some people, ideas or things are better than others that usually results in treating some people unfairly
BLS	Bureau of Labor Statistics

Botheration	The act or state of bothering or the state of being bothered
Bothering	Annoying or pestering someone
Bottom-up change	Change that is implemented gradually and involves managers and employees at all levels of an organization
Browbeating	Intimidating by overbearing looks or words
Burnout	A state of emotional, physical and mental exhaustion caused by excessive and prolonged stress
Bystander	A person who witnesses bias or B≈H
Capital	Anything that confers value or benefit to its owners, such as its equipment or machinery, intellectual property like patents, financial assets, or its employees
Career	A sequence of attitudes and behaviors that a person perceives to be related to work experience during his or her life. The sum total of work-related experiences throughout a person's life
Career counseling	Advice and assistance provided informally or formally to the individual regarding his career development and planning
Career development	A careful, systematic approach to assuring that sound career choices are made; involves both career planning (an individual element) and career management (an organizational element)
Career information systems	The combination of internal job markets with formal career counseling and the maintenance of a career information center for employees
Career management	The organizational element of career development, involving career counseling, career pathing, career resources planning, and career information systems
Career pathing	Identifying coherent progressions of jobs (tracks, routes or paths) that are of particular interest to the organization
Career planning	Making detailed and specific decisions and plans about career goals and how to achieve them
Career plateau	A position from which the chances of being promoted or obtaining a more responsible job are slight
Career stages	Spans of years during which an individual has different types of concerns about job and career, sometimes labeled as the stages of career exploration, establishment, maintenance, and decline
CDC	Centers for Disease Control
CEA	Council of Economic Advisers
Civil lawsuit	A court-based process through which Person A can seek to hold Person B liable for some type of harm or wrongful act
Climate	The social environment of the organization
Codes of conduct	Meaningful symbolic statements about the importance of adhering to high ethical standards in business

Coercion	Using power or force to impose an unwanted behavior
Cohesiveness	The extent to which members of the group are motivated to remain together
Coming out	Disclosing a lesbian, gay, bisexual or transgender/gender-expansive identity within themselves first, and then choosing to reveal it to others
Compensation	Wages and salaries paid to employees for their services
Competitive advantage	The ability of one organization to outperform other organizations because it produces desired goods or services more efficiently and effectively than they do. The component of strategy that specifies the advantages that the organization holds relative to its competitors
Complainant	A person, group or company that makes a complaint, as in a legal action (see also plaintiff)
Complaint	A complaint is an allegation of illegal discrimination
Compliance	Going along with the boss's request but without any stake in the result
Compromise	An agreement or a settlement of a dispute that is reached by each side making concessions
Conflict	Active disagreement between people with opposing opinions or principles
Conflict of interest	A situation where the employee's decision may be compromised because of competing loyalties
Constructive discharge	Conditions are so hostile that the target is forced to leave work
Corroborate	Person or information that confirms or gives support to a statement, theory or finding
Credibility	Reputation as to believability
Crisis Management Team	Group assembled at the top of an organization to develop plans and actions to prevent workplace violence
Cyberbullying	Willful and repeated harm inflicted through the use of computers, cell phones or other electronic devices
Damages	A remedy in the form of a monetary award to be paid to a claimant as compensation for loss or injury
Defaming	Making a false statement that injures someone's reputation or standing within a group
Defendant	A person, company, or entity against whom a claim or charge is brought in a court; person or entity being sued (see plaintiff)
Denigration	Sending or posting gossip or rumors about a person that damages that person's reputation or friendships
Discipline	Punishment inflicted by way of correction and training

Discovery	Obtaining and disclosing evidence and the position of each side of a case so that all parties involved can decide whether to move to trial or negotiate an early settlement
Discrimination	Unfair treatment of one person or group of people because of the person or group's identity (e.g., race, gender, ability, religion, culture)
Disparaging terms	Words used to degrade individual characteristic
Disparate impact	One group receives less favorable results than another
Disparate treatment	One group is subjected to inconsistent application of rules and policies relative to others
Disruptive	Behavior that causes difficulties that interrupt performance or prevent it from continuing
Diversity	Differences among people in age, gender, race, ethnicity, religion, sexual orientation, socioeconomic background and capabilities/ disabilities
DOL	Department of Labor
Downsizing	A reduction in organizational size and operating costs implemented by management in order to improve organizational efficiency, productivity, and/or the competitiveness of the organization
Dual-career families	Households in which both the husband and the wife are pursuing careers, not merely earning an income
Dual-income families	Households in which both the husband and the wife earn a paycheck
Due diligence	Reasonable steps taken by a person in order to satisfy parties and to avoid harm to those involved
Duress	Threats, violence, constraints or other action brought to bear on an individual to do something against their will or better judgment
EBSA	Employee Benefits Security Administration
ECAB	Employees' Compensation Appeals Board
EEOC	The U.S. Equal Employment Opportunity Commission is responsible for enforcing federal laws that make it illegal to discriminate
Effectiveness	Doing the right things in the right way at the right times. A measure of the appropriateness of the goals an organization is pursuing and of the degree to which the organization achieves those goals
Empathy	The ability to identify and share feelings with someone
Employment at will	Freedom of the organization to employ someone when it desires and therefore to dismiss the employee at any time for any reason
Empowerment	Expanding employees' tasks and responsibilities
Enabling Factors	Those things that improve your ability to manage B≈H
Enticement	Attracting by arousing hope or desire
EPA	Equal Pay Act

Equal Employment Opportunity Commission (EEOC)	Agency responsible for enforcing federal laws regarding discrimination or harassment against job applicants or employees in the United States
Equality	Having the same or similar rights and opportunities as others
Equity	The quality of being fair or just
Eroding factors	Those things that impede your ability to reduce B≈H
ESA	Employment Standards Administration; Economics and Statistics Administration
ETA	Employment and Training Administration
Ethical dilemma	A situation where the manager is faced with two or more conflicting ethical issues
Ethics	A moral philosophy or code of morals practiced by a person or group of people
Ethnic Group	People who share a common religion, color or national origin
Evade	To endeavor to set aside truth or to escape punishment
Evidence	The means by which any alleged matter is established or disproved
Exclusion	Intentionally excluding someone from a group or its activities
Fair labor practices	Equitable practices concerning hiring, wages, union relations, etc.
FDA	Food and Drug Administration
Feedback	Response from the receiver of a message to the sender of that message; for instance, telling the employee the results of his or her performance appraisal
Filtering	Withholding part of a message out of the belief that the receiver does not need, will not want the information, or to intentionally deprive the receiver of important information
Financial redress	Compensation for injuries sustained; recovery or restitution for harm or injury; damages or equitable relief
FLRA	Federal Labor Relations Authority
FMCS	Federal Mediation and Conciliation Service
FMLA	Family and Medical Leave Act
Front pay	Money awarded for lost compensation during the period between judgment and reinstatement, or if reinstatement is not feasible, instead of reinstatement
Gender identity	One's deeply held core sense of being a girl/woman, boy/man, some of both, or neither
Glass ceiling	A metaphor alluding to the invisible barriers that prevent minorities and women from being promoted to top corporate positions
Grievance	A written statement or complaint filed by an employee with the union concerning the employee's alleged mistreatment by the company
Group	Two or more people who interact regularly to accomplish a common goal

Group cohesiveness	The degree to which members are attracted or loyal to a group
Group decision-making	Choosing among alternatives by teams, committees or other types of groups rather than by one individual
Group norms	Shared guidelines or rules for behavior that most group members follow
Groupthink	Phenomenon which happens when the maintenance of cohesion and good feelings overwhelms the purpose of the group. A pattern of faulty and biased decision-making that occurs in groups whose members strive for agreement among themselves at the expense of accurately assessing information relevant to a decision
Grudge	A feeling of ill will or resentment
Harassment	A simple definition would be repeatedly sending offensive, rude and insulting messages
Harm	Physical or psychological damage or injury
Hazing	Imposing humiliating or painful tasks
HIPAA	Health Insurance Portability and Accountability Act
HIV	Human Immuno-deficiency Virus
Hostile work environment	The workplace creates an environment that is difficult or uncomfortable for another person to work in, due to discrimination
HPV	Human papillomavirus
Human resource management (HRM)	Activities that managers engage in to attract and retain employees and to ensure that they perform at a high level and contribute to the accomplishment of organizational goals
Humiliation	To reduce an individual to a lower position in one's own eyes or others' eyes
ICE	Immigration and Customs Enforcement
Ignore	Refuse to take notice of or acknowledge; disregard intentionally
ILAB	Bureau of International Labor Affairs
ILO	International Labor Organization
Inconsistency	A communication problem that exists when a person sends conflicting messages
Inequality	An unfair situation when some individuals have more rights or better opportunities than others
Inequity	Lack of fairness
Informal organization	The overall pattern of influence and interaction defined by all the informal groups within an organization. The system of behavioral rules and norms that emerge in a group
Initiative	The ability to act on one's own, without direction from a superior
Injunction	A court order requiring a person to do or cease doing a specific action
Injustice	A situation in which the rights of a person or a group of people are ignored, disrespected, or discriminated against

Innuendo	An indirect derogatory statement
Intention	Something that you want and plan to do
Internal terrorism	Behavior that involves the intent to evoke fear or extreme stress for the purpose of bringing about a change that benefits the perpetrator
Interpersonal communication	Communication between people, especially small numbers of people, either orally, in writing or nonverbally
Intimidation	To force into or deter from some action by inducing fear
Involvement	Taking part in something
Jealousy	Feeling or showing envy of someone or their achievements and advantages
LGBTQ	An acronym that collectively refers to individuals who are lesbian, gay, bisexual, transgender or queer. It is sometimes stated as LGBT (lesbian, gay, bisexual and transgender), GLBT (gay, lesbian, bisexual and transgender)
Life stress	Events or experiences that produce severe strain, for example, bullying or harassment on the job
Litigation	The process of resolving disputes by filing or answering a complaint through the court system
Longevity	Suggests how long any given effort to deal with B≈H might be sustained
MBDA	Minority Business Development Agency
Mediation	A process wherein the parties meet with a mutually selected impartial and neutral person who assists them in the negotiation of their differences
Menace	A person whose actions, attitudes, or ideas are considered dangerous or harmful
Mentor	An experienced and trusted adviser
Merit Systems Protection Board (MSPB)	Federal agency responsible for dealing with personnel actions and appeals
Minority	A smaller group within a state, region, or country that differs in race, religion or national origin from the dominant group
Molestation	Sexual assault or abuse of a person, especially a woman or a child
Molesting	Assault or abuse (of a person, especially a woman) sexually
Name-calling	The use of words to hurt, belittle or be mean to someone or a group
Negotiation	A method of conflict resolution in which the parties in conflict consider various alternative ways to allocate resources to each other in order to come up with a solution acceptable to them all
Negotiator	The role that a manager plays when attempting to work out agreements and contracts that operate in the best interests of the organization

Networking	The exchange of information through a group or network of interlinked computers
NIH	National Institutes of Health
NIOSH	The National Institute for Occupational Safety and Health is part of the CDC charged with developing new knowledge in the field of occupational safety and health and transferring that knowledge into practice
NLRB	National Labor Relations Board
NMB	National Mediation Board
Nonverbal communication	Gestures and facial expressions, which do not involve speaking but can also include nonverbal aspects of speech (tone and volume of voice, etc.)
Norm	A standard of behavior that the group develops for its members
Normality	The condition or state of being usual, typical, or expected (normal)
OBL	Office of Business Liaison
Occupational crime	Offenses that are committed by someone during the course of his or her employment
Occupational deviant behavior	Self-serving deviant acts that occur at the workplace
Offense	A perceived insult to or disregard for an individual
OLMS	Office of Labor Management Standards
On notice	Has received a notification so that one cannot claim to be unaware of a situation
Organizational culture	Values and behaviors that contribute to the unique social and psychological environment of a business
Organizational environment	The set of forces and conditions that operate beyond an organization's boundaries but affect a manager's ability to acquire and utilize resources
Organizational politics	Activities that individuals engage in to increase their power and to use power effectively to achieve their goals and overcome resistance or opposition
OSBP	Office of Small Business Programs
OSDBU	Office of Small and Disadvantaged Business Utilization
OSHA	Occupational Safety and Health Administration charged with ensuring safe and healthful working conditions for workers by setting and enforcing standards and by providing training, outreach, education and assistance
Outplacement	Support service provided by some organizations to help former employees transition to new jobs
Overt discrimination	Knowingly and willingly denying diverse individuals access to opportunities and outcomes in an organization
OWBO	Office of Women's Business Ownership

OWCP	Office of Workers' Compensation Programs
Pain and suffering	The physical or emotional distress resulting from an injury
Participative management	Giving employees a voice in how things are done in organizations
Perception	The recognition and interpretation of sensory information
Perpetrator	A person who engages in B≈H or who carries out a harmful, illegal or immoral act
Persecution	Persistent annoyance, hostility or ill-treatment, especially because of race or political or religious beliefs
Pestering	Troubling or annoying an individual with frequent or persistent requests or interruptions
Plaintiff	A person or entity filing a lawsuit (see defendant)
Positive approaches	Methods that stress prevention and support rather than punishment
Power	An individual's ability to control or direct others
Power imbalance	A situation where one person or group has an advantage over others
Predispositions	The tendency to perceive or act in a certain way because of previous experiences in one's background or environment
Prejudice	Judging or having an idea about someone or a group of people before you actually know them
Prima facie	Latin for "on first view," or "at first appearance." In EEO cases, complainants present evidence and arguments to support a claim of discrimination
Professional ethics	Standards that govern how members of a profession are to make decisions when the way they should behave is not clear-cut
Protected class	Groups protected from employment discrimination by law
Public apology	Apologizing in the presence of others
Punishment	Administering an undesired or negative consequence when dysfunctional behavior occurs; reprimands, discipline, fines, etc. that are used to shape behavior by causing a reduction in unwanted behaviors
Punitive damages	Damages assessed in the legal process to punish a defendant and to prevent him or her from hurting others by the same or similar actions
Quid pro quo	A manager or other authority figure offers or merely hints that he or she will give the employee something (a raise or a promotion) in return for that employee's satisfaction of a sexual demand
Racism	Prejudice and/or discrimination against people because of their racial group
Rareness	The capability of managing the contributing factors to B≈H within the organization
Reasonable Person Standard	A test in personal injury cases that jurors use to determine if a defendant acted like other people would have in the same situation

Recruiting	The process of attracting a pool of qualified applicants who are interested in working for the company
Redress	The setting right of what is wrong
Remedies	A form of court enforcement of a legal right resulting from a successful civil lawsuit
Resistance	The negative, uncooperative response of persons when their boss attempts to influence them
Retaliation	An employer punishes an employee for engaging in legally protected activity
Rumors	Unofficial pieces of information of interest to organizational members but with no identifiable source
SBA	Small Business Administration
Self-efficacy	Your belief in your own abilities to deal with various situations
Sexting	Sending sexually explicit photographs or messages via mobile phone or other electronic means
Sexual harassment	Unwelcome sexual advances, requests for sexual favors, or other verbal or physical conduct of a sexual nature
Shunning	An act of social rejection or emotional distancing
Smoothing	Downplaying the importance of a problem
Stalking	Following someone stealthily to cause them fear
Stereotype	False idea that all group members are the same and/or think and behave in the same way
Stress	A feeling of emotional strain and pressure
Strict liability	Imposes legal responsibility for damages or injuries even if the person who was found strictly liable did not act with fault or negligence
Target	Someone who is subject to B≈H or treated in hurtful ways by a person or a group on purpose and over and over
Team	A group whose members work intensely with each other to achieve a specific, common goal or objective
Team building	A series of activities and exercises designed to enhance the motivation and satisfaction of people in groups by fostering mutual understanding, acceptance, and group cohesion
Teasing	Persistently annoying someone, especially with jokes that may even be about them
Terror	Violence or threats of violence used for intimidation or coercion
Terrorism	Intimidation or coercion by instilling fear
Third-party harassment	Harassment by someone who is not a member of the organization (e.g., customer, supplier)
Threat	Suggestion that something unpleasant or violent will happen if a particular action or order is not followed

Title VII	Part of the Civil Rights Act of 1964 is a federal law that protects employees against discrimination based on certain specified characteristics
Tolerance	The willingness to accept opinions, behaviors and characteristics different from one's own
Traits	Characteristics of a person
Transgender	Term for people whose gender identity differs from that assigned at birth (e.g., assigned female or male)
Turnover	The number or percentage of workers who leave an organization and are replaced by new employees
Unwelcome conduct	Any behavior by subordinates, peers or superiors that is deemed offensive or unwelcome by an employee
Value	The organization's productivity and its value to customers, clients and employees
Vengeance	Infliction of injury, harm, humiliation, or the like, on a person by another who has been harmed by that person
V-REEL®	Framework, originally developed for strategic analysis in organizations (Flint, 2018), provides a unique way of thinking about the causes of B≈H and how to eradicate it. It consists of five components: value, rareness, eroding factors, enabling factors and longevity
Vulnerable individuals	Those who are or may be for any reason unable to take care of themselves, or unable to protect themselves against significant harm or exploitation
Whistle-blower	A person who reports illegal or unethical behavior
Withdrawal	Avoiding people and activities you would usually enjoy; social isolation

Bibliography

Abulaish, M., Islamia, J. M., & Anwar, T. (2013). A keyphrase-based tag cloud generation framework to conceptualize textual data. *International Journal of Adaptive, Resilient and Autonomic Systems*, 4(2), 72–91.

Ahuja, K. K., & Padhy, P. (2021). The cyber avatar of sexual harassment at the workplace: media analysis of reports during COVID-19. *Journal of Psychosexual Health*, OnlineFirst. Available at https://doi.org/10.1177/26318318211047832.

AlertFind (2021). Workplace violence statistics 2018, a growing problem. Available at https://alertfind.com/workplace-violence-statistics/.

Ambrose, M. L., & Ganegoda, D. B. (2020). Abusive according to whom? Manager and subordinate perceptions of abusive supervision and supervisors' performance. *Journal of Organizational Behavior*, 41(8), 737–56.

Asamani, L. (2016). Organizational and individual consequences of workplace violence. *Public Policy and Administration Research*, 6(9), 47–58.

Ashed, G. (2012). Fighting sexual harassment in the field. Available at www.huffingtonpost.com/greg-asbed/fighting-sexual-harassmen_b_1702880.html.

Astrauskaite, M., Notelaers, G., Medisauskaite, A., & Kern, R. M. (2015). Workplace harassment: deterring role of transformational leadership and core job characteristics. *Scandinavian Journal of Management*, 31(1), 121–35.

Atenstaedt, R. (2012). Word cloud analysis of the BJGP. *The British Journal of General Practice*, 62(596), 148. https://doi.org/10.3399/bjgp12X630142.

Baillien, E., De Cuyper, N., & De Witte, H. (2011). Job autonomy and workload as antecedents of workplace bullying: a two-wave test of Karasek's Job Demand Control Model for targets and perpetrators. *Journal of Occupational and Organizational Psychology*, 84(1), 191–208. https://doi.org/10.1348/096317910X508371.

Balleck, B. J. (2019). *Hate Groups and Extremist Organizations in America: An Encyclopedia*. Santa Barbara, CA: ABC-CLIO, LLC.

Bennett, J. (2014). The migrant workers experience. Available at https://prezi.com/rio2xjyzaft0/the-migrant-workers-experience/.

Berry, P. A., Gillespie, G. L., Fisher, B. S., Gormley, D., & Haynes, J. T. (2016). Psychological distress and workplace bullying among registered nurses. *The Online Journal of Issues in Nursing*, 21(3). Available at www.nursingworld.org/MainMenuCategories/ANAMarketplace/ANAPeriodicals/OJIN/TableofContents/Vol-21-2016/No3-Sept-2016/Articles-Previous-Topics/Psychological-Distress-and-Workplace-Bullying.html.

Boland, M. L. (2005). *Sexual Harassment in the Workplace*. Naperville, IL: Sphinx Publishing.

Boone, G. (2015). Labor law highlights, 1915–2015. *Monthly Labor Review*, U.S. Bureau of Labor Statistics, October 2015. https://doi.org/10.21916/mlr.2015.38.

Borg, I., & Groenen, P. J. F. (2005). The four purposes of multidimensional scaling. In Borg & Groenen, *Modern Multidimensional Scaling*, 3–18. Springer Series in Statistics. New York: Springer. https://doi.org/10.1007/0-387-28981-X_1.

Carbo, J., & Hughes, A. (2010). Workplace bullying: developing a human rights definition from the perspective and experiences of targets. *WorkingUSA*, 13(3), 387–403.

Chabowski, B. R., Samiee, S., & Hult, G. T. M. (2015). Cross-national research and international business: an interdisciplinary path. *International Business Review*, 26(1), 89–101.

Chan, C., Wong, J., Yeap, L., Lee, L., Jamil, N., & Nantha, Y. (2019). Workplace bullying and psychological distress of employees across socioeconomic strata: a cross-sectional study. *BMC Public Health*, 19, 608. https://doi.org/10.1186/s12889 -019-6859.

Cobb, E. P. (2013). *Bullying, Violence, Harassment, Discrimination and Stress*. Scotts Valley, CA: CreateSpace Independent Publishing Platform.

Cohen, A., & Vigoda, E. (1999). Politics and the workplace: an empirical examination of the relationship between political behavior and work outcomes. *Public Productivity & Management Review*, 22(3), 389–406. https://doi.org/10.2307/3380710.

Cook, C. R., William, K. R., Guerra, N. G., Kim, T. E., & Sadek, S. (2010). Predictors of bullying and victimization in childhood and adolescence: a meta-analytic investigation. *School Psychology Quarterly*, 25(2), 65–83.

Cook, W. L., & Sheppard, L. (2017). The impact of witnessing online harassment of executive role models. *Academy of Management Proceedings*, 2017(1), 16476.

Corniou, T. S., & Gyorgy, M. (2013). Mobbing in organizations: benefits of identifying the phenomenon. *Procedia – Social and Behavioral Sciences*, 78, 708–71.

Cowie, H., Jennifer, D., Neto, C., Angula, J. C., Pereira, B., del Barrio, C., & Ananiadou, K. (2000). Comparing the nature of workplace bullying in two European countries: Portugal and the UK. In M. Sheehan, S. Ramsey, & J. Patrick (eds.), *Transcending the Boundaries: Integrating People, Processes and Systems*, 128–33. Proceedings of the 2000 Conference, September. Brisbane, Queensland, Australia: Griffith University.

Cox, M., & Cox, T. (2008). Multidimensional scaling. In Chun-houh Chen, Wolfgang Härdle, & Antony Unwin (eds.), *Handbook of Data Visualization*, 315–47. Berlin, Heidelberg: Springer. https://doi.org/10.1007/978-3-540-33037-0_14.

Cox, T. F., & Cox, M. A. A. (2001). *Multidimensional Scaling*. New York: Chapman and Hall.

Crawshaw, L. (2009). Workplace Bullying? Mobbing? Harassment? Distraction by a thousand definitions. *Consulting Psychology Journal: Practice and Research*, 61(3), 263–7.

Crothers, L. M., & Lipinski, J. (2014). *Bullying in the Workplace: Causes, Symptoms, and Remedies*. New York: Routledge/Taylor & Francis.

Crowell, L. (1955). The building of the "four freedoms" speech. *Speech Monographs*, 22(5), 266–83. https://doi.org/10.1080/03637755509375153.

Cutting Edge Recruiting Solutions (2012). The average employee lawsuit costs $250,000 … how safe is your company? Available at https://www.cersnow.com/ blog/the-average-employee-lawsuit-costs-250000how-safe-is-your-company/.

DaPaolo, C. A., & Wilkinson, K. (2014). Get your head into the clouds: using word clouds for analyzing qualitative assessment data. *Tech Trends*, 58(3), 38–44. https:// doi.org/10.1007/s11528-014-0750-9.

Davenport, N. Z., Schwartz, R. D., & Elliott, G. P. (2005). *Mobbing, Emotional Abuse in the American Workplace*, 3rd edition. Ames, IA: Civil Society Publishing.

Deloitte Access Economics (2019). The economic costs of sexual harassment in the workplace. Available at https://www2.deloitte.com/content/dam/Deloitte/au/

Documents/Economics/deloitte-au-economic-costs-sexual-harassment-workplace
-240320.pdf.

Desrumaux, P., Machado, T., Przygodzki-Lionet, N., & Lourel, M. (2015). Workplace bullying and victims' prosocial or antisocial behaviors: what are the effects on equity, responsibility judgments, and help giving? *Journal of Human Behavior in the Social Environment*, 25(6), 509–21. https://doi.org/10.1080/10911359.2014 .988318.

Djurkovic, N., McCormack, D., & Casimir, G. (2005). The behavioral reactions of victims to different types of workplace bullying. *International Journal of Organization Theory & Behavior*, 8(4), 439–60. https://doi.org/10.1108/IJOTB-08 -04-2005-B001.

Does, S., Gundemir, S., & Shih, M. (June 11, 2018). Research: how sexual harassment affects a company's public image. *Harvard Business Review*. Available at https://hbr .org/2018/06/research-how-sexual-harassment-affects-a-companys-public-image.

Dover, L. (2020). What is a "protected class?" Kimball, Tirey & St. John LLP. Available at https://www.kts-law.com/what-is-a-protected-class/.

Dray, P. (2010). *There Is Power in a Union: The Epic Story of Labor in America*. New York: Doubleday.

Dubofsky, M., & McCartin, J. A. (2017). *Labor in America: A History*, 9th edition. Hoboken, NJ: John Wiley & Sons, Ltd.

Edyburn, D. (2010). Word clouds: valuable tools when you can't see ideas through the words. *Journal of Special Education Technology*, 25(2), 68–72.

EEOC.gov (2021). Harassment. Available at https://www.eeoc.gov/harassment.

Einarsen, S. (1999). The nature and causes of bullying at work. *International Journal of Manpower*, 20, 16–27. https://doi.org/10.1108/01437729910268588.

Einarsen, S. V., Hoel, H., & Cooper, C. L. (2002). *Bullying and Emotional Abuse in the Workplace: International Perspectives in Research and Practice*. New York: Taylor & Francis.

Einarsen, S. V., Hoel, H., Zapf, D., & Cooper, C. L. (eds.) (2011). *Bullying and Harassment in the Workplace: Development in Theory and Practice*, 2nd edition. Boca Raton, FL: Taylor and Francis.

Einarsen, S. V., Hoel, H., Zapf, D., & Cooper, C. L. (eds.) (2020). *Bullying and Harassment in the Workplace*, 3rd edition. Boca Raton, FL: CRC Press.

Equal Employment Opportunity Commission (2016). Questions and answers: enforcement guidance on retaliation and related issues. Available at https://www.eeoc .gov/laws/guidance/questions-and-answers-enforcement-guidance-retaliation-and -related-issues.

ERC (2013). 20 subtle signs of bullying at work. Available at https://www.yourerc .com/blog/post/20-subtle-signs-of-workplace-bullying.

Espelage, D. L., & Swearer, S. M. (2003). Research on school bullying and targetization: what have we learned and where do we go from here? *School Psychology Review*, 32(3), 365–83.

Feijó, F. R., Gräf, D. D., Pearce, N., & Fassa, A. G. (2019). Risk factors for workplace bullying: a systematic review. *International Journal of Environmental Research Public Health*, 16(11), 1945. https://doi.org/10.3390/ijerph16111945.

Feldblum, C. R., & Lipnic, V. A. (2016). Select task force on the study of harassment in the workplace, report of co-chairs. Available at https://www.eeoc.gov/select-task -force-study-harassment-workplace.

Fevre, R., Robinson, A., Jones, T., & Lewis, D. (2010). Researching workplace bullying: the benefits of taking an integrated approach. *International Journal of Social Research Methodology*, 13(1), 71–85.

Fischer, T., Tian, A. W., Lee, A., & Hughes, D. J. (2021). Abusive supervision: a systematic review and fundamental rethink. *The Leadership Quarterly*. Available at https://doi.org/10.1016/j.leaqua.2021.101540.

Flint, D. (2018). *Think Beyond Value: Building Strategy to Win*. New York: Morgan James Publishing.

Fonseca, F. (2017). Survey: park service rife with harassment. *The Arizona Republic* (Sunday, October 15), p. 22A.

Francioli, L., Høgh, A., Conway, P. M., Costa, G., Karasek, R., & Hansen, A. M. (2015). Do personal dispositions affect the relationship between psychosocial working conditions and workplace bullying? *Ethics & Behavior*. https://doi.org/10.1080/10508422.2015.1043367.

Friedrichs, D. O. (2002). Occupational crime, occupational deviance, and workplace crime: sorting out the difference. *Criminology and Criminal Justice*, 2(3), 243–56.

Furnham, A., Chan, P. S., & Wilson, E. (2013). What to wear? The influence of attire on the perceived professionalism of dentists and lawyers. *Journal of Applied Social Psychology*, 43(9), 1838–50. https://doi.org/10.1111/jasp.12136.

Giacalone, R. A., & Greenberg, J. (1997). *Antisocial Behavior in Organizations*. Thousand Oaks, CA: Sage Publications.

Glasø, L., Matthiesen, S. B., Nielsen, M. B., & Einarsen, S. (2007). Do targets of workplace bullying portray a general victim personality profile? *Scandinavian Journal of Psychology*, 48, 313–19.

Goldman, T., & Weil, D. (2021). Who's responsible here? Establishing legal responsibility in the fissured workplace. *Berkeley Journal of Employment and Labor Law*, 42(1), 55–116.

Goldsmid, S., & Howie, P. (2014). Bullying by definition: an examination of definitional components of bullying. *Emotional and Behavioural Difficulties*, 19(2), 210–25.

Gordon, S. (2021). 8 signs your boss is a bully. *Verywellfamily*. Available at https://www.verywellfamily.com/signs-your-boss-is-a-bully-460785.

Greenberg, J. (1990). Employee theft as a reaction to underpayment inequity: the hidden cost of pay cuts. *Journal of Applied Psychology*, 75(5), 561–8.

Greenberg, J. (1998). The cognitive geometry of employee theft: negotiating 'the line' between taking and stealing. In R. W. Griffin, A. O'Leary-Kelly, & J. M. Collins (eds.), *Dysfunctional Behavior in Organizations: Violent and Deviant Behavior*, 147–93. Stamford, CT: JAI Press.

Greenwald, J. (2010). Broad definition of bullying poses problem for firms. Available at http://www.businessinsurance.com/article/20100613/ISSUE01/306139987.

Griffin, R. W., & Lopez, Y. P. (2005). "Bad behavior" in organizations: a review and typology for future research. *Journal of Management*, 31(6), 988–1005. https://doi.org/10.1177/0149206305279942.

Grigoryan, L., & Honnen-Weisdorn, G. (2019). Bullying before sexual harassment. *Graziadio Business Review*, 22(2). https://gbr.pepperdine.edu/2019/08/bullying-before-sexual-harassment/.

Gronau, Q. F., & Lee, M. D. (2020). Bayesian inference for multidimensional scaling representations with psychologically interpretable metrics. *Computational Brain & Behavior*, 3(3), 322–40. https://doi.org/10.1007/s42113-020-00082-y.

Gumbus, A., & Lyons, B. (2011). Workplace harassment: the social costs of bullying. *Journal of Leadership, Accountability and Ethics*, 8(5), 72–90.

Harper, J., & Adkins, A. (2015). Employees want a lot more from their managers. *Workplace*. Available at https://www.gallup.com/workplace/236570/employees-lot -managers.aspx.

Haynes, M. (2013). Workplace violence: why every state must adopt a comprehensive workplace violence prevention law. *Cornell HR Review*. Available at www.cornellhrreview.org/workplace-violencewhy-every-state-must-adopt -acomprehensive-workplace-violence-prevention-law/.

Heathfield, S. M. (2019). What's in a comprehensive employee benefits package. *The Balance Careers*. Available at https://www.thebalancecareers.com/what-s-in-a -comprehensive-employee-benefits-package-1917860.

Hecker, T. E. (2007). Workplace mobbing: a discussion for librarians. *The Journal of Academic Librarianship*, 33(4), 439–45.

Henderson, T. J. (2019). Is it a hostile work environment or evidence of other workplace discrimination? Sanford Heisler Sharp, LLP. Available at https://sanfordheisler.com/ is-it-a-hostile-work-environment-or-evidence-of-other-workplace-discrimination/.

Hersch, J. (2018). Valuing the risk of workplace sexual harassment. *Journal of Risk and Uncertainty*, 57(2), 111–31.

Hiscox (2018). Workplace harassment study. Available at https://www.hiscox.com/ documents/2018-Hiscox-Workplace-Harassment-Study.pdf.

History.com Editors (2022). Labor movement. Available at https://en.wikipedia.org/ wiki/List_of_strikes#Seventeenth_century.

Hoel, H., & Einarsen, S. (2010). The effectiveness of anti-bullying regulations: the case of Sweden. *European Journal of Work and Organizational Psychology*, 19, 30–50.

Holcombe, M. (2021). At least 20 mass shootings have taken place in the two weeks since the metro Atlanta spa attacks left 8 dead. Available at https://www.cnn.com/ 2021/04/01/us/two-weeks-20-mass-shootings-trnd/index.html.

Hollis, L. P. (2016). Bullying: harassment by another name, yet still very much the same. *Journal of Black Sexuality and Relationships*, 2(3), 1–10.

Holtfreter, K. (2005). Employee crimes. In L. M. Salinger (ed.), *Encyclopedia of White-Collar & Corporate Crime*, Vol. 1, 284–8. Thousand Oaks, CA: Sage Publications.

Homans, M., & Johnson, I. D. (2008). Employer-led efforts to accommodate faith in the workplace. *Employment Rights and Responsibilities Mid-Winter Meeting*, 16–19. American Bar Association, April 2.

Houck, N. M., & Colbert, A. M. (2016). Patient safety and workplace bullying: an integrative review. *Journal of Nursing Care Quality*. https://doi.org/10.1097/NCQ .0000000000000209.

Hout, M. C., Papesh, M. H., & Goldinger, S. D. (2013). Multidimensional scaling. *Wiley Interdisciplinary Reviews: Cognitive Science*, 4(1), 93–103. https://doi.org/ 10.1002/wcs.1203.

Howard, J. L., Johnston, A. C., Wech, B. A., & Stout, J. (2016). Aggression and bullying in the workplace: it's the position of the perpetrator that influences employees' reactions and sanctioning ratings. *Employee Responsibilities and Rights Journal*, 28(2), 79–100.

Hughes, S. (2001). Violence in the workplace: identifying costs and preventative solutions. *Security Journal*, 14, 67–74. https://doi.org/10.1057/palgrave.sj.8340074.

Human Rights Watch (2012). Cultivating fear: the vulnerability of immigrant farmworkers in the U.S. to sexual violence and sexual harassment. New York:

Human Rights Watch. Available at https://www.hrw.org/sites/default/files/reports/us0512ForUpload_1.pdf.

Hundley, D. (2020). Here's who you can turn to when you can't count on HR (or your boss). Available at https://www.themuse.com/advice/who-to-turn-to-no-hr-department-solve-workplace-issue.

Hurjui, I., & Stefan, I. G. (2016). The relevance of the organizational environment in workplace bullying processes. *Journal of Self-Governance and Management Economics*, 4(2), 83–9.

Hutchins, J. (2019). Results from MaineCanDo workplace harassment survey released. Available at https://www.nonprofitmaine.org/blog/results-from-mainecando-workplace-harassment-survey-released/.

Jaworska, N., & Chupetlovska-Anastasova, A. (2009). A review of multidimensional scaling (MDS) and its utility in various psychological domains. *Tutorials in Quantitative Methods for Psychology*, 5(1), 1–10.

Jenkins, M. (2013). *Preventing and Managing Workplace Bullying and Harassment: A Risk Management Approach*. Samford Valley, Queensland: Australian Academic Press.

Jones, A. L. (2017). Experience of protagonists in workplace bullying: an integrated literature review. *International Journal of Nursing & Clinical Practices*, 4, 246. https://doi.org/10.15344/2394-4978/2017/246

Kane, S. (2019). Who is a workplace bully's target? Available at https://www.thebalancecareers.com/who-is-a-workplace-bully-s-target-2164323.

Karabulut, A. T. (2016). Bullying: harmful and hidden behavior in organizations. 5th International Conference on Leadership, Technology, Innovation and Business Management. *Procedia – Social and Behavioral Sciences*, 229 (2016), 4–11.

Karl, K. A., Hall, L. M., & Peluchette, J. V. (2013). City employee perceptions of the impact of dress and appearance: you are what you wear. *Public Personnel Management*, 42(3), 452–70. https://doi.org/10.1177/0091026013495772.

Kearl, H., Johns, N. E., & Raj, A. (2019). Measuring #metoo: a national study on sexual harassment and assault. Available from Stop Street Harassment at http://www.stopstreetharassment.org/wp-content/uploads/2012/08/2019-MeToo-National-Sexual-Harassment-and-Assault-Report.pdf.

Keegan, S. M. (2015). *The Psychology of Fear in Organizations*. London: Kogan Page.

Keim, J., & McDermott, J. C. (2010). Mobbing: workplace violence in the academy. *The Educational Forum*, 74(2), 167–73. https://doi.org/10.1080/00131721003608505.

Kets De Vries, M. (2018). What can be done about bullies at work? Leadership & Organizations – Blog. Available at https://knowledge.insead.edu/blog/insead-blog/what-can-be-done-about-bullies-at-work-9121.

Kinney, J. A. (1995). *Violence at Work*. Englewood Cliffs, NJ: Prentice-Hall.

Lapierre, L. M., Spector, P. E., & Leck, J. D. (2005). Sexual versus nonsexual workplace aggression and victims' overall job satisfaction: a meta-analysis. *Journal of Occupational Health Psychology*, 10(2), 155–69.

LaVan, H. (2009). What legal protections do victims of bullies in the workplace have? *Journal of Workplace Rights*, 14(2), 143–56.

Lewis, D., Sheehan, M., & Davies, C. (2008). Uncovering workplace bullying. *Journal of Workplace Rights*, 13(3), 281–301.

Li, Y., Chen, P. Y., Tuckey, M. R., McLinton, S. S., & Dollard, M. F. (2019). Prevention through job design: identifying high-risk job characteristics associated with workplace bullying. *Journal of Occupational Health Psychology*, 24(2), 297–306.

Littler® Annual Employer Survey Report (2021). Available at https://www.jdsupra.com/legalnews/the-littler-r-annual-employer-survey-2738047/.

Loh, J., Restubog, S. L. D., & Zagenczyk, T. J. (2010). Consequences of workplace bullying on employee identification and satisfaction among Australians and Singaporeans. *Journal of Cross-Cultural Psychology*, 41(2), 236–52.

Lopez, Y. P., & Griffin, R. W. (2004). A person-situation model of organizational violence. *Proceedings of the Southern Management Association*, 3–8. San Antonio.

Lucas, L. (2019). Tips about dealing with problems when there is no HR. Available at https://www.thebalancecareers.com/coping-without-hr-1917668.

Lucero, M. A., Allen, R. E., & Elzweig, B. (2013). Managing employee social networking: evolving views from the national labor relations board. *Employee Responsibilities and Rights Journal*, 25(3), 143–58.

Luo, A. (2019). What is content analysis and how can you use it in your research? *Scribbr*. Available at https://www.scribbr.com/methodology/content-analysis/.

Luo, A. (2021). Content analysis: a step-by-step guide with examples. *Scribbr*. Available at https://www.scribbr.com/methodology/content-analysis/.

Lutgen-Sandvik, P. (2013). *Adult Bullying*. St. Louis, MO: ORCM Academic Press.

Lutgen-Sandvik, P., Tracy, S. J., & Alberts, J. K. (2007). Burned by bullying in the American workplace: prevalence, perception, degree, and impact. *Journal of Management Studies*, 44(6), 837–62. https://doi.org/10.1111/j.1467-6486.2007.00715.x.

Lytle, T. (2019). Marijuana and the workplace: it's complicated. Available at https://www.shrm.org/hr-today/news/hr-magazine/fall2019/pages/marijuana-and-the-workplace-its-complicated.aspx.

MacLaury, J. (n.d.). A brief history: the U.S. Department of Labor. Available at www.dol.gov/general/aboutdol/history/dolhistoxford#.

Main, A. M. (2021). Measuring workplace harassment based on gender nonconformity. *International Journal of Business and Management Research*, 9(1), 11–19.

Mainiero, L., & Jones, K. (2013). Sexual harassment versus workplace romance: social media spillover and textual harassment in the workplace. *Academy of Management Perspectives*, 27(3), 187–203.

Mantell, M. R., & Albrecht, S. (1994). *Ticking Bombs: Defusing Violence in the Workplace*. Burr Ridge, IL: Irwin Professional Publishing.

Matias, J. N. (2019). Preventing harassment and increasing group participation through social norms in 2,190 online science discussions. *Proceedings of the National Academy of Sciences*, 116(20), 9785–9. https://doi.org/10.1073/pnas.1813486116.

Matthiesen, S. B. (2004). When whistleblowing leads to bullying at work. *Occupational Health Psychologist*, 1(1), 3.

McCann, C., Tomaskovic-Devey, D., & Lee, B. (2018). Employers' responses to sexual harassment. *SSRN Electronic Journal*, 10.2139/ssrn.3407960. Available at https://papers.ssrn.com/sol3/papers.cfm?abstract_id=3407960.

McCurley, S., & Vineyard, S. (1998). *Handling Problem Volunteers*. Downers Grove, IL: Heritage Arts Publishing/VMSystems.

McGurie, J. M., & O'Keefe, B. M. (2014). When must employers permit union activities on company property? Available at https://www.laboremploymentreport.com/2014/01/23/1132/.

Miller, E. M., Jr., & Mondschein, E. S. (2012). Sexual harassment and bullying: similar, but not the same. *Education Law Association's 58th Annual Conference*, Hilton Head, S.C.

Misawa, M., Andrews, J. L., & Jenkins, K. M. (2019). Women's experiences of workplace bullying: a content analysis of peer-reviewed journal articles between 2000 and 2017. *New Horizons in Adult Education & Human Resource Development*, 31(4), 36–50.

Montalbán, F. M., & Durán, M. A. (2005). Mobbing: a cultural approach of conflict in work organizations. IACM 18th Annual Conference. Available at http://ssrn.com/abstract=735105.

Morgan, L. A. (2013). Workplace violence statistics and information. Available at https://work.chron.com/workplaceviolence-statistics-information-13144.html.

Morrison, R. N. (2017). *Activate Human Capital: A New Attitude*. Bloomington, IN: Archway Publishing.

Moskowitz, E. (2018). Can I prevent my employees from saying that? Free(ish) speech in the workplace. *Texas Contractor*. Available at https://www.acppubs.com/articles/7432-can-i-prevent-my-employees-from-saying-that-freeish-speech-in-the-workplace.

Mugavin, M. E. (2008). Multidimensional scaling. *Nursing Research*, 57(1), 64–8. https://doi.org/10.1097/01.NNR.0000280659.88760.7c.

Mulder, R., Bos, A. E. R., Pouwelse, M., & van Dam, K. (2017). Workplace mobbing: how the victim's coping behavior influences bystander responses. *The Journal of Social Psychology*, 157(1), 16–29. https://doi.org/10.1080/00224545.2016.1152213.

Munir, M., & Zafar, M. Z. (2020). Can incidence of workplace bullying really be reduced? Application of the transtheoretical model as tertiary stage anti-bullying intervention. *Pakistan Business Review*, 21(4), 762–77.

Mutz, D. C., & Mondak, J. J. (2006). The workplace as a context for cross-cutting political discourse. *The Journal of Politics*, 68(1), 140–56. https://doi.org/10.1111/j.1468-2508.2006.00376.x.

Namie, G. (2017). 2017 WBI U.S. Workplace Bullying Survey. Available at https://workplacebullying.org/download/2017-wbi/.

Namie, G. (2021). 2021 WBI U.S. Workplace Bullying Survey. Available at https://workplacebullying.org/wp-content/uploads/2021/04/2021-Full-Report.pdf.

Namie, G., & Namie, R. (2009a). *The Bully at Work*. Naperville, IL: Sourcebooks, Inc.

Namie, G., & Namie, R. (2009b). U.S. workplace bullying: some basic considerations and consultation interventions. *Consulting Psychology Journal: Practice and Research*, 61(3), 202–19. https://doi.org/10.1037/A0016670.

Namie, G., & Namie, R. (2011). *The Bully Free Workplace*. Hoboken, NJ: John Wiley & Sons.

Needham, A. W. (2003). *Workplace Bullying: A Costly Business Secret*. New York: Penguin Books.

Neuman, J., & Baron, R. (2003). Social antecedents of bullying: a social interactionist perspective, in S. Einarsen et al. (eds.), *Bullying and Emotional Abuse in the Workplace: International Perspectives in Research and Practice*. New York: Taylor & Francis.

Nichols, T. (1997). *The Sociology of Industrial Injury*. London: Mansell Publishing.

Nielsen, M. B., & Knardahl, S. (2015). Is workplace bullying related to the personality traits of victims? A two-year prospective study. *Work & Stress*, 29(2), 128–49. http://doi.org/10.1080/02678373.2015.1032383.

O'Leary-Kelly, A. M., Bowes-Sperry, L., Bates, C. A., & Lean, E. R. (2009). Sexual harassment at work: a decade (plus) of progress. *Journal of Management*, 35(3), 503–36. https://doi.org/10.1177/0149206308330555.

Olson, L. G. (1983). Portraits in praise of a people: a rhetorical analysis of Norman Rockwell's icons in Franklin D. Roosevelt's "four freedoms" campaign. *Quarterly Journal of Speech*, 69(1), 15–24. https://doi.org/10.1080/00335638309383631.

OSHguide (2020). Available at https://ohsguide.worksafenb.ca/topic/rights.html.

Parzefall, M., & Salin, D. (2010). Perceptions of and reactions to workplace bullying: a social exchange perspective. *Human Relations*, 63(6), 761–80.

Peluchette, J., Karl, K., & Rust, K. (2006). Dressing to impress: beliefs and attitudes regarding workplace attire. *Journal of Business and Psychology*, 21, 45–63.

Peterson, L. (2019). What is mobbing at the workplace? Available at https://smallbusiness.chron.com/mobbing-workplace-43426.html.

Pino, N. W. (2001). Occupational deviance. In Patricia A. Adler, Peter Adler, & Jay Corzine (eds.), *Encyclopedia of Criminology and Deviant Behavior. Volume I: Historical, Conceptual, and Theoretical Issues*, 260–65. Philadelphia, PA: Brunner–Routledge.

Porter, M. E. (1985). *Competitive Advantage: Creating and Sustaining Superior Performance*. New York: Free Press.

Porter, M. E. (2001). The value chain and competitive advantage. In D. Barnes (ed.), *Understanding Business Processes*, 50–66. New York: Routledge.

Porter, M. E., & Kramer, M. R. (2011). Creating shared value. *Harvard Business Review*, 89(1–2), 62–77.

Price, L. W. (2021). 23 signs you're being bullied at work – and what you can do about it. Available at https://fairygodboss.com/career-topics/signs-of-being-bullied-at-work#.

Rayner, C., & Cooper, C. L. (2006). Workplace bullying. In E. K. Kelloway, J. Barling, & J. J. Hurrell, Jr. (eds.), *Handbook of Workplace Violence*, 121–45. Sage Publications, Inc. https://doi.org/10.4135/9781412976947.n7.

Rayner, C., Hoel, H., & Cooper, C. L. (2002). *Workplace Bullying: What We Know, Who Is to Blame, and What Can We Do?* London: Taylor & Francis.

Rayner, C. and Keashley, L. (2005). Bullying at work: a perspective from Britain and North America. In S. Fox & P. E. Spector (eds.), *Counterproductive Work Behavior: Investigations of Actors and Targets*, 271–96, Washington, DC: American Psychological Association. https://doi.org/10.1037/10893-011.

Riffe, D., Lacy, S., & Fico, F. G. (2005). *Analyzing Media Messages Using Quantitative Content Analysis in Research*, 2nd edition. Mahwah, NJ: Lawrence Erlbaum Associates.

Rigglo, R. E. (2013). Are you an easy target for bullies? *Psychology Today* online. Available at https://www.psychologytoday.com/us/blog/cutting-edge-leadership/201301/are-you-easy-target-bullies.

Roberts, C. W. (ed.) (1997). *Text Analysis for the Social Sciences: Methods for Drawing Statistical Inferences from Texts and Transcripts*. Mahwah, NJ: Lawrence Erlbaum Associates.

Robinson, B. (2019). New study says workplace bullying on rise: what you can do during national bullying prevention month. *Forbes*. Available at https://www.forbes.com/sites/bryanrobinson/2019/10/11/new-study-says-workplace-bullying-on-rise-what-can-you-do-during-national-bullying-prevention-month/?sh=7ab64b732a0d.

Robinson, S. L., & O'Leary-Kelly, A. M. (1998). Monkey see, monkey do: the influence of work groups on the antisocial behavior of employees. *Academy of Management Journal*, 41(6), 658–72.

Roehling, M. V. (2002). Weight discrimination in the American workplace: ethical issues and analysis. *Journal of Business Ethics*, 40, 177–89. https://doi.org/10.1023/A:1020347305736.

Romo, V. (2021). We're seeing a spike in workplace shootings: here's why. Available at https://www.npr.org/2021/05/27/1000745927/why-were-seeing-a-spike-in-workplace-shootings.

Rosenthal, P., & Budjanovcanin, A. (2011). Sexual harassment judgments by British employment tribunals 1995–2005: implications for claimants and their advocates. *British Journal of Industrial Relations*, 49(2), 236–57.

Rospenda, K. M., Richman, J. A., Ehmke, J. L. Z., & Zlatoper, K. W. (2005). Is workplace harassment hazardous to your health? *Journal of Business and Psychology*, 20(1), 95–110. http://doi.org/10.1007/s10869-005-6992-y.

Ryan, L. (2017). Ten unmistakable signs of a fear-based workplace. Available at https://www.forbes.com/sites/lizryan/2017/03/07/ten-unmistakable-signs-of-a-fear-based-workplace/#4ac047401e26.

Saguy, A. C. (2011). French and US legal approaches to sexual harassment. *Travail genre et societes*, 49(2), 236–57.

Salin, D. (2003). Ways of explaining workplace bullying: a review of enabling, motivating and precipitating structures and processes in the work environment. *Human Relations*, 56(10), 1213–32.

Sansone, R. A., & Sansone, L. A. (2015). Workplace bullying: a tale of adverse consequences. *Innovations in Clinical Neuroscience*, 12(1–2), 32–7.

Schat, A. C., Frone, M. R., & Kelloway, E. K. (2006). Prevalence of workplace aggression in the U.S. workforce: findings from a national study. In E. K. Kelloway, J. Barling, & J. J. Hurrell (eds.), *Handbook of Workplace Violence*, 47– 89. Thousand Oaks, CA: Sage Publications.

Schneider, B., Ashworth, S. D., Higgs, A. C., & Carr, L. (1996). Design, validity, and use of strategically focused employee attitude surveys. *Personnel Psychology*, 49(3), 695–705. https://doi.org/10.1111/j.1744-6570.1996.tb01591.x.

Schneider, K. T., Swan, S., & Fitzgerald, L. F. (1997). Job-related and psychological effects of sexual harassment in the workplace: empirical evidence from two organizations. *Journal of Applied Psychology*, 82(3), 401–15.

Schooley, S. (2020). Workplace harassment: how to recognize and report it. *BusinessNewsDaily*. https://www.businessnewsdaily.com/9426-workplace-harassment.html.

Scott, V. C., & Wolfe, S. M. (2016). *Community Psychology*. Thousand Oaks, CA: Sage Publications.

Seiner, J. A. (2021). Plausible harassment. *UC Davis Law Review*, 54, 1295–352.

Sepler, Fran (2015). Workplace bullying: what it is and what to do about it. *Journal of Collective Bargaining in the Academy*, Proceedings, 0(42), 1–19. Available at https://thekeep.eiu.edu/jcba/vol0/iss10/42.

Sewell, G., & Barker, J. R. (2006). Coercion versus care: using irony to make sense of organizational surveillance. *Academy of Management Review*, 31, 934–61. https://doi.org/10.5465/AMR.2006.22527466.

Sharp, S., & Smith, P. K. (1994). *School Bullying: Insights and Perspectives*. Abingdon: Routledge.

Skurzynski, G. (2009). *Sweat and Blood: A History of U.S. Labor Unions*. Minneapolis, MN: Twenty-First Century Books.

Smith, G. (2004). An evaluation of the corporate culture of Southwest Airlines. *Measuring Business Excellence*, 8(4), 26–33. https://doi.org/10.1108/13683040410 569389.

Smith, P. K., Cowie, H., Olafsson, R. F., & Liefooghe, A. P. D. (2002). Definitions of bullying: a comparison of terms used, and age and gender differences, in a fourteen-country international comparison. *Child Development*, 73, 1119–33.

Smokowski, P. R., & Kopasz, K. H. (2005). Bullying in school: an overview of types, effects, family characteristics, and intervention strategies. *Children & Schools*, 27(2), 101–10.

Stanciu, S. (2020). Racial discrimination at work: the signs and responses. *Lawyer Monthly*. Available at https://www.lawyer-monthly.com/2018/11/racial-discrimination -at-work-the-signs-and-responses/.

Statista (2021). Number of victims of workplace shootings in the United States between 1982 and March 2021. Available at https://www.statista.com/statistics/476400/ workplace-shootings-in-the-us-by-victim-count/.

Stemler, S. (2000). An overview of content analysis. *Practical Assessment, Research, and Evaluation*, 7(17). https://doi.org/10.7275/z6fm-2e34. Also available at https:// scholarworks.umass.edu/pare/vol7/iss1/17.

Stephenson-Laws, J. (2018). Increase workplace wellness to decrease workplace violence. *EHSToday*. Available at https://www.ehstoday.com/safety/article/21919595/ increase-workplace-wellness-to-decrease-workplace-violence.

Stricker, H. (2006). Assembly on private property. Freedom Forum Institute. Available at https://www.freedomforuminstitute.org/first-amendment-center/topics/freedom -of-assembly/assembly-on-private-property/.

Swartz Swidler, LLC (2019). What are the most common types of harassment in the workplace? Available at https://swartz-legal.com/what-are-the-most-common-types -of-harassment-in-the-workplace/.

Sygnatur, E. F., & Toscano, G. A. (2000). Work-related homicides: the facts. *Compensation and Working Conditions*, 5(1), 3–8.

Tabak, F., & Smith, W. P. (2005). Privacy and electronic monitoring in the workplace: a model of managerial cognition and relational trust development. *Employee Responsibilities and Rights Journal*, 17, 173–89. https://doi.org/10.1007/s10672 -005-6940-z.

Tepper, B. J. (2000). Consequences of abusive supervision. *Academy of Management Journal*, 43(2), 178–90.

Tepper, B. J., Moss, S. E., & Duffy, M. K. (2011). Predictors of abusive supervision: supervisor perceptions of deep-level dissimilarity, relationship conflict, and subordinate performance. *Academy of Management Journal*, 54(2), 279–94.

Tessem, B., Bjørnestad, S., Chen, W., & Nyre, L. (2015). Word cloud visualisation of locative information. *Journal of Location Based Services*, 9(4), 254–72. https://doi .org/10.1080/17489725.2015.1118566.

Totenberg, N. (2020). Supreme Court delivers major victory to LGBTQ employees. Available at https://www.npr.org/2020/06/15/863498848/supreme-court-delivers -major-victory-to-lgbtq-employees.

Tzeng, J., Lu, H. H., & Li, W. (2008). Multidimensional scaling for large genomic data sets. *BMC Bioinformatics*, 9, 179.

Unknown (2017). Costs of workplace bullying. Available at https://shr.ucsc.edu/elr/ abusive-conduct-and-bullying-in-the-workplace/costs-of-workplace-bullying.html.

U.S. Department of Education (2005). Common components of state anti-bullying laws and regulations, by state. stopbullying.gov. Available at https://www.stopbullying .gov/sites/default/files/StopBullying-Law-Policies-Regulations.pdf.

U.S. Department of Labor, Bureau of Labor Statistics (2017). The economics daily: homicides in retail trade, 2003–2008. Available at https://www.bls.gov/opub/ted/ 2012/ted_20120104.htm.

USLegal.com (2021). Harassment law and legal definition. Available at https:// definitions.uslegal.com/h/harassment/.

Van Fleet, D. D. (2017). Human capital, workplace violence, and human resource management in agribusiness: review and recommendations. *Journal of Agribusiness*, 35(1), 53–74.

Van Fleet, D. D. (2018). Human capital and inappropriate behavior: review and recommendations. *Journal of Human Resource and Sustainability Studies*, 6(4), 275–93. http:doi.org/10.4236/jhrss.2018.64042.

Van Fleet, D. D., & Van Fleet, E. W. (1996). Curriculum module, "Workplace violence: moving toward minimizing risks." Minerva Education Institute. Available from the Institute or its home page at http://www.minerva.org/ [no longer available].

Van Fleet, D. D., & Van Fleet, E. W. (2006). Internal terrorists: the terrorists inside organizations. *Journal of Managerial Psychology*, 21(8), 763–74.

Van Fleet, D. D., & Van Fleet, E. W. (2010). *The Violence Volcano: Reducing the Threat of Workplace Violence*. Charlotte, NC: Information Age Publishing.

Van Fleet, D. D., & Van Fleet, E. W. (2012). Towards a behavioral description of managerial bullying. *Employee Responsibilities and Rights Journal*, 24(3), 197–215.

Van Fleet, D. D., & Van Fleet, E. W. (2014a). Future challenges and issues of bullying in the workplace. In Laura M. Crothers & John Lipinski (eds.), *Bullying in the Workplace: Causes, Symptoms, and Remedies*, 550–77. New York: Routledge/ Taylor & Francis.

Van Fleet, D. D., White, L., & Van Fleet, E. W. (2018). Baseballs or cricket balls: on the meanings of bullying and harassment. *Journal of Human Resource and Sustainability Studies*, 6(1), 131–48.

Van Fleet, E. W., & Van Fleet, D. D. (2007). *Workplace Survival: Dealing with Bad Bosses, Bad Workers, Bad Jobs*. Frederick, MD: PublishAmerica.

Van Fleet, E. W., & Van Fleet, D. D. (2014b). *Violence at Work: What Everyone Should Know*. Charlotte, NC: Information Age Publishing.

Vardi, Y., & Weitz, E. (2016). *Misbehavior in Organizations: A Dynamic Approach*, 2nd edition. New York: Routledge.

Vartia, M. (1996). The sources of bullying: psychological work environment and organizational climate. *European Journal of Work and Organizational Psychology*, 5(2), 203–14. https://doi.org/10.1080/13594329608414855.

Vega, G., & Comer, D. R. (2005). Bullying and harassment in the workplace. In R. E. Kidwell & C. L. Martin (eds.), *Managing Organizational Deviance*, 183–204. Thousand Oaks, CA: Sage Publishing.

Vigoda, G., & Talmud, I. (2010). Organizational politics and job outcomes: the moderating effect of trust and social support. *Journal of Applied Social Psychology*, 40(11), 2829–61.

Vuleta, B. (2021a). 27+ alarming workplace violence statistics. Legaljobs. Available at https://legaljobs.io/blog/workplace-violence-statistics/.

Vuleta, B. (2021b). Sexual harassment in the workplace statistics – what you need to know. Available at https://whattobecome.com/blog/sexual-harassment-in-the -workplace-statistics/.

Weil, D. (2014). *The Fissured Workplace: Why Work Became So Bad for So Many and What Can Be Done to Improve It.* Cambridge, MA: Harvard University Press.

Wikipedia.org (2021). List of mass shootings in the United States in 2021. Available at https://en.wikipedia.org/wiki/List_of_mass_shootings_in_the_United_States_in _2021.

Wolf, R. B. (2015). What a difference the word 'accident' makes in sexual assault coverage cases. *Claims Journal.* Available at https://www.claimsjournal.com/news/ west/2015/05/08/263274.htm.

Woolf, M. (2021). Workplace bullying is on the rise [2021 study]. Available at https:// www.myperfectresume.com/career-center/careers/basics/workplace-bullying-in -2021.

Yahnke, K. (2018). 11 types of workplace harassment (and how to stop them). Available at https://i-sight.com/resources/11-types-of-workplace-harassment-and -how-to-stop-them/.

Zhang, S., & Leidner, D. (2018). From improper to acceptable: how perpetrators neutralize workplace bullying behaviors in the cyber world. *Information & Management*, 55(7), 850–65.

Index

abuse of power 34, 55
abusive management 6, 18
action words 21
activating an organization's human
    capital 213
Active Java 18
adequate staffing 94
    see also prevention
aftermath 96
Age Discrimination in Employment Act
    155,159, 160
agents of the organization 133
aggression 1, 2, 5, 7, 8, 14, 89
    see also bullying
aggressive 6, 21, 22, 37, 70,74, 76, 105,
    120, 135, 136, 180
    see also ction words
aggressive management 6
alarm systems 94
    see also prevention
alcohol 72, 73, 74, 156
    see also occupational deviant
        behavior
ambiguous job instructions 56
    see also bad bosses
Americans with Disabilities Act 155,
    160, 165
angry outbursts 59
    see also workstyle
anonymous notes 11, 77, 112
anti-B≈H policy 140, 141, 146,
anti-discrimination policy 140
antisocial and dysfunctional behavior 72
antisocial behavior 5, 40, 71, 74, 77,
anxiety 8, 39, 88, 92, 118
    see also impact
apathy 41
    see also safety issues
assault 21, 32, 43, 84, 124, 137, 190
    see also action words
assign blame 56
    see also poor management skills

await results 124
    see also individual actions

B≈H 11, 17, 24–28, 32–45, 49, 51,
    55–64, 67–72, 75–80, 83, 86, 88,
    90–93, 95–97, 102–112, 114,
    117–119, 121–129, 133–148, 151,
    153–156, 163, 164, 170, 174,
    177–182, 187, 188, 189
backward boss 14, 55
bad boss(es) 49, 51, 52, 53, 55
begin at the top 85, 134
behaviors influenced by environment 69
belittle, demean, or degrade 35, 59
    see also workstyle
belittling 1, 68
    see also bullying
blocking 1, 3, 30, 89, 176
bullying 1–13, 17–24, 25, 27, 30, 32,
    34, 35, 37, 44, 49, 51, 61, 67, 83,
    106–108, 117, 121, 134, 141, 146,
    152–155

campaigning 1
    see also bullying
characteristics of target/victims 105
check with human resources 117
    see also individual actions
Civil Rights Act of 1964 76, 155, 158,
    165, 173
Civil Rights Act of 1991 155, 160, 166
client uses foul language 60
    see also third parties
clogging executive toilets 87
coerce 56
    see also bad bosses
coercion 1, 25, 141
    see also bullying
complacency 42
    see also safety issues
condescension 2, 68

see also aftermath
fear of violence at work 87
fissured workplace 133
forms of bullying 12
forms of harassment 4
four horsemen of safety 41
    see also safety issues
Franklin Roosevelt's Four Freedoms 170
free speech 170
freedom from discrimination 170, 176
freedom from fear 170, 174, 175
freedom from want 170, 172
freedom of assembly 170, 175, 176
freedom of religion 173

gaslighting 3
    see also bullying
Genetic Information Nondiscrimination
    Act of 2008 155, 161,166
gossip 7, 29, 35, 42, 50, 90, 91, 92
government regulations 151

harasser 11, 87,
    see also harassment
harassment 1, 2, 3, 4, 5, 6, 7, 8, 9, 10, 11,
    12, 13, 17, 18, 19, 20, 21, 22, 23,
    24, 25, 27, 30, 32, 34, 37, 44, 47,
    49, 51, 67, 68, 71, 73, 83, 92, 108,
    117, 123, 126, 133, 138, 141, 142,
    143, 144, 145, 146, 152, 154, 155,
    156, 158, 170, 174
hitting 35
human resources (HR) 29, 109, 110, 117,
    120, 123, 126, 127, 134, 141, 146

ignore an employee 57
    see also poor people skills
ignoring 2, 7, 51
    see also bullying
Immigration Act (McCarran-Walter Act)
    of 1952 157
Immigration Act of 1924 156
Immigration and Nationality Act (1965)
    158
impact 1, 8, 20, 21, 69, 71, 76, 88, 92,
    94, 111, 119, 124, 133, 151, 156,
    173, 177, 182, 188
impedes your success 103
    see also individual dispositions

inadequate training for those managers
    55
inappropriately touching 36
    see also sexual B≈H
inattention 42
    see also safety issues
incivility 6, 105
inconsistent policies 50
    see also poor managers
individual actions 117, 141
individual disposition 103
inside forces 72, 97
inside influences 69, 79, 98
    see also behaviors influenced by
        environment
insomnia 8
    see also impact
instill fear 50, 59
    see also poor managers
internal terrorism 74, 91, 92
    see also violent behavior and
        terrorism
intimidation 2, 25, 32, 39, 66, 73, 92,
    141, 162, 178
    see also bullying
intrude on a person's privacy 59, 103
    see also workstyle
intrusion 2
    see also bullying
isolation 2, 185
    see also bullying

joking 10, 35, 50, 130

kicking 35, 84, 86

labeling 19, 21
    see also bullying
Labor Management Relations
    (Taft-Hartley) Act of 1947 153,
    157
Labor-Management Reporting and
    Disclosure Act (1959) 157
larceny 73
    see also occupational crimes
learning objectives 179
    see also develop training
less intensive behavior 67
liaison with local police 94

Printed and bound by CPI Group (UK) Ltd, Croydon, CR0 4YY

16/04/2025

14658491-0002